S0-CYF-608

Annotated Bibliography of Chicago History

Annotated Bibliography of Chicago History

Frank Jewell

CHICAGO HISTORICAL SOCIETY

1979

Library of Congress Catalog Card No.: 79-50317

ISBN: 0-913820-08-3

Manufactured in the United States of America

INTRODUCTION

This bibliography began as an effort at self-help when I started to make a list of books and articles about Chicago prior to joining the staff of the Chicago Historical Society. Once at the Society I found that there was no extensive bibliography of Chicago history and so I decided to take this first step toward a comprehensive work.

All entries in this bibliography have been verified; whenever verification proved impossible the initial entry was replaced by the word "deleted." Changes and additions were accommodated by the addition of letters to the entry numbers in each subject category.

I estimate that there are at least ten times as many books and articles relating to Chicago's history as are listed here. When faced with many items for one topic, I attempted to choose the most useful titles. Much of the excluded material is ephemeral and may be found in:

Poole's Index to Periodical Literature
Nineteenth Century Readers' Guide
Readers' Guide to Periodical Literature
Social Sciences and Humanities Index
International Index
Humanities Index
Social Science Index
Art Index
Public Affairs Information Bulletin (PAIB)
Applied Science and Technology Index
Writings on American History
America: History and Life

Newspaper articles are best traced, albeit with some difficulty, in four unique files held by the Chicago Historical Society:

Newspaper Clipping File
Annals of Labor and Industry
W.P.A. Newspaper Project Index
Bessie Louise Pierce Papers

Additional works of greater substance will be found in the bibliographies listed in Section Z (Z27-57).

Most of the items in the bibliography have their own formal bibliography or bibliographical footnotes. Only when these were of exceptional value have they been noted.

The arrangement of material in this bibliography was determined in large part by the needs and experience of the Society's reference staff. Cross-references should enable readers to use it to best advantage. Readers are advised, in addition, to examine the Table of Contents for related subject areas.

Since a work of this nature is always in process, we invite users of the bibliography to send us their comments, corrections, and suggestions for the next edition.

ACKNOWLEDGMENTS

A project of this kind requires the cooperation and help of numerous individuals. I am grateful to my colleagues for their assistance and forbearance during this project. Ann Billingsley receives a special thanks. She converted thousands of my note cards into camera-ready copy in a remarkable one-and-a-half steps, and shared the tiresome business of verification and indexing. All of this she did with great intelligence, initiative, and good humor.

A number of outside readers also gave their help. Perry R. Duis read all parts of the manuscript. He was generous in sharing both his knowledge and his personal collection of Chicago material. Timothy G. Walch and Glen E. Holt read most or all of the first draft and made helpful comments on particulars and organization. Urban historians Gerald A. Danzer, Harold Platt, and Thomas J. Schlereth supplied me with references. The Society and I also owe a debt to Frank Williams of the University of Illinois Press for excellent technical advice.

Finally, my wife, Mary Beth, put up with this whole business very well. I am grateful to her.

TABLE OF CONTENTS

ABBREVIATIONS

Am. - America, American
arch. - architecture
assoc. - association
bull. - bulletin
CH - Chicago History
comp. - compiler
dept. - department
econ. - economic(s)
ed. - education
geo. - geography
h. - history
illus. - illustrated
ISHS - Illinois State Historical Society
j. - journal
JISHS - Journal of the Illinois State Historical Society
JSAH - Journal of the Society of Architectural Historians
lit. - literature
mag. - magazine
nat. - national
n.s. - new series
pol. - political, politics
q. - quarterly
r. - review
rec. - record
soc. - sociology
tech. - technology
trans. - transactions

Universities and Colleges

B.S.U. - Ball State University
C.-M.U. - Carnegie-Mellon University
Col.U. - Columbia University
C.U. - Cornell University
C.U.N.Y. - City University of New York
C.W.R.U. - Case Western Reserve University
DeP.U. - DePaul University
G.W.U. - George Washington University
Ha.U. - Harvard University
I.I.T. - Illinois Institute of Technology
Ind.U. - Indiana University
J.H.U. - Johns Hopkins University
L.U. - Loyola University
McCormick Theol. Sem. - McCormick Theological Seminary
M.S.U. - Michigan State University
Nash.U. - Nashville University
Neb.U. - Nebraska University
N.E.I.S.C. - Northeastern Illinois State College
N.E.I.U. - Northeastern Illinois University

(Universities and Colleges, cont'd)

N.I.U. - Northern Illinois University
N.U. - Northwestern University
N.Y.U. - New York University
O.S.U. - Ohio State University
P.U. - Princeton University
R.U. - Roosevelt University
S.I.U. - Southern Illinois University
S.L.U. - St. Louis University
S.U. - Stanford University
S.U.Iowa - State University of Iowa
U.C. - University of Chicago
U.C.L.A. - University of California at Los Angeles
U.Col. - University of Colorado
U.H. - University of Houston
U.I. - University of Illinois
U.I.C. - University of Illinois at Chicago Circle
U.I.U. - University of Illinois at Urbana
U.Kan. - University of Kansas
U.Mich. - University of Michigan
U.M. - University of Minnesota
U.Miss. - University of Mississippi
U.Mo. - University of Missouri
U.N.C. - University of North Carolina
U.N.D. - University of Notre Dame
U.Ok. - University of Oklahoma
U.Penn. - University of Pennsylvania
U.T. - University of Texas
U.Tenn. - University of Tennessee
U.Va. - University of Virginia
U.W. - University of Wisconsin
U.Wash. - University of Washington
V.U. - Vanderbilt University
W.I.U. - Western Illinois University

A
GENERAL STUDIES

Before 1837

See also: Y, Indians

A1 Chicago. Commission on Chicago Historical and Architectural Landmarks. *Summary of Information on the Site of Fort Dearborn*. Chicago, 1971.

A short chronology, plan of the Fort, etc.

A2 Clinton, Katherine. "Pioneer Women in Chicago, 1833-1837." *J. of the West*, XII, 2 (Ap. 1973), 317-324.

A lightweight article describing conditions Chicago women had to grapple with.

A3 Cortesi, Lawrence. *Jean duSable: Father of Chicago*. Philadelphia, 1972.

A children's book.

A4 Currey, Josiah Seymour. *The Story of Old Fort Dearborn*. Chicago, 1912.

An old popular history of the coming of the white man, the construction of Fort Dearborn, the early settlers, life in the Fort, and the massacre that destroyed Old Fort Dearborn.

A5 Feldman, Eugene P. R. *Jean Baptiste Point Du Sable*. Chicago, 1973.

A brief biographical sketch which has been issued in many formats, including this pamphlet.

A6 Helm, Linai T. *The Fort Dearborn Massacre*. Chicago, 1912.

Helm was a lieutenant with the garrison that was attacked in 1812. He wrote this account in 1814. It disappeared for almost 100 years, when it was found and edited by Nelly Kinzie Gordon, herself a native Chicagoan born in 1835. She reprints other primary material that bears on the early settlement.

A7 Kirkland, Joseph. *The Chicago Massacre of 1812: A Historical and Biographical Narrative of Fort Dearborn*. Chicago, c1893.

The most detailed account - includes excerpts from various accounts of the massacre, sketches of prominent individuals and families, and records of the War Department about Fort Dearborn, and a list of the dead.

A8 Lee, George R. *The Beaubiens of Chicago.* Canton, Mo., 1973.

The Beaubiens were early settlers engaged in fur trade and hotel business, and leaders in the religious and cultural life of the town. Their role in Chicago's history causes this family-financed study to be mentioned.

A9 Lindsey, David. "The Founding of Chicago." *Am. H. Illus.*, VIII, 8 (Dec. 1973), 24-33.

A popular article that summarizes Chicago's history from the coming of the French into the 1830s.

A10 McLear, Patrick E. "'. . . And Still They Come.' - Chicago From 1832-36." *J. of the West*, VII, 3 (1968), 397-404.

Chicago's population expanded rapidly in the mid-1830s, fueling an economic boom. McLear examines the causes of the increase in numbers.

A11 Meehan, Thomas A. "Jean Baptiste Point du Sable, the First Chicagoan." *JISHS*, LVI, 3 (Autumn 1963), 439-453.

Meehan's two articles are the best biographical sketches of DuSable. The 1963 article is simply a reworking of the material that he used in the earlier study (A12).

A12 __________. "Jean Baptiste Point du Saible the First Chicagoan." *Mid-America*, XIX, 2 (Ap. 1937), 83-92.

A13 Meyer, Alfred Herman. "Circulation and Settlement Patterns of the Calumet Region of Northwest Indiana and Northeast Illinois: The First Stage of Occupance - The Pottawatomie and the Fur Trader, 1830." *Annals of the Assoc. of Am. Geographers*, XLIV, 3 (Sept. 1954), 245-274.

An article of critical importance for an understanding of the relationship between the face of the land and early travel and settlement on it. This relationship is particularly important to Chicago's history because of the role of transportation in Chicago's growth.

A14 Quaife, Milo M. *Checagou: From Indian Wigwam to Modern City, 1673-1835.* Chicago, 1933.

A revised, shortened, popular version of *Chicago and the Old Northwest* (A15).

A15 __________. *Chicago and the Old Northwest: A Study of the Evolution of the Northwestern Frontier, Together with a History of Fort Dearborn.* Chicago, 1913.

A documented, detailed history of the period, with appendixes of primary material on Fort Dearborn. It remains the standard account. Bibliography.

A16 Tilton, Clint Clay. "Gurdon Saltonstall Hubbard and Some of His Friends." *ISHS Trans.*, XL (1933), 83-178.

Hubbard, like the Beaubiens, was an early settler in Chicago and involved in many aspects of the town's, and later the city's, affairs. This friendly biography thus deals with many aspects of Chicago's development.

A17 Vogel, Virgil J. "The Mystery of Chicago's Name." *Mid-America,* XL, 3 (July 1958), 163-174.

Vogel considers the possible meanings for the word "Chicago" and concludes that it meant "wild onions" and that it came from the Miami tribe.

1837 to the Present

See also: Q9

A18 Andreas, Alfred Theodore. *History of Chicago.* 3 vol. Chicago, 1884-1886.

Andreas' is the most often cited of the long 19th century histories of Chicago. He prints many excerpts from primary sources and many illustrations. Much of present-day Chicago was in Cook County and it is necessary to use his *History of Cook County, Illinois,* Chicago, 1884, as well.

A19 Blanchard, Rufus. *Discovery and Conquests of the North-West with the History of Chicago.* Wheaton, Ill., 1881.

Another long history of Chicago. A substantial amount of primary material is printed in the two volumes. Part of it was quoted from records and part was solicited by Blanchard from early settlers. This material is particularly useful for early residents and institutions. The 1898-1903 two volume edition carried the story another two decades, but the editions are different and it is necessary to consult both.

A20 Bronstein, Don. *Chicago, I Will.* Text by Tony Weitzel. Cleveland, 1967.

A photographic essay.

A21 Chatfield-Taylor, H. C. *Chicago.* Boston, 1917.

Treats the history of the city by the south, north, and west sides from the point of view of an important social figure.

A21a Chicago. Dept. of Public Works. *Chicago.* Edited by Daphne Christiansen. Chicago, 1973.

A broad view of much of Chicago's built environment, transportation, sanitation, public buildings, etc. Published by the city, it has a boostering flavor.

A22 Chicago Herald and Examiner. *Illustrated History of Chicago . . .* Chicago, 1887.

A few line drawings not found elsewhere.

A23 *Chicago: Transformations of an Urban System.* Edited by Brian J. L. Berry. Cambridge, c1976.

An important, wide-ranging study of population, housing, residential patterns, transportation, etc. The product of team research, the study concluded that "the processes of change described . . . unfold in a particular way, reflecting an intricate interweaving of the metabolic rhythms of the growing metropolis with longer term upturns and downswings of the Chicago building cycle and with the unexpected occurrence of a variety of outside shocks. The result is pulsating, reverberating growth and change, beginning in the ways in which new growth is accommodated and ended in the ways in which the costs and benefits filter to the disadvantaged."

A24 Colbert, Elias. *Chicago: Historical and Statistical Sketch of the Garden City . . . from the Beginning until Now, . . . with Full Statistical Tables.* Chicago, 1868.

A good source for early statistical information and lists of officers, early settlers, institutions, etc.

A25 Condit, Carl W. *Chicago, 1910-29: Building, Planning and Urban Technology.* Chicago, 1973.

A26 __________. *Chicago, 1930-70: Building, Planning, and Urban Technology.* Chicago, 1974.

Condit established his reputation as a student of the skyscraper. He became the leading exponent of the "Chicago School" in a series of works noted in the section on architecture. In these two volumes he expanded his scope to cover other aspects of the physical city, urban planning, and transportation. The bibliographies, arranged by chapter, include newspaper articles as well as traditional sources.

A27 Currey, Josiah Seymour. *Chicago: Its History and Its Builders.* 5 vol. Chicago, 1912.

Three volumes of detailed narrative history and two volumes of biographical sketches.

A28 Cutler, Irving. *Chicago: Metropolis of the Mid-Continent.* 2nd ed. Chicago, c1976.

Cutler is a well-known Chicago geographer. His account of the city is topical, showing how the physical features of the area mixed with the influx of a new, varied population, changing transportation technology, and a growing, diverse economy. He describes urban growth and planning and concludes with lists of historic sites, Chicago "firsts," significant dates and selected statistics. The bibliography is well organized and useful. The best short introduction to Chicago.

A29 __________. *The Chicago-Milwaukee Corridor: A Geographic Study of Inter-Metropolitan Coalescence.* Evanston, 1965.

An excellent study of a large area tracing its evolution and growth from c1830.

A30 Dedmon, Emmett. *Fabulous Chicago.* New York, 1953.

A well-written work, it is a popular one-volume history.

A31 Duis, Perry. *Chicago: Creating New Traditions.* Chicago, 1976.

A well illustrated catalog of an exhibition at the Chicago Historical Society. The perceptive essay reflects current scholarship in the six areas of concern: architecture, urban planning, reform, culture, merchandising, and literature.

A32 Farr, Finis. *Chicago: A Personal History of America's Most American City.* New Rochelle, 1973.

A recent popular history which takes the story up to 1968.

A33 Furer, Howard B. *Chicago: A Chronological and Documentary History, 1784-1970.* Dobbs Ferry, 1974.

The chronology extends beyond Winslow (A53, 54), but it is sometimes wrong. The index is not well organized. Documents are generally short excerpts. Bibliography.

A34 Gilbert, Frank. *Centennial History of the City of Chicago: Its Men and Institutions.* Chicago, 1905.

Boostering, topical history, published by the *Inter-Ocean* newspaper.

A35 Gilbert, Paul and Charles Lee Bryson. *Chicago and Its Makers. A Narrative of Events from the Day of the First White Man to the Inception of the Second World's Fair.* Chicago, 1929.

One third of the text is devoted to a narrative, the middle section to landmarks and buildings, and the last two to biographies. The principal value is the extensive collection of pictures and biographical detail.

A36 Ginger, Ray. *Altgeld's America: The Lincoln Ideal Versus Changing Realities.* Chicago, 1965 (c1958).

A survey of the period 1892-1905. Ginger argues that Lincoln had established the ideal of rural, individualistic, self-governing society existing to serve the whole man, a sort of balanced humanity, but that Chicago of the period was urban, organized into large groups and corporations, governed by corrupt leaders in pursuit of the single goal of profit. The reformers or "rebels" against the reality sought to re-work the ideal to fit the reality of the period.

A37 Harper, William H., ed. *Chicago, A History and Forecast.* Chicago, 1921.

A38 Hayes, Dorsha. *Chicago, Crossroads of American Enterprise.* New York, 1944.

A general history with a strong economic and booster bias.

A39 Kirkland, Joseph. *The Story of Chicago.* 2 vol. Chicago, 1892-94.

Another long 19th century history, particularly useful for its illustrations (which are indexed) and its detailed chapter on newspapers.

A40 Kogan, Herman and Lloyd Wendt. *Chicago: A Pictorial History.* New York, 1958.

The photographs cover many topics, not just buildings. The narrative is undistinguished.

A41 Kogan, Herman and Rick. *Yesterday's Chicago.* Miami, 1976.

Photographs and captions.

A42 Korth, Fred G. *The Chicago Book, Photographs.* Chicago, 1949.

A43 Laughlin, Clarence John. *Photographs of Victorian Chicago.* New York, 1968.

A44 Lieberman, Archie. *Chicago in Color.* New York, 1969.

An undistinguished collection of photographs.

A45 Lewis, Lloyd and Henry Justin Smith. *Chicago: The History of Its Reputation.* New York, 1929.

A readable, popular history.

A46 Longstreet, Stephen. *Chicago, 1860-1919.* New York, 1973.

A popular "social history" in its broadest sense. Longstreet knew many of the people about whom he wrote.

A47 Masters, Edgar Lee. *The Tale of Chicago*. New York, 1933.

The story of Chicago told with important details from the perspective of 1933, by a participant in some of the events.

A48 Mayer, Harold M. *Chicago: City of Decisions*. Chicago, 1955.

Two short speeches by Mayer, a leading student of the city.

A49 Mayer, Harold M. and Richard C. Wade. *Chicago: Growth of a Metropolis*. Chicago, 1969.

A narrative of the city's growth to 1969. It is recognized not only as an important, perhaps the most important, book on Chicago, but also as a ground-breaking work in urban history. It was one of the first books to use photographs and other images as a principal source of information, rather than as illustrations. Almost 1000 photographs and 50 maps are used in the book to document and elaborate the argument. The illustrations and captions make it an essential work of reference. Glen E. Holt, a research associate of Mayer and Wade, has written an interesting article on Chicago's picture resources in *Chicago History*, n.s., I, 3 (Spring 1971), 158-169.

A50 Moses, John and Joseph Kirkland. *History of Chicago*. 2 vol. Chicago, 1895.

A long, detailed narrative. Fewer illustrations than Andreas' work (A18).

A51 Pierce, Bessie L. *A History of Chicago*. 3 vol. Chicago, 1937-1957.

The most important work yet published on Chicago in the 19th century. The book is a synthesis based on extensive research by a team of assistants. It is a product of the 1930s and this is reflected in its lack of balance and treatment of important themes. See Perry R. Duis' comments in *Chicago History*, n.s., V, 3 (Fall 1976), 130-140.

A52 Smith, Henry Justin. *Chicago's Great Century 1833-1933*. Chicago, 1933.

Another medium length narrative.

A52a Wagenknecht, Edward Charles. *Chicago*. Norman, 1964.

Topical, short.

A53 Winslow, Charles S. *Historical Events of Chicago*. Chicago, 1937.

A good chronology to 1935. The index is cross-referenced to the chronology.

A54 Winslow, Charles S. *Historical Events of Chicago.* 3 vol. Typescript. [Chicago?, n.d.]

The most detailed chronology from 1679-1913. There is no index in the book but a card index is located in the Chicago Historical Society.

B
DESCRIPTION

There are many works of description in other sections of this bibliography. Accounts listed here are general in nature and are drawn only from the Chicago Historical Society's collections.

General

B1 Pierce, Bessie L., ed. *As Others See Chicago: Impressions of Visitors, 1673-1933*. Chicago, 1933.

Probably the best-known collection of descriptions of Chicago from Marquette to the World's Fair of 1933.

Before 1860

B2 Arnold, Issac N. *William B. Ogden and Early Days in Chicago*. Chicago, 1882.

Ogden came to the city in 1835 and quickly became a leading citizen.

B3 Benton, Colbee C. *A Visitor to Chicago in Indian Days: Journal to the 'Far-Off West'*. Chicago, 1957.

Record of a trip from Vermont to Chicago in the summer of 1833 and of his tour of the Indian villages in the area.

B4 Cleaver, Charles. *Early Chicago Reminiscences*. Chicago, 1882.

Personal, rambling narrative covering the 1830s-1850s. He also wrote *History of Chicago*, Chicago 1892.

B5 Ekman, Ernst. "Frederika Bremer in Chicago in 1850." *Swedish Pioneer H. Q.*, XIX, 4 (Oct. 1968), 234-244.

Translations of a Swedish settler's letters.

B6 Gale, Edwin O. *Reminiscences of Early Chicago and Vicinity*. Chicago, 1902.

An easy-to-read account which touches many of the important events in early Chicago history. Mostly social material.

B7 Hoffman, Charles Fenno. *A Winter in the West: Letters Descriptive of Chicago and Vicinity in 1833-34*. 2 vol. Chicago, 1882.

Several of the letters are from Chicago.

B8 Hollister, John Hamilcar. *Memories of Eighty Years: Autosketches, Random Notes and Reminiscences*. Chicago, 1912.

Dr. Hollister practiced medicine in Chicago from 1855 to about 1899.

B9 Hubbard, Gurdon Saltonstall. *The Autobiography of Gurdon Saltonstall Hubbard, Pa-pa-ma-ta-be, "The Swift Walker."* Chicago, 1911.

Hubbard was an important early settler of Chicago.

B10 Hurlbut, Henry Higgins. *Chicago Antiquities . . .* Chicago, 1881.

He prints letters, extracts, other documents, with annotations. It is an essential volume for the study of early Chicago.

B11 Kinzie, Julliette Augusta. *Wau-Bun, the 'Early Day' in the Northwest*. Chicago, 1857.

Chapters on early Chicago and Ft. Dearborn, the Massacre, etc. A well-known and much used source.

B12 Lasswell, David. "Chicago Before the Fire: Some People, Places and Things." *CH*, n.s., I, 4 (Fall 1971), 196-203.

Photographs and some description of Chicago before the Fire.

B13 McCague, James. *When Chicago Was Young*. Champaign, 1971.

B14 McIlvaine, Mabel, comp. *Reminiscences of Chicago During the Forties and Fifties*. Chicago, 1913.

Reprints accounts by: William Bross, 1813-1890; Charles Cleaver, 1814-1893; Joseph Jefferson, 1829-1905; and Alfred Andreas on the railroads.

B15 Mason, Edward Gay. *Early Chicago and Illinois*. Chicago, 1890.

Biographical sketches of early citizens with some documents relative to them.

B16 Ossoli, Sarah Margaret (Fuller) Marchesa d'. *Summer on the Lakes in 1843*. Boston, 1844.

A well-known account. At the time of her visit Chicago had a population of over 7000.

B17 Quaife, Milo Milton, ed. *The Development of Chicago, 1674-1914: Shown in a Series of Contemporary Original Narratives*. Chicago, 1916.
An interesting series of excerpts.

1860-1916

B18 Casey, Robert Joseph. *Chicago Medium Rare: When We Were Both Younger.* Indianapolis, 1952.

Stories about Chicago from the late 1890s to, roughly, the early 1930s.

B19 Clark, Herma. *The Elegant '80s: When Chicago Was Young.* Chicago, 1941.

A description, in the form of letters, of social life and customs in the 1880s.

B20 Cook, Frederick Francis. *Bygone Days in Chicago: Recollections of the 'Garden City' of the Sixties.* Chicago, 1910.

Cook was a newspaperman and wrote these stories for the *Times* under the name "By-Gone Days." The columns are supplemented by some of Cook's own recollections. Many illustrations are reproduced.

B21 Coyne, F. E. *In Reminiscence: Highlights of Men and Events in the Life of Chicago.* Chicago, 1941.

Coyne was a Republican political figure who wrote an anecdotal account of his and Chicago's life before WWI.

B22 "The Gay Nineties in Chicago, A French View." *CH,* VII, 11 (Spring 1966), 341-348.

B23 Gregory, Addie. *A Great-Grandmother Remembers.* Chicago, 1940.

There is material here for social history in post-Civil War Chicago to the 1940s.

B24 Harrison, Edith. *"Strange to Say": Recollections of Persons and Events in New Orleans and Chicago.* Chicago, 1949.

Memoirs of the wife of a long-time Chicago mayor.

B25 Hollister, John Hamilcar.

See B8.

B26 Howells, William Dean. *Letters of an Altrurian Traveller, 1893-94.* Gainesville, 1961.

Some of these concern Chicago, particularly the 1893 Fair.

B27 McClure, James Baird. *Stories and Sketches of Chicago: An Interesting, Entertaining and Instructive Sketch of the Wonderful City "By the Sea."* Chicago, 1880.

Many illustrations, some description of history prior to 1880. In some ways, more of a guidebook.

B28 McIlvaine, Mable, comp. *Reminiscences of Chicago During the Civil War*. New York, 1967 (c1914).

Reprints newspaper accounts, etc.

B29 Peterson, William S. "Kipling's First Visit to Chicago." *JISHS,* LXIII, 3 (Autumn 1970), 290-301.

Describes Kipling's visit and his unfavorable reaction.

B30 Simon, Andreas. *Chicago, the Garden City. Its Magnificent Parks, Boulevards and Cemeteries. Together with Other Descriptive Views and Sketches*. Chicago, 1893.

Descriptions and illustrations as of 1893.

B31 Staudenraus, P. J., ed. "'The Empire City of the West' - A View of Chicago in 1864." *JISHS,* LVI, 2 (Summer 1963), 340-349.

B32 Zochert, Donald. "Heinrich Schliemann's Chicago Journal." *CH,* n.s., II, 3 (Spring-Summer 1973), 173-181.

Schliemann, famous as the man who re-discovered Troy, visited Chicago in 1867.

1916-1942

B33 Beck, Frank Orman. *Hobohemia*. Rindge, NH, 1956.

Short essays of many people he met early in the 20th century in Chicago - hobos, radicals, reformers, etc.

B33a Casey, Robert Joseph. See B18.

B34 Greenlaw, Lowell Mason. *Georgia Faye: Story of an American Family*. New York, 1954.

Some material on Chicago post-1900.

B34a Gregory, Addie. See B23.

B35 Halper, Albert. *On the Shore: Young Writer Remembering Chicago*. New York, 1934.

Describes the period before and after WWI.

B36 Halper, Albert, ed. *This is Chicago: An Anthology.* New York, 1952.

Short essays in description by a variety of well-known residents of Chicago.

B36a Harrison, Edith. See B24.

B37 Lewis, Lloyd. *It Takes All Kinds.* New York, 1928.

A collection of his columns.

B38 Meeker, Arthur. *Chicago, with Love: A Polite and Personal History.* New York, 1955.

A history of Chicago from 1902 hung on an autobiographical framework. Meeker came from a well-to-do family and his account reflects that circumstance.

B39 Morley, Christopher D. *Old Loopy: A Love Letter for Chicago.* Chicago, 1935.

A short, friendly memoir.

B40 Starrett, Helen Ekin. *Cottage Grove Avenue: Chicago. A Study of Life on One of the Typically Ugly Streets in the Typically "Ugly City."* Typescript. Chicago, 1920.

1945 -

B41 Algren, Nelson. *Chicago: The City on the Make.* Garden City, 1951.

An essay and poem that conveys Algren's powerful feelings about Chicago.

B42 Dubkin, Leonard. *My Secret Places: One Man's Love Affair with Nature in the City.* New York, 1972.

Dubkin, a nature writer, describes his favorite places in Chicago.

B43 Fitzpatrick, Tom. *Fitz: All Together Now.* New York, 1972.

A Pulitzer Prize winning journalist's columns.

B44 Greene, Bob. *Johnny Deadline, Reporter: The Best of Bob Greene.* Chicago, 1976.

A collection of his columns.

B45 Harris, Sydney J. *The Best of Sydney J. Harris.* Boston, 1975.

B46 __________. *Strictly Personal.* Chicago, 1953.

Two collections of his columns.

B47 Kupcinet, Irv. *Kup's Chicago.* Cleveland, 1962.

An autobiographical account of some of the people he has met and the events he has reported.

B48 Liebling, Abbott Joseph. *Chicago: The Second City.* Westport, 1974 (c1952).

Three essays by a visitor who viewed the city with a critical eye. Often cited.

B49 Royko, Mike. *I May be Wrong, But I Doubt It.* Chicago, 1968.

B50 __________. *Slats Grobnik and Some Other Friends.* New York, 1973.

B51 __________. *Up Against It.* Chicago, 1967.

This and the above two entries are collections of Royko's work.

B52 Terkel, Louis "Studs". *Division Street: America.* New York, 1967.

A collection of interviews making an oral history.

C
CLIMATE, TOPOGRAPHY, ETC.

See also: F, Transportation (water); A29; H165, 166

C1 Alden, W. C. *Description of the Chicago District, Illinois-Indiana: Chicago (Riverside, Chicago, Des Plaines, and Calumet Quadrangles)*. [Washington?], 1902.

The first major mapping of the geology of the Chicago area. Superseded by Bretz (C3, 4).

C2 Atwood, Wallace W. and James Goldthwait. *Physical Geography of the Evanston-Waukegan Region*. Urbana, 1908.

Describes the general geographic features of the area, the geological formations, the shoreline in 1907, previous geological features, and settlement from the geographer's point of view.

C3 Bretz, J. Harlan. *Geology of the Chicago Region: Part I - General*. Urbana, 1955.

C4 __________. *Geology of the Chicago Region: Part II - The Pleistocene*. Urbana, 1955.

The two parts make up the best geological description of Chicago and the area around it. Part I was intended "for the use of schools and the layman. Part II . . . more technical in nature . . . include[s] the details needed by geologists, engineers, and others . . .". Part II, however, is quite clear to a non-geologist and repays study. Both parts are well illustrated with charts and photographs. The fifteen color maps that accompany the work are fundamental to a study of the area.

C5 Cowles, Henry C. *The Plant Societies of Chicago and Vicinity*. Chicago, 1901.

An early description of vegetation in the area. Mostly superseded by Schmid (C14).

C6 Cox, Henry J. and John H. Armington. *The Weather and Climate of Chicago*. Chicago, 1914.

They describe the extremes, mean, and seasonal fluctuations of temperature, precipitation, humidity, sunshine, wind, and barometric pressure in great detail. The sources of Chicago's weather and storm tracks are also discussed. Much of the information is in tabular form.

C7 Ford, Edward Russell. *Birds of the Chicago Region*. Rev. ed. Chicago, 1956.

An annotated list revised from a shorter list published in 1934. It provides information about the seasons particular birds appear in the area, references to sightings, and citations to other literature.

C8 Fryxell, F. M. *The Physiography of the Region of Chicago*. Chicago, 1927.

Written to describe " . . . in a broad way the outstanding natural features of the region and emphasize especially such as have bearing upon regional planning" in preparation for making a sound base map of the Chicago area. The metropolitan area is divided for this purpose by the nature of land use (e.g., "The Lake Plain, a Great Industrial Area," "The Outer Upland, an Agricultural Area"). This division and the book's simple, clear prose have made it a classic but one that is now dated because of changing patterns of land use.

C9 Goode, John Paul. *The Geographic Background of Chicago*. Chicago, c1926.

A geography in the proper sense, that is not a geology but an explanation of how Chicago's situation in regard to certain natural features determined aspects of the city's growth. Among the natural features discussed are: coal, iron ore, timber, grain production, livestock production, and Chicago's location at the hub of an important transportation network.

C10 Pepoon, H. S. *An Annotated Flora of the Chicago Area*. Chicago, 1927.

A long essay describes the flora of the region in six subareas. This is followed by a long list of plants observed in the area, their location, other information, with references to the relevant literature.

C11 Pope, Clifford Hillhouse. *Amphibians and Reptiles of the Chicago Area*. [Chicago, 1947].

A clearly written guide for the layman, well organized with more than 60 illustrations.

C12 Salisbury, Rollin D. and William C. Alden. *The Geography of Chicago and Its Environs*. Rev. ed. Chicago, 1920.

An old standard text, more of a geology than a geography, however. It remains a clear summary of the state of knowledge in 1920.

C13 Schmid, James A. *Urban Vegetation: A Review and Chicago Case Study*. Chicago, 1975.

A model study describing the physical environment of the Chicago area, native vegetation, the effects of urban- and suburbanization on the native vegetation, and current residential landscaping. The actual and potential benefits of urban vegetation are assessed. Finally, Chicago's situation is set in a broader context of American and West European cities. Bibliography.

C14 Shelford, Victor E. *Animal Communities in Temperate America, as Illustrated in the Chicago Region: A Study in Animal Ecology*. Chicago, c1913.

Shelford wrote this book as a model for field zoology. As such, it treats environments and the animal groups within them, e.g., "Animal Communities of Large Lakes (Lake Michigan)," "Animal Communities of the Tension Lines Between Land and Water." It was thus a pioneer work in ecology but not organized for ready reference.

C15 Swink, Floyd A. *A Guide to the Wild Flowering Plants of the Chicago Region*. Chicago, 1953.

An attempt to aid laymen in finding the names of flowering plants that they find in the Chicago area. There are only a few line drawings which makes the rather complicated arrangement difficult to use.

C16 __________. *Plants of the Chicago Region: A Checklist of the Vascular Flora of the Chicago Region with Notes on Local Distribution and Ecology*. 2nd ed. Lisle, Ill., 1974.

The standard work. A list of more than 2000 plants that have been found in the Chicago area. Each entry is annotated with a description of the general areas where the plant may be found, with some specific locations, plants that it is found with, and references to relevant literature. A map showing locations is included for most entries. Arrangement is by scientific name with a list of common names for cross reference. A problem is the absence of photographs.

C17 U.S. Geological Survey. *Chicago and Vicinity*. Compiled in 1966. Washington, 1968.

C18 U.S. Weather Bureau. *Climatic Guide for Chicago, Illinois Area*. Washington, 1962.

The standard update for Cox and Armington's work (C6).

C19 Willman, N. B. *Summary of the Geology of the Chicago Area*. Illinois State Geological Survey Circular, #467.

An update of Bretz (C3, 4) covering an area 80 miles long and 50 miles wide (compared to 55 by 25 miles in Bretz' work). Compression to 77 pages makes reading for those untrained in geology more difficult than in Bretz, but by no means impossible. A clear, well-designed color map accompanies the text. Bibliography.

D
CITY PLANNING

City planning in Chicago has produced a plethora of documents from a bewildering number of bodies. The first and fundamental document, Burnham's *Plan of Chicago,* was published by the Commercial Club of Chicago.

The success of the Plan led the city to approve the creation of the Chicago Plan Commission to study and implement the Plan. The Commission had more than 300 members and the work in large part fell to its Chairman, Charles Wacker, and the Managing Director, Walter Moody. Much of the money to support the efforts to win public acceptance came from the Commercial Club.

In the period of the Depression, the vigor of the Commission waned and it was reconstituted in 1939 by the city with broader responsibilities. By the mid-1950s, however, the Commission was dormant. It was replaced by a city agency in 1956, the Department of City Planning, which was in turn reorganized as the Department of Development and Planning.

The Chicago Regional Planning Association was established in the mid-1920s to promote area-wide cooperation in planning. The Metropolitan Housing and Planning Council was established in 1934 for this same purpose. In 1956 the State of Illinois created the Northeastern Illinois Metropolitan Area Planning Commission, later shortened to Northeastern Illinois Planning Commission, as the firt state body to promote regional planning in the Chicago area. In the city of Chicago the Chicago Central Area Committee was formed to improve the Loop.

Many of the documents of these quasi-official and official bodies pertain more to other subjects than to planning and have been listed elsewhere in this bibliography. Listed below are the principal documents, histories and analyses of planning in Chicago that relate directly to planning the city of Chicago. Many critical studies on planning were published in newspapers or magazines. Condit's two volumes, *Chicago 1910-1929* and *1930-1970* (A25, 26), Field's thesis (D32), and the periodical indexes cited above in the introduction are the best guides to this literature.

In general, see also these chapters: F, Transportation (air, mass transit, automobiles); G, Government (health and sanitation, park district); and H, Economics (real estate).

Documents

D1 Bennett, Edward H. *The Axis of Chicago.* Chicago, 1929.

Bennett, the co-author of the 1909 Plan, presented an anlysis of the various proposals for a super highway running west.

D2 Burnham, Daniel H. and Edward H. Bennett. *Plan of Chicago*. Edited by Charles Moore. Chicago, 1909.

The first comprehensive plan for a city of more than a million population in the western world. The Plan of 1909 is the fundamental document for urban planning in Chicago.

D3 Chicago. Department of City Planning. *Basic Policies for the Comprehensive Plan of Chicago*. Chicago, 1964.

This was designed to stimulate widespread public debate by outlining some major considerations in a sort of interim document.

D4 __________. *Basic Policies for the Comprehensive Plan of Chicago. A Summary for Citizen Review*. Chicago, 1965.

D5 __________. *Development Plan for the Central Area of Chicago: A Definitive Text for Use with Graphic Presentation*. Chicago, 1958.

The first major document of the newly created Department of City Planning. It dealt with the core of the city, arguing that the core had been the area that made Chicago vital in the past.

D6 Chicago. Department of Development and Planning.
Far North Development Area. Chicago, 1968.
Far Northwest Development Area. Chicago, 1968.
Far South Development Area. Chicago, 1968.
Far Southeast Development Area. Chicago, 1968.
Far Southwest Development Area. Chicago, 1968.
Far West Development Area. Chicago, 1968.
Illinois Central Air Rights Development. Chicago, 1968.
Mid-South Development Area. Chicago, 1968.
Mid-West Development Area. Chicago, 1967.
Near South Development Area. Chicago, 1967.
Near West Development Area. Chicago, 1967.
North Development Area. Chicago, 1967.
Northwest Development Area. Chicago, 1968.
O'Hare Development Area. Chicago, 1968.
Southeast Development Area. Chicago, 1968.
Southwest Development Area. Chicago, 1968.

A series of area plans designed to work out the implications of the 1966 Comprehensive Plan.

D7 __________. *The Comprehensive Plan of Chicago*. Chicago, 1966

This was the central document that the Department of Development and Planning had worked towards since 1957. It was a major restatement of Chicago's goal to replace the Burnham Plan.

D8 Chicago. Department of Development and Planning. *The Comprehensive Plan of Chicago: Summary Report*. Chicago, 1967.

D9 __________. *Joint Capital Improvements Program for Chicago*. Chicago, 1954- .

Reports for other years have been issued by the Engineering Board of Review, the Capital Improvements Program Division, Department of City Planning, and later by the Department of Development and Planning. The city is required to report on how its public works projects relate to the plan. Issued annually.

D10 __________. *The Lakefront Plan of Chicago*. Chicago, 1972.

D11 __________. *The Riveredge Plan of Chicago*. Chicago, 1974.

D12 Chicago. Plan Commission. *Building New Neighborhoods: Subdivision Design and Standards*. Chicago, 1943.

D13 __________. *Chicago's Greatest Issue: An Official Plan*. Chicago, 1911.

The first crucial vote by the citizens of Chicago on issues raised by the Plan of 1909 came over bonds to widen 12th Street. The Plan Commission distributed over 175,000 copies of this summary of the Plan to prepare for the election.

D14 Deleted

D15 __________. *Master Plan of Residential Land Use of Chicago*. Chicago, 1943.

In four parts: 1. framework of non-residential uses; 2. the residential pattern of Chicago; 3. types of planning areas and their treatment; 4. pattern of residential Chicago in 1965.

D16 __________. *The Outer Drive Along the Lake Front, Chicago*. Chicago, 1929.

An interesting text with documents.

D17 Chicago. Zoning Commission. *[Base Use Map of Chicago]*. [Chicago, 1923].

A fundamental document.

D18 Moody, Walter D. *Wacker's Manual of the Plan of Chicago: Municipal Economy*. Chicago, 1911.

Written for distribution in the public schools. It and later revisions were read by hundreds of thousands of children and their parents.

D19 Moody, Walter D. *What of the City?* Chicago, 1919.

Moody was the chief publicist for the Chicago Plan Commission. This was an important publication by him towards the end of his tenure. It contains material not found elsewhere.

D20 Northeastern Illinois Planning Commission. *The Comprehensive Plan for the Development of the Northeastern Illinois Counties Area*. Chicago, 1968.

D21 Putnam, Rufus W. *Harbor Plan of Chicago*. Chicago, 1927.

One of the last publications of the propaganda wave of the 1909 Plan.

D22 Skidmore, Owings & Merrill for the Chicago Area Committee. *Chicago 21, a Plan for the Central Area Communities, September 1973*. Chicago, 1973.

This plan was paid for by Loop businessmen.

History and Analysis

See also: A23, 25, 26, 31, 49: E48, 49; L32; V37

D23 Akeley, Roger P. "Implementing the 1909 Plan of Chicago: An Historical Account of Planning Salesmanship." U.T. unpub. M.S. thesis, 1973.

Akeley's is a long thesis, well researched and organized. He argues that the Burnham Plan was one of the best implemented plans in the United States and that this was due to the techniques of Charles Wacker and Walter Moody. Good, long bibliography and an appendix of bond issues.

D24 Bach, Ira J. "A Reconsideration of the 1909 'Plan of Chicago'." *CH*, n.s., II, 3 (Spring-Summer 1973), 132-141.

A good summary of the Plan.

D25 Baron, Harold M., ed. *The Racial Aspects of Urban Planning: Critique of the Comprehensive Plan of the City of Chicago*. Chicago, 1968.

An important group of critical articles on the 1966 Comprehensive Plan.

D26 Baum, Alvin, Jr. "Chicago and the City Beautiful: 1890-1910." Ha.U. unpub. Honors thesis, 1952.

D27 Deleted

D28 Burnham, Daniel H. and Robert Kingery. *Planning the Region of Chicago*. Chicago, 1956.

There is a short overview of planning in Chicago followed by descriptions of the geography, demography, transportation, etc. of the area in relation to planning.

D29 Chicago. Department of City Planning. *The Chicago Plan Commission. A Historical Sketch: 1909-1960*. Chicago, 1961.

A clear, short narrative of the publications and public bodies that grew out of the Plan of 1909. It is useful for finding important publications that are listed in other parts of this bibliography.

D30 Costonis, John J. "The Chicago Plan: Incentive Zoning and the Presentation of Urban Landmarks." *Harvard Law R.*, LXXXV, 3 (Jan. 1972), 574-634.

D31 __________. *Space Adrift: Saving Urban Landmarks Through the Chicago Plan*. Urbana, [1974].

Costonis' proposal is to transfer the unused development rights of landmark buildings to another developer to obtain what is in effect a zoning variance. Many Chicago references; good, long bibliography.

D32 Field, Cynthia. "The City Planning of D. H. Burnham." Col.U. unpub. Ph.D. thesis, 1974.

A long, careful analysis of Burnham's work in planning. She studies the 1893 Fair, his work on Washington's McMillan Commission Plan, the Group Plan for Cleveland, the Plan for West Point and his plan for Manila, to show the development of certain of his key ideas. These came together in the Plan of Chicago. In all of these plans Burnham worked from 19th century values which gave no new ideas for the solution of 20th century problems.

D33 Flint, Barbara J. "Zoning and Residential Segregation: A Social and Physical History, 1910-40." U.C. unpub. Ph.D. thesis, 1977.

A comparative study of St. Louis, Atlanta and Chicago.

D34 Glaab, Charles Nelson and A. Theodore Brown. *A History of Urban America*. New York, [1967].

Sets the Burnham Plan in the context of the City Beautiful movement.

D35 Hays, James F. "Chicago Zoning Administration and the City Council." U.C. unpub. M.A. thesis, 1955.

A useful collection of history, ordinances, statistics, reports and law cases.

D36 Hillman, Arthur and Robert J. Casey. *Tomorrow's Chicago*. Chicago, 1953.

A popular but reasoned look at the past history of planning in Chicago and a call to plan and organize the city for the future. Hillman and Casey hoped to do for the 1960s what Wacker and Moody had done for an earlier time.

D37 Jacobs, Jane. *The Death and Life of Great American Cities*. New York, 1961.

Another national study but one hostile to the Burnham Plan.

D38 *Journal of the American Institute of Planners*. XXXIII, 5 (Sept. 1967), 353-359.

A series of critiques of the new plan.

D39 King, Andrew Jay. "Law and Land Use in Chicago: A Prehistory of Modern Zoning." U.W. unpub. Ph.D. thesis, 1976.

The 19th century assumed that the market would provide for the best use of land. ". . . urbanization in the United States profoundly affected society's perception of land in cities." As perceptions changed, society sought to regulate land use. The changes that led up to zoning are the focus of this study.

D40 McCarthy, Michael P. "Chicago Businessmen and the Burnham Plan." *JISHS*, LXIII, 3 (Autumn 1970), 228-256.

An account of the role of the Chicago business community in urging Burnham to write the plan and in overcoming opposition to it.

D41 Miller, John J. B. *Open Land in Metropolitan Chicago*. Chicago, 1962.

A publication of the Open Land Association which was formed in 1959 to acquire undeveloped land for public use. This was their first publication and it described the situation at that time.

D42 Neufeld, Maurice Frank. "The Contributions of the World's Columbian Exposition to the Idea of a Planned Society in the United States." U.W. unpub. Ph.D. thesis, 1935.
See his article in *JISHS*, **XXVII**, 1 (Ap. 1934), 71-93, "The White City: The Beginnings of a Planned Civilization in America." It is somewhat dated but is still sound in many aspects.

D43 Pattison, William D. "Cemeteries of Chicago: A Phase of Land Utilization." *Assoc. of Am. Geographers*, XLV, 3 (Sept. 1955), 245-257.

D44 __________. "Land for the Dead of Chicago." U.C. unpub. M.A. thesis, 1952.

D45 Peterson, Jon A. "The Origins of the Comprehensive City Planning Ideal in the United States - 1840-1911." Ha.U. unpub. Ph.D. thesis, 1967.

D46 Platt, Rutherford H. *Open Land in Urban Illinois: Roles of the Citizen Advocate*. DeKalb, Ill., 1971.

Primarily a "how to" book but there is some material on planning for open space in Chicago.

D47 Schroeder, Douglas. *The Issue of the Lakefront: An Historical Critical Survey*. Chicago, 1963.

D48 Scott, Mellier G. *American City Planning Since 1890*. Berkeley, 1969.

The single best volume on the subject. There is much material on early Chicago planning. Good bibliography.

D49 Walker, Robert Averill. *The Planning Function in Urban Government*. 2nd ed. Chicago, 1950.

There is a long important chapter on the Plan of 1909 and its aftermath.

D50 Wille, Lois. *Forever Open, Clear and Free: The Historic Struggle for Chicago's Lakefront*. Chicago, 1972.

A popular account of the effort to maintain the lakefront in Chicago.

D51 Wisdom, Lloyd Charles. "Community Planning as an Outgrowth of the Park Movement: Frederick Law Olmsted and Urban Design." U.W. unpub. M.A. thesis, 1971.

E
ARCHITECTURE

There is a great deal more literature on Chicago's architectural history than is found in this list. Only the most useful items have been cited. Most general histories have passages on architecture; in particular see Condit (A25, 26), Mayer and Wade (A49), Cutler (A28), and the Department of Public Work's *Chicago* (A21a).

General

See also: A31; Q1, 8, 9; W, Columbian Exposition Architecture

E1 Andrews, Wayne. *Architecture in Chicago and Mid-America: A Photographic History*. New York, 1968.

Essay and photographs.

E2 *Architectural Review*. "Chicago." CLXII, 968 (Oct. 1977).

An entire issue treating the city's architecture.

E3 "Architecture." *Chicago*, II, 2 (Spring 1965), 22-73.

Most of the issue was given over to contemporary Chicago architecture.

E4 Burchard, John and Albert Bush-Brown. *The Architecture of America: A Social and Cultural History*. Boston, 1961.

The fame of the Chicago School disappeared for a time after WWI. Pevsner, Mumford, the MOMA show, and Giedion gave it renewed scholarly recognition. These works help to see the School in context, as do the works of Collins, Hitchcock, and this book by Burchard and Bush-Brown.

E5 Cohen, Stuart E. *Chicago Architects: Documenting the Exhibition of the Same Name Organized by Laurence Booth, Stuart E. Cohen, Stanley Tigerman, and Benjamin Weese*. Chicago, 1976.

An important revisionist publication. The exhibition presented ". . . work by Chicago architects which is mostly unknown today because it represents a diversity of formal, spatial, symbolic, and technological ideas which cannot be discussed as the work of a school." The premise of the show is that histories of architecture have been written to validate theories of a "Chicago skyscraper" and the "Prairie School." As a result, ". . . that which fits neither the theory nor the historical narrative will be discarded."

E6 Drury, John. *Old Chicago Houses*. Chicago, 1941.

Less an architectural study than it is one of the people who were famous or lived in famous houses in Chicago. There are, however, many details not found elsewhere.

E7 Giedion, Sigfried. *Space, Time and Architecture*. 3rd ed. Cambridge, 1954 (1st ed., 1941).

A sweeping study of architecture in the west from the 17th century which helped revive respect for Chicago architecture. See E4.

E8 Grube, Oswald, Peter Pran and Franz Schulze. *One Hundred Years of Architecture in Chicago*. Chicago, 1976.

An exhibition catalog with a great many details about the buildings listed.

E9 Historic American Buildings Survey. *Historic American Buildings Survey: Chicago and Nearby Illinois Areas; List of Measured Drawings, Photographs, and Written Documentation in the Survey, 1966*. Compiled by J. William Rudd. Park Forest, Ill., 1966.

E10 __________. *Northern Illinois 1716-1872. Comprising a Series of Fifty Plates of Measured Drawings of Pioneer Architecture in Northern Illinois, Selected as Characteristic of Those Made by a Group of Architects and Draftsmen in Chicago from January to May 1934*. 3 vol. [Chicago], 1934.

Photographs and drawings, some of which are Chicago-related.

E11 Hitchcock, Henry Russell. *Architecture: Nineteenth and Twentieth Centuries*. Baltimore, 1958.

A classic study which presents a balanced review of the Chicago School in an American context.

E12 Jones, John H. and Fred A. Britten, ed. *A Half Century of Chicago Building: A Practical Reference Guide*. Chicago, 1910.

Still a good survey, arranged by types of buildings, problems, etc. Illustrations of buildings, some interiors and a few of building techniques. Detailed section on building codes.

E13 Koeper, Frederick. *Illinois Architecture from Territorial Times to the Present: A Selective Guide*. Chicago, 1968.

A good, general survey.

E14 Leonard, H. Stewart. "The History of Architecture in Chicago." U. C. unpub. M.A. thesis, 1934.

The most useful feature of this paper is the appendix of biographical sketches which give a partial annotated list of the work of Van Osdel, Boyington, Burling, Carter and Adler.

E15 Mumford, Lewis. *The Brown Decades: A Study of the Arts in America, 1865-1895*. New York, 1931.

See E4.

E16 Museum of Modern Art. *Early Modern Architecture: Chicago, 1870-1910*. 2nd ed. New York, 1940.

See E4.

E17 Orear, George W. *Commercial and Architectural Chicago*. Chicago, 1887.

E18 Pevsner, Nikolaus. *Pioneers of Modern Design from William Morris to Walter Gropius*. Baltimore, 1960 (c1936).

See E4.

E19 Randall, Frank Alfred. *History of the Development of Building Construction in Chicago*. New York, 1972 (c1949).

The most important reference work on Chicago building between North Avenue and 12th Street and the River to the Lake, up to 1946. There is an introductory essay, a detailed list of milestones in building construction to 1931 arranged by year of construction, an annotated presentation of part of Rand McNally's 1898 *View of Chicago*, and indexes to architects and engineers, buildings, and locations. A very detailed bibliography is supplied in each building description.

E20 "Special Issue - Chicago Architecture." *Inland Arch.*, n.s., XIII, 6 (June 1969).
A review of many aspects, past and present.

E21 Tallmadge, Thomas. *Architecture in Old Chicago*. Chicago, 1964 (c1941).
This is part of a larger manuscript that Tallmadge was at work on when he was killed. It is still the best account of pre-Fire architecture and his good sense and balance repay reading the later sections.

Periodicals

Chicago architects wrote about their work and the work of their contemporaries. The leading journals reported most major buildings. These and rich collections of scholarly articles will be found in the following journals:

E22 *Architectural Forum.*
E23 *Architectural Record.*
E24 *Architectural Review.*
E25 *Inland Architect.* On which, see: Robert Vincent Prestiano, "The Inland Architect: A Study of the Contents, Influence, and Significance of Chicago's Major Late Nineteenth-Century Architectural Periodical," N.U. unpub. Ph.D. thesis, 1973. This long study of the journal found that its approach was basically conservative, e.g., in not paying much notice to Wright; but it did provide an open forum for discussion which was much used by architects in the area.
E26 *Journal of the Society of Architectural Historians.*
E27 *The Prairie School Review.* Devoted to the study of the Prairie School.

Major Schools

Three major architectural schools have developed in Chicago: the Chicago School of commerical building; the Prairie School; and the Second Chicago School, led by Mies van der Rohe. For a good discussion of the terms, see: H. Allen Brooks, "'Chicago School': Metamorphosis of a Term," *JSAH,* XXV, 2 (May 1966), 115-118.

(Chicago School)

E28 "The Chicago School of Architecture: A Symposium." *The Prairie School R.,* IX, 1 and 2 (1972).

Winston Wiseman argued that ". . . we are being led to believe, erroneously I think, that Chicago was the birthplace of the skyscraper, the skeleton frame, and indeed of modern architecture. These are bold and great claims which, I hold, cannot be substantiated. They are exaggerated, half-truths which, when accepted uncritically, distort history." Carl Condit argued for the Chicago School. Comment was offered from Sir John Summerson, Henry-Russell Hitchcock, and H. Allen Brooks.

E29 Condit, Carl W. "The Chicago School and the Modern Movement in Architecture." *Art in Am.,* XXXVI, 1 (Jan. 1948), 19-36.

E30 __________. *The Chicago School of Architecture: A History of Commercial and Public Building in the Chicago Area, 1875-1925.* Revised and enlarged from *The Rise of the Skyscraper.* Chicago, 1964.
Carl Condit is the most visible proponent of the "Chicago School," and this is the longest statement of his argument. It is important to note that Condit is a student of technology. This point of view pervades his argument about all aspects of the change from load bearing walls to steel frame construction. See also his two volume study of Chicago (A25, 26).

E31 Jordy, William H. "The Commercial and the 'Chicago School'." *Perspectives in Am. H.*, I (1967), 390-400.

E32 Miller, Hugh C. *The Chicago School of Architecture: A Plan for Preserving a Significant Remnant of America's Architectural Heritage.* Washington, D.C., 1973.

A good short study of the Chicago School based on existing buildings.

(Prairie School)

E33 Brooks, H. Allen. *The Prairie School: Frank Lloyd Wright and His Midwest Contemporaries.* Toronto, 1972.

A well researched, ably illustrated synthesis of the entire School. A standard work, but one that assumes some prior knowledge. He argues that the link between the Chicago School and the Prairie School was through Sullivan and that the Prairie School ". . . devised a mode universally applicable to every building type."

E34 __________. "Steinway Hall. Architects and Dreams." *JSAH*, XXII, 3 (Oct. 1963), 171-175.

A study of the early years of some of the important members of the School.

E35 Peisch, Mark L. *The Chicago School of Architecture: Early Followers of Sullivan and Wright.* New York, 1964.

Really his 1959 Columbia Ph.D. thesis. This is a study of Walter Burley Griffin and others in the Prairie School. It is included because of its material on lesser figures, but beware of errors of fact. *Cf.*, review *JSAH*, XXV, 3 (Oct. 1966), 225-226.

E36 *Prairie School Architecture: Studies from "The Western Architect."* Edited with an introduction by H. Allen Brooks. Toronto, 1975.

Reprints a series of important early articles.

E37 Scully, Vincent J. *The Shingle Style: Architectural Theory and Design from Richardson to the Origins of Wright.* New Haven, 1955.

(Second Chicago School)

There is very little on the School as a school; much more on the individual members.

E38 Chermayeff, Serge. "L'Architecture au Bauhaus de Chicago." *L'Architecture d'Aujourd'hui*, 28 (Feb. 1950), 50-68.

E39 Darnall, Margaretta Jean. "From the Chicago Fair to Walter Gropius: Changing Ideals in American Architecture." C.U. unpub. Ph.D. thesis, 1975.

A study in architectural values with many examples drawn from Chicago.

E40 Newman, Roslyn. "The Development of the Department of Architecture Begun at the Bauhaus and Its Continuation in the Illinois Institute of Technology." N.U. unpub. M.A. thesis, 1971.

The only introduction to the topic. A short narrative and an analysis of the three major figures.

E41 Schulze, Franz. "The New Chicago Architecture." *Art in Am.*, LVI, 3 (May-June 1968), 60-71.

An excellent introduction in a short pictorial format.

E42 Wingler, Hans Maria. *The Bauhaus: Weimar, Dessau, Berlin, Chicago*. Translated by Wolfgang Jabs and Basil Gilbert. Edited by Joseph Stein. Cambridge, 1969.

A collection of photographs and excerpts from source material.

Biography - Individuals and Firms

The literature on architects and their firms is large. The following are only a sample, especially on major figures such as Mies, Sullivan and Wright. Some important figures, such as Van Osdel, have no biography. See also, below, Skyscrapers and Individual Works.

(Adler, Dankmar)

E43 Elstein, Rochelle S. "The Architectural Style of Dankmar Adler." U.C. unpub. M.A. thesis, 1963.

She rejects the argument that Adler had no real architectural style. Her analysis is rooted in a study of his buildings rather than in the written accounts of his work. She publishes a new list of his work with 43 photographs. More accessible but shorter is her article, "The Architecture of Dankmar Adler," *JSAH,* XXVI, 4 (Dec. 1967), 242-249.

(Adler, David)

E44 Pratt, Richard. *David Adler*. New York, 1970.

An essay with photographs and captions about one of Chicago's important eclectic architects.

(Bock, Richard)

E45 Hallmark, Donald Parker. "Richard W. Bock: Sculptor for Frank Lloyd Wright and the Architects of the Chicago School." U.Iowa unpub. M.A. thesis, 1970.

The best work on Bock. The second volume is wholly photographs.

(Boyington, William)

E46 Sloan, Tom L. B. "The Architecture of William W. Boyington." N.U. unpub. M.A. thesis, 1962.

A chronological account with lists of buildings.

(Burnham, Daniel)

See also: D2, 13, 23, 24, 34, 40;

E47 Hines, Thomas S. *Burnham of Chicago: Architect and Planner.* New York, 1974.

Sees Burnham in many ways as representative of Republican Progressivism, and the imperialist movement in this country. Thus, "Burnham was alternately archaic and progressive." He argues that Burnham's influence was horizontal, i.e., widespread at the time, as contrasted to Sullivan's, which was vertical and affected architects only in future years.

E48 Moore, Charles H. *Daniel Hudson Burnham, Architect, Planner of Cities.* 2 vol. Boston, 1921.

Moore was a close friend of Burnham, and the book reflects this bias, but he was also able to supply much primary materia

(Burnham and Root)

E49 Rebori, A. N. "The Work of Burnham and Root." *Arch. Rec.*, XXXVIII, 1 (July 1915), 33-168.

Details, plans, photographs. Cf., Elstein (E43), Nickel (E89) and Hoffman (E78).

E50 Wade, Louise Carroll. "Burnham and Root's Stockyards Connection." *CH*, n.s., IV, 3 (Fall 1975), 139-147.

The story of how John B. Sherman helped Burnham and Root become well-known to the packers. The origins of many buildings projects are thus explained.

(Byrne, Barry)

E51 Chappell, Sally Anderson. "Barry Byrne: Architecture and Writings." N.U. unpub. Ph.D. thesis, 1968.

A study of the work of one of Wright's important students.

(Cobb, Henry)

E52 Lewis, Julius. "Henry Ives Cobb and the Chicago School." U.C. unpub. Ph.D. thesis, 1954.

Argues that Cobb has not been described as fully as he should have been. Cobb, he maintains, was original but original within an eclectic context that never broke "with the grammar of historical reference." Cobb was very popular and to understand him is to give an added dimension to the understanding of the Chicago School.

(Ericsson, Henry)

E53 Ericsson, Henry. *Sixty Years a Builder: The Autobiography of Henry Ericsson*. Chicago, 1942.

Autobiography by a man who participated in the heyday of Chicago building.

(Graham, Anderson, Probst and White)

E54 *The Architectural Work of Graham, Anderson, Probst and White, Chicago and Their Predecessors D. H. Burnham & Co. and Graham, Burnham & Co.* 2 vol. London, 1933.

E55 *Graham, Anderson, Probst, White*. Chicago, [1976?].

Photographs and a list of recent works.

(Griffin, Walter)

E56 Birrell, James. *Walter Burley Griffin*. Brisbane, 1964.

Only about one-third of the book is devoted to Chicago.

(Jenny, William LeBaron)

E57 Bannister, Turpin C. "Bogardus Revisited." *JSAH*, XV, 4 (Dec. 1956), 12-22; XVI, 1 (Mar. 1957), 11-19.

The last half of this very well-documented article discusses the possible sources that inspired Jenney to use the steel frame.

E58 Turak, Theodore. "Jenney's Lesser Works: Prelude to the Prairie Style?" *The Prairie School R.*, VII, 3 (3rd Q. 1970), 5-20.

Another side of Jenney's work. See his other articles in this journal.

E59 __________. "William LeBaron Jenney: A Nineteenth Century Architect." U.Mich. unpub. Ph.D. thesis, 1966.

Argues that Jenney was well trained as an engineer *and* as an architect. He was schooled to the notion that the structural dynamics of a building be expressed. Thus, Jenney designed buildings from need, from the best technical knowledge of the day, and from that came his aesthetic. Jenney's writings and teachings also show that he was a master architect as well as a master engineer. See also his article in *JSAH*, XXIX, 1 (March 1970), 40-47.

(Jensen, Jens)

E60 Collier, Malcolm. "Jens Jensen and Columbus Park." *CH*, n.s., IV, 4 (Winter 1975-1976), 225-234.

An overview of his work in Chicago.

E61 Eaton, Leonard K. "Jens Jensen and the Chicago School." *Progressive Arch.*, XLI (Dec. 1960), 144-150.

Argues the case that ". . . Jensen stood for most of the same qualities in landscape architecture that Sullivan and Wright represented in the building art . . ."

E62 __________. *Landscape Artist in America: The Life and Work of Jens Jensen*. Chicago, 1964.

Jensen created Chicago's West Park System among other important work in the area. Essays introduce each section of this photographic essay which records his extant work and some that has been destroyed. Good bibliography.

(Mies van der Rohe, Ludwig)

E63 Blake, Peter. *Mies van der Rohe: Architecture and Structure*. Baltimore, 1964.

E64 Blaser, Werner. *Mies van der Rohe: The Art of Structure*. New York, 1965.

E65 Carter, Peter. *Mies van der Rohe at Work*. New York, 1974.

An analysis of many of his major works. The pictures, plans, specifications and list of works make the book valuable.

E66 Drexler, Arthur. *Ludwig Mies van der Rohe*. New York, 1960.

A short essay, photographs, list of works, good bibliography.

E67 Hilberseimer, Ludwig. *Mies van der Rohe*. Chicago, 1956.

A photographic essay.

E68 Johnson, Philip C. *Mies van der Rohe*. New York, 1947.

E69 "The Legacy of Mies van der Rohe." *Inland Arch.*, XIV, 7 (Aug. 1970), 10 *passim*.

Discusses his firm as well as Mies in a series of articles.

E70 Pawley, Martin. *Mies van der Rohe*. New York, 1970.

Essay, photographs, history of buildings; includes a useful bibliography.

(Nimmons, Carr and Wright)

E71 Stanford, L. O. "American Modernistic Civic Architecture 1917-33: A Case for a Twenties Style." U.N.C. unpub. Ph.D. thesis, 1976.

She uses five national firms, one of which is Nimmons, Carr and Wright of Chicago, to describe a style that, while new, was not radical and that symbolized the American economy.

(Olmsted, Frederick)

See also: D51

E72 Olmsted, Frederick Law. *The Papers of Frederick Law Olmsted*. Edited by Charles C. McLaughlin and Charles E. Beveridge. I- . Baltimore, 1977- .

E73 Ranney, Victoria Post. *Olmsted in Chicago*. Chicago, 1972.

A good, short essay with many photographs and some plans.

E74 Roper, Laura. *FLO: A Life of Frederick Law Olmsted*. Baltimore, 1973.

The standard life.

(Purcell and Elmslie)

E75 Gebhard, David S. "William Gray Purcell and George Grant Elmslie and the Early Progressive Movement in American Architecture from 1900 to 1920." U.M. unpub. Ph.D. thesis, 1959.

An important study of two men of the second rank. See also his "Louis Sullivan and George Grant Elmslie," *JSAH*, XIX, 2 (May 1960), 62-68.

E76 Walker Art Center. *Purcell and Elmslie, Architects, 1910-1922*. Minneapolis, 1953.

Very short catalog with photographs and a list of buildings.

(Richardson, Henry)

E77 Hitchcock, Henry Russell. *The Architecture of H. H. Richardson and His Times*. 1st ed 1936. New York, 1975.

Not a Chicago architect, but his Glessner House and much more importantly, the Marshall Field Wholesale Store, brought masonry architecture to its highest point in Chicago. Hitchcock's book is good, but the arrangement of the new material is a bad one. Bibliography.

(Root, John Welborn)

E78 Hoffmann, Donald. *The Architecture of John Welborn Root*. Baltimore, [1973].

Well researched and illustrated. Hoffman argues that Root understood the economics of his day - intense concentration and corporate organization - and that his expression of this understanding in architecture made him the principal figure of the Chicago School. Bibliography.

E79 Monroe, Harriet. *John Welborn Root, Architect . . .* Chicago, 1898.

A long life by Root's sister-in-law.

E80 Root, John Wellborn. *The Meanings of Architecture: Buildings and Writings by John Wellborn Root*. Edited by Donald Hoffman. New York, [1967].

(Skidmore, Owings and Merrill)

See also: D22

E81 *Architecture of Skidmore, Owings and Merrill, 1950-1962*. Text by Ernst Danz. Introduction by Henry Russell Hitchcock. Translated by Ernst van Haagen. New York, 1963 (c1962).

E82 Woodward, Christopher. *Skidmore, Owings and Merrill.* New York, [1970].

Photographs, notes, essay. A few Chicago buildings.

(Sullivan, Louis)

E83 Andrew, David S. "Louis Sullivan and the Problem of Meaning in Architecture." Wash.U. unpub. Ph.D. thesis, 1977.

"The thesis argues against the validity of the organic analogy and tries to show that Sullivan asked his buildings to bear a crushing weight of extra-architectural significance. Instead of treating architecture as the palpable and iconic expression of the ideals and convictions of the various institutional bodies of society, Sullivan looked upon building largely from the point of view of a private, socially unintegrated individual. His highly personal ornamental style is a result of this viewpoint . . ."

E84 Bush-Brown, Albert. *Louis Sullivan.* New York, 1960.

A good, short life, but Morrison's book is still the best.

E85 Connely, Willard. *Louis Sullivan as He Lived.* New York, 1960.

An effort to fill in the personal side of Sullivan's life. Study and preparation seem to have gone into the work, but there is no documentation. No illustrations. Bibliography.

E86 Crook, David H. "Louis Sullivan, the World's Columbian Exposition and American Life." Ha.U. unpub. Ph.D. thesis, 1964.

An important study, particularly in light of Sullivan's later remarks on the Fair. See also his "Louis Sullivan and the Golden Doorway," *JSAH,* XXVI, 4 (Dec. 1967), 250-258.

E87 Hope, H. R. "Louis Sullivan's Architectural Ornament." *Mag. of Art,* XL, 3 (Mar. 1947), 111-117.

Seeks to redress the emphasis on the elements of modernity in Sullivan's work and show that he held ornament as a highly important function.

E88 Morrison, Hugh. *Louis Sullivan: Prophet of Modern Architecture.* New York, 1935.

The standard account. Includes a bibliography of the writings of Dankmar Adler and Louis Sullivan. The bibliography is updated in later printings and in *Louis Sullivan and the Architecture of Free Enterprise,* a catalog of an Art Institute of Chicago show.

E89 Nickel, Richard. "A Photographic Documentation of the Architecture of Adler and Sullivan." I.I.T. unpub. M.A. thesis, 1957.

The work of a gifted photographer and Sullivan student who gave his life to preserve architectural fragments. On Nickel see: Norman Mark, "On the Adler and Sullivan Trail with the Tireless Richard Nickel," *Inland Arch.*, XIII, 6 (June 1969), 44-49.

E90 Paul, Sherman. *Louis Sullivan, an Architect in American Thought*. Englewood Cliffs, 1962.

An analysis of Sullivan's ideas, the influences on them, and his influence.

E91 Sprague, Paul. "Architectural Ornament of Louis Sullivan and His Chief Draftsmen." 2 vol. P.U. unpub. Ph.D. thesis, 1969.

A careful analysis of Sullivan's ornament which he believed was necessary for a building to achieve its full artistic expression. The origin of his ornament and the influence of the chief draftsmen - Wright, Elmslie and Parker Berry - on Sullivan's work, are examined.

E92 Sullivan, Louis. *The Autobiography of an Idea*. New York, 1924.

E93 __________. *The Testament of Stone: Themes of Idealism and Indignation from the Writings of Louis Sullivan.* Edited by Maurice English. Evanston, 1963.

Essays in this work were ". . . selected to illustrate, not Sullivan the architect . . . but Sullivan as Jeremiah . . . Architecture . . . as an index and expression of social health or disease."

E94 Szarkowski, John. *The Idea of Louis Sullivan*. Minneapolis, 1956.

An essay and many photographs.

E95 Wright, Frank Lloyd. *Genius and the Mobocracy*. New York, 1949.

As interesting for what it says about Wright as it is for what it says about Sullivan.

(Weissenborn, Leo)

E96 Weissenborn, Leo Julius. *Backlog of Happenstances.* New York, 1955.

Autobiography of a Chicago architect.

(Wright, Frank L.)

E97 Chicago. Art Institute. Burnham Library of Architecture. *Buildings by Frank Lloyd Wright in Seven Middle Western States, 1887-1959.* Chicago, 1963.

An easy-to-use checklist.

E98 Farr, Finis. *Frank Lloyd Wright.* New York, 1961.

A standard popular account.

E99 Hitchcock, Henry Russell. *In the Nature of Materials: 1887-1941. The Buildings of Frank Lloyd Wright.* New foreword and bibliography. New York, 1973 (c1942).

E100 Manson, Grant C. *Frank Lloyd Wright.* New York, 1958.

Possibly the best life, but only the first volume was published.

E101 Scully, Vincent, Jr. *Frank Lloyd Wright.* New York, 1960.

A good selection of photographs and a very perceptive essay lay out the architectural influences on Wright.

E102 Smith, Norriss Kelly. *Frank Lloyd Wright: A Study in Architectural Content.* Englewood Cliffs, 1966.

E103 Starosciak, Kenneth and Jane. *Frank Lloyd Wright, a Bibliography.* New Brighton, Minn., 1973.

E104 Storrer, William Allin. *The Architecture of Frank Lloyd Wright, a Complete Catalog.* Cambridge, 1974.

Photographs and captions.

E105 Twombly, Robert C. *Frank Lloyd Wright: An Interpretive Biography.* New York, [1973].

A good, general biography with the most useful bibliography.

E106 Wright, Frank Lloyd. *An Autobiography.* New York, 1932.

E107 Wright, Frank Lloyd. *The Buildings, Plans and Designs of Frank Lloyd Wright*. 1st ed., 1910. New York, 1963.

E108 __________. *A Testament*. New York, 1957.

Skyscrapers

E109 Christison, Muriel B. "How Buffington Staked His Claim." *Art Bull.*, XXVI, 1 (Mar. 1944), 13-24.

Leroy Buffington claimed priority for his writings on the iron frame. His claims were exploded in these articles: Hugh Morrison, "Buffington and the Skyscraper," *Art Bull.*, XXVI, 1 (Mar. 1944), 1-2; Dimitris Tselos, "The Enigma of Buffington's Skyscraper," *Art Bull.*, XXVI, 2 (Mar. 1944), 3-12; E. M. Upjohn, "Buffington and the Skyscraper," *Art Bull.*, XVII, 1 (Mar. 1935), 48-70.

E110 Condit, Carl W. "Sullivan's Skyscrapers as the Expression of Nineteenth Century Technology." *Technology and Culture*, I, 2 (Winter 1959), 78-93.

Condit's viewpoint as a student of technology is clear in this article. He concludes that, "In the last analysis Sullivan's civic architecture is a celebration of technique, as is most contemporary architecture . . ."

E111 Jenney, William LeBaron. "The Chicago Construction, or Tall Buildings on a Compressible Soil." *Inland Arch.*, XVIII, 4 (Nov. 1891), 41.

A clear, illustrated explanation.

E112 Morrison, Elizabeth Newman. "The Development of Skyscraper Style 1874-1922." U.C. unpub. M.A. thesis, 1931.

Two useful items: a list of "important buildings 1874-1922," with a picture of each and an indication of comment in an architectural review; and a long bibliography of articles on this subject.

E113 Mujica, Francisco. *History of the Skyscraper*. New York, 1930.

E114 Newton, Roger Hale. "New Evidence on the Evolution of the Skyscraper." *Art Q.*, IV (Winter 1941), 56-70.

E115 Peck, Ralph B. *History of Building Foundations in Chicago*. Urbana, 1948.

A clear summary.

E116 Rowe, Colin. "Chicago Frame." *The Arch. R.*, CXX, 718 (Nov. 1956), 285-289.

A revisionist article. He argues that the Chicago Frame was the result of a particular need and that it therefore created no archetype. Mies (e.g., the Glass House) created an ideal solution to an abstract problem and did create an archetype.

E117 Shultz, Earle and Walter Simmons. *Offices in the Sky*. Indianpolis, 1959.

A popular history of the skyscraper with much material on Chicago.

E118 **Deleted**

E119 Tallmadge, Thomas E. "Was the Home Insurance Building the First Skyscraper of Skeleton Construction? *Arch. Rec.*, LXXVI, 2 (Aug. 1934), 113-118.

E120 Webster, J. Carson. "The Skyscraper: Logical and Historical Considerations." *JSAH*, XVIII, 4 (Dec. 1959), 126-139.

A clear explanation of what a skyscraper is. He lays out several criteria to define a true skyscraper.

Individual Works

Most major buildings are described and their plans reproduced in one of the major periodicals (E23-27).[1] Randall (E19) lists most secondary references to Chicago buildings before 1948. See also: A1, 21; P64.

E121 Chicago. Commission on Chicago Historical and Architectural Landmarks. See below for a list of pamphlets on individual buildings.

The Commission on Chicago Historical and Architectural Landmarks was established in 1968 by city ordinance, and was given the responsibility of recommending to the City Council that specific landmarks be preserved and protected by law. The Commission makes its recommendations to the City Council only after extensive study. As part of this study, the Commission's staff prepares detailed documentation

---

[1] The Chicago Historical Society has a large collection of ephemeral literature on these and many more buildings.

on each potential landmark. This public information brochure is a synopsis of various research materials compiled as part of the designation procedure. Obviously, the list grows continually.

Astor Street District
Francis J. Dewes House
Jane Addams' Hull House
Monadnock Building
The Rookery
Union Stock Yard Gate
Hutchinson Street District
Samuel M. Nickerson House
Chicago Board of Trade Building
John J. Glessner House
Old Colony Building
Jackson Boulevard District
McCormick Row House District
Old Town Triangle District
Krause Music Store
Chicago Public Library Cultural Center
Fisher Building
Fine Arts Building
The Emil Bach House
860-880 Lake Shore Drive
Manhattan Building
Carson, Pirie, Scott & Co. Building

E122 Chicago Tribune. *The International Competition for a New Administration Building for the Chicago Tribune, MCMXXII.* Chicago, 1923.

A collection of the drawings entered in the contest.

E123 Condit, Carl W. "The Structural System of Adler and Sullivan's Garrick Theater Building." *Technology and Culture,* V, 4 (Winter 1964), 523-540.

"The structural system of the Garrick Theater Building (Chicago) reveals to us the dual role that the building has played in the history of the structural arts. On the one hand, it is a major pioneer work of contemporary architecture . . . the creation of trained engineers as well as an imaginative architect. On the other hand, the very complexity of the structural system reveals the extent to which the engineers relied on the empirical and pragmatic approach that the earlier builder in iron once followed exclusively."

E124 Denson, Wilbur Thurman. "A History of the Chicago Auditorium" U.W. unpub. Ph.D. thesis, 1974.

He argues that the Auditorium was Adler's work, not Sullivan's, and that it was not a financial success.

E125 Duis, Perry R. "'Where is Athens Now?': The Fine Arts Building 1898-1918." *CH,* n.s., VI, 2 (Summer 1977), 66-78.

A physical and social history of the building. The concluding part appears *ibid.,* VII, 1 (Spring 1978), 40-53.

E126 Estate of Marshall Field. *Report of the Committee Appointed by the Marshall Field Estate for the Examination of the*

Structure of the Home Insurance Building. Chicago, 1931.

The estate commissioned a study to investigate claims of priority in the development of skeleton construction before the demolition of the building destroyed the evidence. The report supports the claim advanced for the building.

E127 Frueh, Erne R. and Florence. "Stained Glass Windows at the Second Presbyterian Church." *CH,* n.s., VI, 4 (Winter 1977-1978), 210-217.

E128 Fuller, Ernest. "Famous Chicago Buildings." *Chicago Tribune,* Nov. 29, 1958-May 30, 1959.

A long series on important Chicago buildings.

E129 Glessner, John J. *The House at 1800 Prairie Avenue*. Chicago, 1978.

As much an insight into his personality as a study of the house.

E130 Hoffman, Donald. "John Root's Monadnock Building." *JSAH,* XXVI, 4 (Dec. 1967), 269-278.

A detailed discussion of the formation of the idea for the building.

E131 Lillibridge, Robert M. "Pullman: Town Development in the Era of Eclecticism." *JSAH,* XII, 3 (Oct. 1953), 17-22.

E132 Murphy (C.F.) Associates. *Historical American Building Survey of the Cable Building, 57 East Jackson, Chicago, Illinois, 1899, Holabird & Roche, Architects*. Chicago, 1961.

E133 Roosevelt University. *The Auditorium Building: Its History and Architectural Significance*. Chicago, 1976.

E134 Van Zanten, David T. "Richardson's Glessner House, Chicago 1886-1887." *JSAH,* XXIII, 2 (May 1964), 107-111.

Argues that Glessner House had little impact on architectural style at the time of its construction.

E135 Vinci, John. "The Chicago Stock Exchange Building." *CH,* n.s., III, 1 (Spring-Summer 1974), 23-27.

E136 __________. "Graceland: The Nineteenth Century Garden Cemetery." *CH,* n.s., VI, 2 (Summer 1977), 86-98.

E137 __________. *The Stock Exchange Trading Room*. Chicago, 1977.

E138 Wright, Frank Lloyd. *The Robie House*. Palos Park, Ill., 1968.

Other Studies of Special Topics

See also: A21a, 23; F3, 4; O67, 73, 80, 95, 115; P64; L25

E139 Adrian, Dennis. *Seven Chicago Architects*. Chicago, 1976.

E140 Block, Jean F. *Hyde Park Houses*. Chicago, 1978.

An illustrated guide book to a neighborhood with a significant architectural past.

E141 Brooks, H. Allen. "Chicago Architecture: Its Debt to the Arts and Crafts." *JSAH,* XXX, 4 (Dec. 1971), 312-317.

Although the article centers on Wright, it is one of the few attempts to treat this subject.

E142 Bushnell, George D. "Chicago's Magnificent Movie Palaces." *CH,* n.s., VI, 2 (Summer 1977), 99-106.

A short narrative of the rise and fall of the opulent movie theatres in Chicago's past.

E143 Dull, Elizabeth Helsing. "The Domestic Architecture of Oak Park, Illinois: 1900-1930." N.U. unpub. Ph.D. thesis, 1973.

Most of Chicago's architects designed houses in Oak Park. She studies them all, not just the Prairie School. Many photographs and plans are reproduced.

E144 Eaton, Leonard K. *Two Chicago Architects and Their Clients: Frank Lloyd Wright and Howard Van Doren Shaw*. Cambridge, 1969.

A study of the clients of Wright, the *avant garde*, and Shaw, the traditionalist. It raises the question, who paid for the architecture?

E145 Field, Walker. "A Re-examination into the Invention of the Balloon Frame." *JSAH*, II, 4 (Oct. 1942), 3-29.

A fairly detailed discussion of the forerunners of St. Mary's of Chicago, the erection of the church, and the technique used.

E146 Gayle, Margot. "A Heritage Forgotten: Chicago's First Cast Iron Buildings." *CH,* n.s., VII, 2 (Summer 1978), 98-108.

A survey of the rise and fall of cast iron buildings in Chicago.

E147 Deleted

E148 Kaufmann, Edgar. "Some American Architectural Ornament of the Arts and Crafts Era." *JSAH,* XXIV, 4 (Dec. 1965), 285-291.

E149 Kihlstedt, Folke Tyko. "Formal and Structural Innovations in American Exposition Architecture: 1901-1939." N.U. unpub. Ph.D. thesis, 1973.

Sets the architecture of the 1933 World's Fair in a national and international context.

E150 Lowe, David. "Greek Revival Architecture in Chicago." *CH,* n.s., IV, 3 (Fall 1975), 157-166.

The illustrations are useful for early Chicago architecture, but the essay is inferior to Tallmadge's treatment (E21) of the same subject.

E151 __________. *Lost Chicago.* Boston, 1975.

A photographic essay on buildings in Chicago that have been destroyed or altered out of recognition. The text is much less useful than the photographs.

E152 Meeks, Carroll Louis V. *The Railroad Station: An Architectural History.* New Haven, 1956.

An important study of a type in which Chicago architects played a major role.

E153 Pew, Celia, *et.al. Chicago Women Architects: Contemporary Directions.* Chicago, 1978.

E154 Szuberla, Guy. "Three Chicago Settlements: Their Architectural Form and Social Meaning." *JISHS,* LXX, 2 (May 1977), 114-129.

He argues that settlement house architecture reflected a desire to "Americanize" immigrants. Studies the work of Irving H. Pond, Allen B. Pond, and Dwight Heald Perkins.

E155 Wight, Peter B. "Public School Architecture at Chicago: The Work of Dwight H. Perkins." *Arch. Record,* XXVII, 6 (June 1910), 494-512.

Perkins was briefly in charge of school building in Chicago; his work is some of the best in the city.

Guides to Notable Architecture

E156 Chicago. Art Institute. Burnham Library. *Guide to Chicago and Midwestern Architecture*. Chicago, 1963.

E157 Bach, Ira J. *Chicago on Foot*. 3rd ed. Chicago, 1977.

The best set of architectural walking tours.

E158 Illinois Institute of Technology. Department of Architecture. *Chicago Architecture*. Chicago, n.d.

Available through the Department of Architecture.

E159 Landmarks Preservation Council and Service. *Chicago's Landmark Structures: An Inventory. Central Area . . .* Chicago, 1975.

E160 __________. *Chicago's Landmark Structures: An Inventory. Loop Area*. Chicago, 1974.

E161 Randall, John D. *A Guide to Significant Chicago Architecture of 1872 to 1922*. Glencoe, Ill., 1958.

E162 Siegel, Arthur S., ed. *Chicago's Famous Buildings: A Photographic Guide to the City's Architectural Landmarks and Other Notable Buildings*. 2nd ed. Chicago, 1969.

Good maps, plans of many buildings, and an authoritative text make this an excellent guide.

E163 Sprague, Paul. *Guide to Frank Lloyd Wright and Prairie School Architecture in Oak Park*. Oak Park, 1976.

E164 Webster, James Carson. *Architecture of Chicago and Vicinity*. [Media?, Penn.], 1965.

Guidebook with pictures and some plans. Bibliography.

F
TRANSPORTATION

See also: D, City Planning; A2la, 23, 25, 26, 28, 29, 49; H15

Roads Before the Automobile

F1 Quaife, Milo M. *Chicago's Highways Old and New: From Indian Trail to Motor Road*. Chicago, 1923.

The basic text for Chicago's major roads.

Water

See also: D21; G63, 64, 69, 71; I138

F2 Becht, J. Edwin. *Commodity Origins, Traffic, and Markets Accessible to Chicago Via the Illinois Waterway*. Chicago, c1952.

F3 Becker, Donald N. "Development of the Chicago Type Bascule Bridge." *Trans. of the Am. Soc. of Civil Engineers*, CIX (1945), 995-1046.

A thorough, illustrated study.

F4 __________. "The Story of Chicago's Bridges." *Midwest Engineer*, II, 5 (Jan. 1950), 3-9.

F5 Chicago. Department of the Port. *The Seaport of Chicago*. Chicago, 1962.

F6 Chicago. Department of Public Works. *Straightening the Chicago River*. Chicago, 1926.

See also the second edition, 1930. History, maps and documents relating to this civic improvement.

F7 Chicago. Department of Public Works. Bureau of Engineering. Division of Bridges and Viaducts. *Bataan-Corregidor Memorial Bridge*. Chicago, 1949.

A detailed account of the bridge, with diagrams and pictures. Includes information on the previous State Street bridges, and a short history of bridges in Chicago.

F8 __________. *The Movable Bridges of Chicago*. [Chicago, 1969?]

A short description of the bridges and a general explanation of bridge building in Chicago.

F9 Clayton, John. "How They Tinkered with a River." *CH*, n.s., I, 1 (Spring 1970), 32-46.

Describes changes and suggestions for changes in the Chicago River from the time of the French to the current day.

F10 Dornfeld, A. A. "Chicago's Age of Sail." *CH*, n.s., II, 3 (Spring-Summer 1973), 156-165.

Describes the types of ships used on the Great Lakes in the mid-19th century.

F11 __________. "Steamships: A Hundred Years Ago." *CH*, n.s., IV, 3 (Fall 1975), 148-156.

Describes the types of steamships that drove sailing vessels off of the lakes.

F12 __________. "Steamships After 1871." *CH*, n.s., VI, 1 (Spring 1977), 12-22.

F13 Fleming, George J., Jr. "Canal at Chicago: A Study in Political and Social History." Catholic U. of Am. unpub. Ph.D. thesis, 1951.

F14 Gray, James. *The Illinois*. New York, 1940.

A volume in the series *Rivers of America*.

F15 Hansen, Harry. *The Chicago*. New York, 1942.

A sound history of the River, including much general Chicago history.

F16 Hartshorne, Richard. "The Lake Traffic of Chicago." U.C. unpub. Ph.D. thesis, 1924.

There is some historical content but the heart of this thesis is a description of conditions at the time, a period when the decline of the economic importance of the River as a harbor was being recognized. This paper is also useful to those studying a particular commodity as the major trades are described fully.

F17 Howe, Walter A., comp. *Documentary History of the Illinois and Michigan Canal*. Springfield, 1957.

F18 Illinois. International Trade Division. *Seaport - Chicago*. Chicago, 1971.

F19 Knight, Robert and Lucius H. Zeuch. *The Location of the Chicago Portage Route of the Seventeenth Century*. Chicago, 1928.

The definitive work on the subject.

F20 Kogan, Bernard R. "Chicago's Pier." *CH,* n.s., V, 1 (Spring 1976), 28-38.

A description and history of Navy Pier.

F21 Krenkel, John H. *Illinois Internal Improvements 1818-1848.* Cedar Rapids, 1958.

Some material on the Illinois-Michigan Canal.

F22 Lamb, John M. "Canal Boats on the Illinois and Michigan Canal." *JISHS,* LXXI, 3 (Aug. 1978), 211-224.

A general narrative with pictures and excerpts from source material.

F23 __________. "Early Days on the Illinois & Michigan Canal." *CH,* n.s., III, 3 (Winter 1974-1975), 168-176.

A collection of anecdotes.

F24 Lee, Henry W. "The Calumet Portage." *ISHS Trans.,* XVII (1912), 24-43.

F25 Mansfield, John Brandt. *History of the Great Lakes.* 2 vol. Chicago, 1899.

A long, detailed, 19th century history useful for details.

F26 Maurice White, O.S.F., Sister Mary. "History of the Illinois Waterway System from 1822 to 1956." DeP.U. unpub. M.A. thesis, 1957.

F27 Mayer, Harold M. *The Port of Chicago and the St. Lawrence Seaway.* Chicago, 1957.

Some historical background, a description of the Port, and proposals to deal with increased traffic that will result from the St. Lawrence Seaway. Bibliography.

F28 Piehl, Frank J. "Shall We Gather at the River." *CH,* n.s., II, 4 (Fall-Winter 1973), 196-205.

A description of bridging the Chicago River.

F29 Putnam, James W. *The Illinois and Michigan Canal: A Study in Economic History.* Chicago, 1918.

A sound, detailed account.

F30 Rice, Mary Jane Judson. *Chicago, Port to the World.* Chicago, 1969.

F31 Richheimer, Robert Horace. "The Northwest River and Harbor Convention Held at Chicago, July 5, 1847." U.C. unpub. M.A. thesis, 1963.

An issue in national politics, the meeting was important in identifying Chicago as a convention center.

F32 Russell, Joseph Albert. *The St. Lawrence Seaway: Its Impact by 1965 Upon Industry of Metropolitan Chicago and Illinois Waterway Associated Areas.* 2 vol. Chicago, 1959-1960.

F33 Smith, Hermon Dunlap. *The Des Plaines River, 1673-1940: A Brief Consideration of Its Names and History.* Lake Forest, Ill., 1940.

F34 Deleted

F35 U. S. Board of Engineers for Rivers and Harbors. *The Ports of Chicago, Ill., Indiana Harbor, Ind., and Muskegon, Mich.* Washington, 1953.

F36 Williams, Mentor L. "The Background of the Chicago River and Harbor Convention, 1847." *Mid-America,* XIX, 4 (Oct. 1948), 219-232.

A well researched, sound article.

F37 __________. "The Chicago River and Harbor Convention, 1847." *Miss. Valley H. R.,* XXXV, 4 (Mar. 1949), 607-626.

The best brief account.

Railroads

(General)

There is no historical study of the railroads in Chicago. Since Chicago was a major center, most histories of railroads have some material on the city and most general histories of Chicago have material on railroads. The books listed below are general studies of American railroads or biographies of railroads that ran into Chicago. All have something to say about Chicago. The quality of the books varies greatly.

F38 Boylan, Josephine. "The Illinois Railroad and Its Successors." *JISHS,* XXX, 2 (July 1937), 180-192.

F39 Campbell, Edward G. *The Reorganization of the American Railroad System, 1893-1900.* New York, 1938.

F40 Campbell, G. M. "A Historical Sketch of the Baltimore & Ohio Chicago Terminal Railroad Company and Its Predecessor Companies." *Railway and Locomotive H. Soc. Bull.*, LXXIII, (May 1948), 54-62.

F41 Casey, Robert J. and William A. S. Douglas. *Pioneer Railroad: The Story of the Chicago and North Western System.* New York, 1948.

F42 Chicago and Northwestern Railway Company. *Yesterday and Today: A History.* Chicago, 1905.

F43 Clark, Stewart Alan. "Illinois Shortline Railroads: 1840-1962." U.C. unpub. M.S. thesis, 1962.

A compilation of material on the Chicago and Northwestern Railway. Useful for details.

F44 Cochran, Thomas C. *Railroad Leaders, 1845-1890. The Business Mind in Action.* Cambridge, 1953.

F45 Corliss, Carlton J. *Main Line of Mid-America: The Story of the Illinois Central.* New York, 1950.

F46 Derleth, August. *The Milwaukee Road: Its First Hundred Years.* New York, 1948.

F47 Dorin, Patrick C. *Everywhere West: The Burlington Route.* Seattle, 1976.

F48 __________. *The Lake Superior Iron Ore Railroads.* Seattle, 1969.

F49 Gates, Paul Wallace. *The Illinois Central Railroad and Its Colonization Work.* Cambridge, 1934.

F50 Hargrave, Frank Flavius. *A Pioneer Indiana Railroad: The Origin and Development of the Monon.* Indianapolis, c1932.

F51 Harlow, Alvin F. *The Road of the Century: The Story of the New York Central.* New York, 1947.

F52 Hayes, William Edward. *Iron Road to Empire: The History of 100 Years of the Progress and Achievements of the Rock Island Lines.* New York, 1953.

F53 Hilton, George W. *The Monon Route.* 2nd ed. Berkeley, 1978.

F54 Hungerford, Edward. *The Story of the Baltimore and Ohio Railroad, 1827-1927.* 2 vol. New York, 1928.

F55 Lewis, Lloyd and S. Pargellis, eds. *Granger County: A Pictorial Social History of the Burlington Railroad.* Boston, 1949.

F56 Lyford, Will Hartwell. *History of Chicago and Eastern Illinoi Railroad Company to June 30, 1913.* Chicago, 1913.

F57 Marshall, James Leslie. *Sante Fe, the Railroad That Built an Empire.* New York, [1945].

F58 Mott, Edward H. *Between the Ocean and the Lakes: The Story of the Erie.* New York, 1901.

F59 Olmsted, Robert P. *Six Units to Sycamore: Chicago Great Western in Illinois.* Janesville, Wisc., 1967.

F60 __________. *Trail of the Zephyrs: The Burlington Route in Northern Illinois.* n.p., c1970.

F61 Overton, Richard C. *Burlington Route: A History of the Burlington Lines.* New York, 1965.

F62 __________. *Burlington West: A Colonization History of the Burlington Railroad.* Cambridge, 1941.

F63 Rice, Herbert W. "The Early History of the Chicago, Milwaukee and St. Paul Railway." U. Iowa unpub. Ph.D. thesis, 1939.

F64 Richardson, Helen R. *Illinois Central Railroad Company: A Centennial Bibliography, 1851-1951.* Washington, 1950.

F65 Schotter, Howard Ward. *The Growth and Development of the Pennsylvania Railroad Company.* Philadelphia, 1927.

F66 Stover, John F. *American Railroads.* Chicago, 1961.

F67 __________. *History of the Illinois Central Railroad.* New York, 1975.

The definitive work.

F68 __________. *The Life and Decline of the American Railroad.* New York, 1970.

F69 Taylor, George Rogers and Irene D. Neu. *The American Railroad Network, 1861-1890.* Cambridge, 1956.

F70 Teweles, Richard Jack. *The Economic History of the Chicago and Eastern Illinois Railroad.* Urbana, 1949.

F71 Turner, Charles W. *Chessie's Road.* Richmond, 1956.

F72 White, John H., Jr. *American Locomotives: An Engineering History, 1830-1880.* Baltimore, 1968.

F73 White, John H. *The American Railroad Passenger Car.* Baltimore, c1978.

F74 __________. *Early American Locomotives.* New York, 1972.

F75 Wood, C. R. and D. M. *Milwaukee Road - West.* Seattle, 1972.

(Special Chicago Railroad Studies)

See also: H7; I116-118, 121, 139.

F76 Brownson, Howard G. *History of the Illinois Central Railroad to 1870.* Urbana, 1915.

Mostly on the finances of the company.

F77 Chicago Association of Commerce. *Smoke Abatement and Electrification of Railway Terminals in Chicago.* Chicago, 1915.

F78 "Chicago Railroad Fair." *State and Local H. News,* IV, 6 (Sept. 1948), 95-99.

F79 Hughel, C. G. "History of Chicago Passenger Stations." *J. of the Western Soc. of Engineers,* XLII, 2 (Ap. 1937), 78-81.

F80 Mayer, Harold M. "The Localization of Railway Facilities in Metropolitan Centers as Typified by Chicago." *J. of Land and Public Utility Econ.,* XX, 4 (Nov. 1944), 299-315.

A condensation of part of his thesis.

F81 __________. *The Railway Pattern of Metropolitan Chicago.* Chicago, 1943.

A thorough description of railroads in Chicago at the peak of their use. Despite the omissions of some material owing to the war, it is still the most useful work on the subject. Bibliography.

F82 __________. "The Railway Terminal Problem of Central Chicago." *Econ. Geography,* XXI, 1 (Jan. 1945), 62-76.

A lucid description of the problem of an excess of capacity wrongly located and a call for action. No notes.

F83 Newton, Albert William. "Chicago, Burlington, & Quincy R. R. Chicago Terminals." *Railway and Locomotive H. Soc. Bull.,* 95 (Oct. 1956), 68-78.

F84 Pinkepank, Jerry A. "The Belt Railway of Chicago: A Railroad's Railroad." *Trains,* XXVI, 11 (Sept. 1966), 36-46.
A survey of what it does, with much historical information and a map.

F85 Pinkepank, Jerry A. "How the Belt Came to Be." *Trains*, XXVI, 12 (Oct. 1966), 42-49.

An historical overview.

F86 Tan, Pei-Lin. "The Belt and Switching Railroads of Chicago Terminal Area." U.C. unpub. Ph.D. thesis, 1931.

A chapter on the belt lines in Chicago, followed by chapters on the physical plant, services, finances and an evaluation. Bibliography.

F87 White, John H. "Chicago Locomotive Builders." Offprint, *Railway Bull.*, 122 (April 1970), 52-59.

Air

See also: H167.

F88 Bushnell, George D. "The International Aviation Meet, 1911." *CH*, n.s., V, 1 (Spring 1976), 12-18.

F89 Caster, Alida, Roger A. Ketcham and David A. NewMyer. *Interim Aviation Plan*. Chicago, 1973.

A study by the Chicago Area Transportation Study.

F90 Chicago Area Transportation Study. *Northeastern Illinois 1995 Airport System: Implementation Study/Priority Statement*. Chicago, 1976.

Another interesting report, with a long bibliography.

F91 Dermody, H. "Chicago's First Flight." *S. P. A. Journal*, XII (Oct. 1949), 84-87.

An account of a balloon flight, the first in Chicago.

F92 Doherty, Richard Paul. "The Origin and Development of Chicago-O'Hare International Airport." B.S.U. unpub. Ph.D. thesis, 1970.

F93 General Airport Company. *Comprehensive Study Relating to Aeronautical Facilities for Metropolitan Area of Chicago Projected to 1970*. Stamford, 1946.

An interesting description of the state of flying in Chicago in the 1940s can be made from this.

F94 Harza Engineering Company. *A Lake Michigan Site for Chicago's Third Major Airport*. Chicago, 1967.

F95 Kirchherr, Eugene Carl. "Airport Land Use in the Chicago Metropolitan Area: A Study of the Historical Development, Characteristics, and Special Problems of a Land Use Type within a Metropolitan Area." N.U. unpub. Ph.D. thesis, 1959.

Divides the era of early airport land use into the periods 1910-1925 when airplanes were still a novelty and 1925-1941 when military use dominated with some thought of air mail. There was, in fact, little regulation of land use for airports, and this created problems. See his article on the same subject in *Bull. of the Ill. Geographical Soc.*, XVI, 2 (Dec. 1974), 22-32.

F96 __________. "Variations in the Number and Distribution of Commercial Airports in the Chicago Region, 1951-1967." *Michigan Academician,* III, 1 (Summer 1970), 83-93.

Considers the period after his thesis. He shows that the number of airports fell from 36 to 29 and that airports tended to be removed farther from the center of the area. It is surprising that there were several new airports built in the period, offsetting some closings.

F97 Scamehorn, Howard L. *Balloons to Jets.* Chicago, 1957.

The basic history of aviation in Illinois.

F98 __________. "The Formative Period of Aviation in Illinois, 1890-1919." U.I.U. unpub. Ph.D. thesis, 1956.

His thesis has more details on the pre-flight period than does his book.

F99 Taaffe, Edward James. "The Air Passenger Hinterland of Chicago." U.C. unpub. Ph.D. thesis, 1952.

Describes the "shadow" area of Chicago's airline business, *i.e.*, the area that Chicago served exclusively, and the outer ring where Chicago was the dominant air city. Chicago in 1952 had more strength to the west than the east due to New York. Already the principal function of Chicago's airlines was to link large metropolitan areas. "In general, the airline pattern has tended to follow the outlines of the railroad pattern . . ."

F100 Taylor, Frank. *High Horizons: United Airlines System.* New York, 1964.

A house history.

F101 Whitehouse, Arthur G. J. *The Sky's the Limit: A History of the U. S. Airlines.* New York, [c1971].

F102 Wood, Alexander Lockhart. "Airport Development and Design: A New Architectural Problem." N.U. unpub. Ph.D. thesis, 1972.

F103 Wray, James Ronald. "Atlas of Chicago Municipal Airport." U.C. unpub. M.A. thesis, 1948.

An excellent detailed study of the physical description of Midway which sets it in its immediate geographical context and in the larger context of its commercial hinterland. The bibliography is very important for the study of early aviation in Chicago.

Mass Transit

(General)

See also: G111a; H170; I5, 60.

F104 Burton, Ralph J. "Mass Transport in the Chicago Region: A Study of Metropolitan Government." U.C. unpub. Ph.D. thesis, 1939.

An ". . . attempt to cover the important aspects of mass transport in the Chicago region as a governmental problem."

F105 Chicago Area Transportation Study. *Final Report*. 3 vol. Chicago, 1959-1962.

The CATS was established by the city, county, state and Federal governments in 1955. Using 1956 as a base line, vol. 1 presents a detailed survey of the movement of people; vol. 2 gives an historical review and projects into the future; vol. 3 provides standards and plans.

F106 __________. *1970 Travel Characteristics: A Staff Report*. Chicago, 1975.

Useful as an update of earlier studies.

F107 Chicago Association of Commerce and Industry. *A Study of Ground Transportation Planning in the Chicago Region*. Chicago, 1970.

F108 Chicago. City Council. Committee on Local Transportation. *A Comprehensive Local Transportation Plan for the City of Chicago*. Chicago, 1937.

A long, detailed report on all areas of Chicago's mass transit in 1937 with recommendations for the future.

F109 Chicago. Transit Authority. *Chicago's Mass Transportation System*. [Chicago, c1957].

A friendly overview.

F109a Chicago. Transit Authority. *Chronological Order of Service Changes*. Typescript. [Chicago], 1961.

An important document in tracing the history of transportation in Chicago.

F110 __________. *Horses to Horsepower: A Pictorial Review of Local Transportation in Chicago Since 1859*. Chicago, 1970.

Pictures and captions.

F111 DeCamp, Roderick Kyle. "The Chicago Transit Authority: A Study in Responsibility." U.C. unpub. Ph.D. thesis, 1958.

A description of how the CTA came to be is followed by sections on administration, policy formulation, revenue, problems and planning.

F112 Harlan, Homer Charles. "Charles Tyson Yerkes and the Chicago Transportation System." U.C. unpub. Ph.D. thesis, 1975.

The scope of the thesis is Chicago transportation in the period for Yerkes' career in Chicago and cannot be treated in any other context. A thorough paper but limited by the absence of sources of Yerkes, who, Harlan concludes, has not been treated fairly by previous work.

F113 Illinois. Governor's Transportation Task Force. *Crisis and Solution: Public Transportation in Northeastern Illinois*. Chicago, 1973.

Recommends a regional transit system.

F114 Rock, Steven Michael. "The Redistributive Effects of Mass Transit in the Chicago Area." N.U. unpub. Ph.D. thesis, 1975.

F115 Sullivan, Joseph V. "Historical Data (Chicago Transportation), Information as to Events Connected with Chicago Transportation Companies - Gathered from Various Sources." Typescript. Chicago, 1930, 1940.

F116 Weber, Harry Perkins, comp. *Outline History of Chicago Traction*. Chicago, 1936.

Not in fact a synthetic work of history, it is a collection of excerpts, etc., strung together by head notes. Useful for details.

F117 Weber, R. David. "Rationalizers and Reformers: Chicago Local Transportation in the 19th Century." U.W. unpub. Ph.D. thesis, 1971.

The single most useful work on the topic. A thorough, sound study of the development of the system and different forces that directed its shape.

(Elevated)

F118 Boyd, H. T. *More Median Transit for Chicago*. Chicago, 1970.

F119 Central Electric Railfans' Association. *Chicago's Rapid Transit*. Chicago, 1973.

F120 __________. *The Great Third Rail*. Chicago, 1961.

F121 Chicago Area Transportation Study. *The Skokie Swift: A Study in Urban Rapid Transit; a Summary of the Chicago Area Transportation Study's Role in the Chicago Transit Authority, Village of Skokie Mass Transit Demonstration Project Sponsored by the Housing and Home Finance Agency*. Chicago, 1968.

F122 Chicago. Transit Authority. Research and Planning Department *Skokie Swift, the Commuter's Friend*. Chicago, 1968.

A short history and description by the Transit Authority.

F123 Davis, James L. *The Elevated System and the Growth of Northern Chicago*. Evanston, 1965.

Settlement patterns centered on the "el" and land values rose. He describes the impact 1895-1914, the background 1848-1894, land values and construction patterns.

F124 Fletcher, Connie. "The Loop El: Love It or Lose It." *Chicago*, XXVI, 11 (Nov. 1977), 192-206.

(Surface)

F125 Bryant, George T. "The Gripman Wore a Sheepskin Coat." *CH*, n.s., I, 1 (Spring 1970), 47-56.

A personal recollection of the changes in public transportation in Chicago.

F126 Central Electric Railfans' Association. *Interurban to Milwaukee*. Chicago, 1962- .

F127 Gruber, John. *Trolleys to Milwaukee: A Pictorial Review of the North Shore Line*. Champaign, 1963.

F128 Hilton, George W. *Cable Railways of Chicago*. Chicago, 1954.

A useful narrative.

F129 Hilton, George W. and John F. Due. *The Electric Interurban Railways in America*. Stanford, 1960.

F130 Johnson, James D. *A Century of Chicago Streetcars, 1858-1958*. Wheaton, Ill., 1964.

A popular book, many pictures.

F131 Lind, Alan R. *Chicago Surface Lines: An Illustrated History*. Park Forest, Ill., 1974.

F132 Middleton, William D. *The Interurban Era*. Milwaukee, 1961.

A popular history of a type of transportation once important to Chicago.

F133 __________. *North Shore: America's Fastest Interurban*. San Marino, 1964.

Many pictures, but with a longer text than the Olmsted book.

F134 __________. *South Shore, the Last Interurban*. San Marino, 1970.

A popular history with many photographs.

F135 Olmsted, Robert P. *Interurbans to the Loop: North Shore Line, South Shore Line*. Janesville, Wisc., 1969.

F136 __________. *Scenes from the Shore Lines: North Shore Line, South Shore Line*. Janesville, Wisc., 1964.

A picture book.

F137 Piehl, Frank J. "Our Forgotten Streetcar Tunnels." *CH*, n.s., IV, 3 (Fall 1975), 130-138.

An account of how the tunnels came about in the mid-19th century and how they became first cable car and then street car tunnels.

F137a Roberts, Sidney I. "Portrait of a Robber Baron: Charles T. Yerkes." *Business H. R.*, XXXV, 3 (Autumn 1961), 344-371.

(Underground)

F138 Chicago. Department of Subways and Superhighways. *The Chicago Subways*. Chicago, 1943.

"Picture story of the construction of Chicago's subways."

F139 *The Chicago Freight Tunnels*. Chicago, 1928.

A friendly description of the tunnel system by the owners. Less detailed than the publication of 1906.

F140 Donaho, John Albert. "The Chicago Subway: A Pattern for the Federal-Municipal Relationship." U.C. unpub. M.A. thesis, 1943.

A description of the P.W.A.-City of Chicago relationship in the construction of the Chicago subway.

F141 Dornfeld, A. A. "The Freight Tunnel Under Chicago." *CH*, n.s., IV, 1 (Spring 1975), 23-31.

A sound, popular account of the system of freight tunnels built in the early 20th century to deal with freight traffic and waste removal in the Loop.

F142 Illinois Tunnel Company. *Chicago Subway System.* Chicago, 1906.

Pictures, diagrams, tables, etc., on the construction of the freight subway system.

Automobiles and Trucks

See also: D1, 16; H173; K20.

F143 Alvord, John W. *A Report to . . . the Commercial Club on the Street Paving Problem in Chicago.* Chicago, 1904.

F144 Barrett, Paul Francis. "Mass Transit, the Automobile, and Public Policy in Chicago, 1900-1930." U.I.C. unpub. Ph.D. thesis, 1976.

A thorough, well-documented study which argues that it was the cast of mind created by the problems of mass transit in the '90s that caused public policies to be badly framed thereafter. The auto was a new device and there were no preconceptions of how to deal with it. Therefore, the problems of the auto were dealt with pragmatically. See also his article in *Business H. R.*, XLIX, 4 (Winter 1975), 473-497.

F145 Barton-Aschman Associates, Inc. *A Parking Program for Chicago Central Area.* Chicago, 1965.

Analysis and projection of need.

F145a Chicago. Continental Illinois National Bank Area Development Division. *Industrial Labor Sheds: Suburban Area of Metropolitan Chicago.* Chicago, 1978.

Based on a sample of automobiles in parking lots of various businesses.

F146 Chicago. Department of Superhighways. *A Comprehensive Superhighway Plan for the City of Chicago . . .* Chicago, 1939.

F146a Ergün, Gökmen. *Development of a Downtown Parking Model.* Chicago, 1971.

Part of the Chicago Area Transportation Study. Bibliography.

F147 Fellman, Jerome D. *Truck Transportation Patterns of Chicago.* Chicago, 1950.

". . . emphasizes the intercity common motor carrier activity which centers upon Chicago and the local traffic and terminal facility patterns consequent upon that intercity movement. It discusses the external traffic relations of Chicago with the middle west and the nation, and stresses the internal relationships between truck traffic and other transportational and economic elements of the urban scene."

F148 Helvig, Magne. *Chicago's External Truck Movements.* Chicago, 1964.

A description of intercity trucking in the area that points out that Chicago's truck system is the largest in the U. S. because Chicago is an overnight trip to more than 25% of the U. S. markets.

F149 Kitch, Edmund W., Marc Isaacson and Daniel Kasper. "The Regulation of Taxicabs in Chicago." *J. of Law and Econ.*, XIV, 2 (Oct. 1971), 285-348.

A hostile review of the Chicago system of licensing.

F150 Walker, Samuel A. *Crosstown Transit Study: Final Report on the 1965 Demand.* Chicago, 1970.

G
GOVERNMENT

Municipal

(General)

See also: A2la; M, Social Reform and Welfare

G1 Chicago. Bureau of Statistics and Municipal Library. *The Chicago City Manual Containing a List of the Executive and Other City Officers, with Descriptions of Their Duties; Lists of the Aldermen and of the Committees of the City Council; and the Rules Regulating that Body and Many Other Matters Relating to the City Government, or That Are of Municipal Concern*. Chicago, 1908-1916.

A basic source for city government information.

G2 Chicago. Bureau of Public Efficiency. *The Nineteen Governments of Chicago* . . . Chicago, 1913, 1915.

A description of the various independent jurisdictions in the area, e.g., Park Districts. The book is reformist, e.g., in proclaiming that: "Chicago's greatest needs are the unification of its local governments and a short ballot."

G3 Grosser, Hugo S. *Chicago: A Review of Its Governmental History from 1837 to 1906*. Chicago, 1906.

G4 Holt, Glen E. "Will Chicago's Itinerant City Hall Be Moved Once More?" *CH*, n.s., VI, 3 (Fall 1977), 155-166.

An account of the seven moves made by City Hall in the city's first 75 years.

G5 James, Edmund Janes. *The Charters of the City of Chicago*. Chicago, 1898, 1899.
The text of the charters, related law and commentary.

G6 Karlen, Harvey M. *The Governments of Chicago*. Chicago, 1958.

"This book is designed to introduce the reader to the maze of political and administrative relationships that are the governments of Chicago . . . It is . . . an accurate and organized account of the history and structure of functions of the government . . . of Chicago."

G7 League of Women Voters of Chicago. *The Key to Our Local Government: Chicago, Cook County Metropolitan Area*. 4th ed. Chicago, 1978.
An evenhanded survey of the structure of government. Earlier editions are useful in tracking changes in the government. A revised edition is issued at irregular intervals.

G8 Parsons, Malcolm B. *The Use of the Licensing Power by the City of Chicago*. Urbana, 1952.

Treats Chicago's power to license, licensing for public health, public safety, morals and revenues from licenses. Bibliography.

G9 Proudfoot, Malcolm Jarvis. "Chicago's Fragmented Political Structure." *Geo. R.*, XLVII, 1 (June 1957), 106-117.

A short discussion of the variety of jurisdictions in Chicago.

G10 Simpson, Herbert D. *Tax Racket and Tax Reform in Chicago*. Chicago, 1930.

A description of the tax system in the years 1925-1930 and proposals for change.

G11 Sparling, Samuel E. *Municipal History and Present Organization of the City of Chicago*. Madison, 1898.

An early history of the structure and workings of Chicago's government. It can be used with various reform group publications to indicate the course of Chicago's municipal government.

G12 Winchell, Samuel Robertson. *Chicago, Past and Present: A Manual for the Citizen, the Teacher and the Student; History, Government, Officials, Their Duties and Salaries*. Chicago, 1906.

A very simple description of the government of Chicago.

G13 Winfree, Gail M. *A Directory of City Services*. Chicago, 1977.

There are several older, similar directories.

(City Council)

G14 Gable, William Russell. "The Chicago City Council: A Study of Urban Politics and Legislation." U.C. unpub. Ph.D. thesis, 1953.

A clear description of the formal and informal organization of the Council and the parties. The actual workings of the Council are described with examples from public housing, fiscal policy, and utility regulations. Some biographical sketches, e.g., Thomas Keane, are included.

G15 Slayton, William Larew. "Chicago's House of Lords: A Study of the Function of the Finance Committee of the Chicago City Council." U.C. unpub. M.A. thesis, 1943.

(Fire Department)

See also: V, Disasters (Fire of 1871)

G16 Bushnell, George D. "Chicago's Rowdy Firefighters." *CH*, n.s., II, 4 (Fall/Winter 1973), 232-241.

An account of organized fire protection in Chicago before a salaried department was established.

G17 Little, Kenneth. *Chicago Fire Department Engines: Sixty Years of Motorized Pumpers, 1912-1972*. Chicago, 1972.

G18 __________. *Chicago Fire Department Hook & Ladder Tractors, 1914-1971*. Chicago, 1971.

This and the book above are mostly pictures.

G19 McQuade, James S. *A Synoptical History of the Chicago Fire Department* . . . Chicago, 1908.

The only history available.

(Home Rule)

G20 Chicago. Home Rule Commission. *Report and Recommendations: A Report to Mayor Richard J. Daley and the Chicago City Council*. Chicago, 1972.

A massive update of the report to Kennelly.

G21 __________. *Chicago's Government, Its Structural Modernization and Home Rule Problems: A Report to Mayor Martin H. Kennelly and the Chicago City Council*. Chicago, 1954.

A good description of the work of the Council, the legislative-executive relationship, recommendations about "home rule," and conclusions.

G22 Lepawsky, Albert. *Home Rule for Metropolitan Chicago*. Chicago, 1935.

An early argument in favor of "home rule." Lepawsky tries to lay out the practical problems that arose because Chicago was subordinated to the State of Illinois.

(Law Department)

G23 Siebenschuh, Robert W. *The Administration of Municipal Legal Services: The Chicago Law Department*. Chicago, 1942.

(Park District)

Prior to 1934 there had been several separate park districts, e.g., the West Park District. See also: D, City Planning; E60-62, 72-74; H184

G24 *The Brookfield Zoo, 1934-54*. Chicago, 1954.

A short history of the institution; brief description and histories of the animal collections.

G25 Duis, Perry R. and Glen E. Holt. "Chicago's Green Crown: The Parks." *Chicago,* XXVI, 8 (Aug. 1977), 84-86.

A short overview of the history of the park district.

G26 Chicago Bureau of Public Efficiency. *The Park Governments of Chicago: An Inquiry into Their Organization and Methods of Administration*. Chicago, 1911.

Describes the divided park districts and argues for their unification.

G27 Chicago Park District. *General Information: Chicago's Parks and Recreation Program*. Chicago, 1934, 1936, 1947 and 1961.

Handbooks which cover some specifics about different aspects of the parks.

G28 __________. *Handbook of Chicago Parks*. Chicago, 1934.

A guide to the parks at the time of the consolidation of the park system.

G29 __________. *Monuments and Memorials*. Mimeograph. Chicago, 1975.

Later edition of *Principal Monuments, Memorials, Fountains, Etc., In the Park District*, published by the Chicago Park District in 1949.

G30 __________. *Table of Parks and Park Facilities, 1971*. Chicago, 1971.

An alphabetical list of parks by name, their size in acres, Ward numbers and indoor and outdoor facilities.

G30a Clayton, John. "A Lincoln Park Legend." *CH,* n.s., II, 2 (Fall 1972), 100-105.

An explanation and description of the Couch tomb in the southwest corner of Lincoln Park.

G31 Cranz, Galen. "Models for Park Usage: Ideology and the Development of Chicago's Public Parks." U.C. unpub. Ph.D. thesis, 1971.

He argues that Chicago's parks developed in response to several national models current at different times.

G32 Griffin, Al. "Chicago's Civilized World of Wild Animals." *CH*, n.s., IV, 4 (Winter 1975-1976), 235-243.

A descriptive overview.

G33 Kiley, Dan. *Chicago Inland Regional Parks. Design Study Report . . . for Department of Development and Planning, Chicago, Illinois*. Charlotte, Ver., 1969.

A modern critique of the inland parks. A map and an historical sketch are enclosed for each park studied.

G34 McCarthy, Michael P. "Politics and the Parks: Chicago Businessmen and the Recreation Movement." *JISHS*, LXV, 2 (Summer 1972), 158-172.

He argues that the success of the movement for parks in Chicago was due to the support of the business community.

G35 Osborn, Marian Lorena. "The Development of Recreation in the South Park System of Chicago." U.C. unpub. M.A. thesis, 1928.

An historical overview 1869-1903, followed by chapters on the small parks, field house program and general developments 1904-1928.

G36 Rauch, John Henry. *Public Parks . . . with Special Reference to the City of Chicago*. Chicago, 1869.

An early argument in support of parks with an appendix of legislation regarding parks.

(Personnel)

G37 Ellison, Ethel. "The Status of Women in the Chicago City Service." U.C. unpub. M.A. thesis, 1927.

A descriptive essay.

G38 Karlen, Harvey M. "Some Political and Administrative Aspects of Municipal Wage Determination in Chicago, 1911-1941." U.C. unpub. Ph.D. thesis, 1950.

A description with recommendations for change.

G39 Kingsbury, Joseph B. "Municipal Personnel Policy in Chicago, 1895-1915." U.C. unpub. Ph.D. thesis, 1923.

Dated but thorough.

(Police and Criminal Justice)

See also: H202; L, Social Conditions; U, Riots

G40 Balbus, Isaac D. *The Dialectics of Legal Repression: Black Rebels Before the American Criminal Courts.* New York, 1973.

Argues from a study of the punishment of blacks in the 1968 riot in Chicago and two riots in other cities that blacks were repressed by the legal system, and that the sanctions imposed represent a delicate balance between American political elites. Balbus is a Marxist whose views have undergone continual change. See also his U.C. Ph.D. thesis, "Rebellion and Response . . .," 1970.

G41 Beeley, Arthur Lawton. *The Bail System in Chicago.* Chicago, 1927.

Beeley's book is based on his research for his Ph.D. thesis. It is a survey with a reformist point of view. There is a long section on the types of prisoners involved.

G42 Beigel, Herbert and Allan. *Beneath the Badge: A Story of Police Corruption.* New York, 1977.

Records the history of a long investigation in police corruption in Chicago, 1970-1976.

G43 Chang, Ching Hui. *Police Administration in New York, Chicago and Philadelphia.* Urbana, 1929.

G44 Chicago. Citizens Committee to Study Police-Community Relations. *Police and Public: A Critique and a Program: Final Report of the Citizens' Committee to Study Police-Community Relations in the City of Chicago to Mayor Richard J. Daley.* Chicago, 1967.

A long report with bibliography.

G45 Chicago. Citizens' Police Committee. *Chicago Police Problems.* Reprinted 1969. Chicago, c1931.

A reforming report.

G46 Chicago. Committee on Criminal Justice. *Strategies for the Seventies: Planning for Criminal Justice, 1972.* Chicago, 1971.

G47 Chicago. Community Trust. *Reports Comprising the Survey of the Cook County Jail*. New York, 1974 (c1922).

A detailed study with photographs. The team was led by George W. Kirchwey, a noted penologist of his day.

G48 Chicago. Police Department. Operations Research Task Force. *Allocations of Resources in the Chicago Police Department*. Washington, 1972.

A technical report of a management analysis of the police department.

G49 *Chicago Police Investigations: Three Reports*. New York, 1971.

Reprints investigations of the police in 1898, 1904, and 1911-1912.

G50 Davis, Kenneth Culp. *Police Descretion*. St. Paul, 1975.

G51 Flinn, John Joseph. *History of the Chicago Police*. New York, 1973 (c1887).

A long book with many details useful for the mid-19th century and before.

G52 Haller, Mark H. "Historical Roots of Police Behavior: Chicago, 1890-1925." *Law and Society R.*, X, 2 (Winter 1976), 303-323.

Haller argues that the police in this period reflected the mores of their time and allowed certain kinds of crime to exist. The police thus enforced mores, not laws.

G53 __________. "Urban Crime and Criminal Justice: The Chicago Case." *J. of Am. H.*, LVII, 3 (Dec. 1970), 619-635.

Somewhat the same theme as above. He describes an informal system of criminal justice resting on the attitudes of the time.

G54 Hopkins, Ernest Jerome. *Our Lawless Police: A Study of the Unlawful Enforcement of the Law*. New York, 1931.
A national study of police misconduct, with many Chicago references.

G55 Jeter, Helen Rankin. *The Chicago Juvenile Court*. Washington, 1922.
A careful description of the court, its jurisdiction, organization and procedures.

G56 John Howard Association, Chicago. *A Study of the Police Lockups in the City of Chicago*. Chicago, 1947- .

An annual publication; title varies.

G57 Johnson, David R. "Crime Fighting in Chicago: An Analysis of Its Leadership, 1919-1927." U.C. unpub. M.A. thesis, 1966.

He describes the Crime Commission, the Ryerson Committee, the structure of elite reform and the attitudes and limitations of reform. He argues that many of the reformers were well meaning, but owing to their limited experience they did not understand the causes of crime. Only after causes became well known in the work of academics and social workers could there be a successful attack on crime.

G58 __________. "The Search for an Urban Discipline: Police Reform as a Response to Crime in American Cities, 1800-1875." U.C. unpub. Ph.D. thesis, 1972.

Extends his analysis to a national scope. See his M.A. thesis above (G57).

G59 Ketcham, George A. "Municipal Police Reform: A Comparative Study of Law Enforcement in Cincinnati, Chicago, New Orleans, New York, and St. Louis, 1844-1877." U.Mo. unpub. Ph.D. thesis, 1967.

American cities did not develop a police system until the English showed the way. New York was the first between 1844 and 1857; other cities soon followed. American police forces were similar and all failed to solve the problem of an efficient force free from excessive political influence.

G60 Levering, Johnson, *et.al*. *Chicago Police Lockups: A History of Reform in Police Handling of Persons in Detention, 1947-1962*. Chicago, 1963.

A report on change and the condition in 1963. A discussion of previous literature on lockups is included.

G61 McClory, Robert. *The Man Who Beat Clout City*. Chicago, c1977.

The story of Renault Robinson who founded the Afro-American Patrolman's League in face of opposition from City Hall.

G62 Miller, Jay A. "Racism Marks Chicago Police." *FOCUS/Midwest*, VI, 40 (1967), 10-14.

He argues that police racism is causing a growing rift between the police and the community.

G63 Muller, Jack. *I, Pig: Or, How the World's Most Famous Cop, Me, Is Fighting City Hall*. New York, 1971.

A long-time Chicago policeman "tells all he knows."

G64 Robertson, Leon S., Robert F. Rich, and H. Laurence Ross. "Jail Sentences for Driving While Intoxicated in Chicago: A Judicial Policy That Failed." *Law and Society R.*, VIII, 1 (Fall 1973), 55-67.

G65 Robinson, Cyril D. *The Mayor and the Police: A Look at the Political Role of the Police in Society.* [Chicago?, 1970?]

He argues that ". . . the police serve as a shield for the mayor's responsibility for long-time neglect of city problems, especially in ghetto communities."

G66 Ruchelman, Leonard I. *Police Politics: A Comparative Study of Three Cities.* Cambridge, 1974.

A study of the police as part of the machine and their political evolution as machines became less effective.

G67 Schiller, Ronald. "No Traffic-Court Jam." *Nat. Civic R.*, LIX, 3 (Mar. 1970), 141-147.

An account of Chicago's remodeled traffic courts.

G68 Stern, Max. "The Chicago House of Correction: A History and Examination of Recent Statistics Regarding Persons Committed to It." U.C. unpub. M.A. thesis, 1932.

A history of the treatment of petty offenders in Chicago and a description of the situation in 1930.

G69 Walker, Samuel. *A Critical History of Police Reform: The Emergence of Professionalism.* Lexington, Mass., c1977.

There are many Chicago references in this national study.

G70 Whittemore, L. H. *Cop! A Closeup of Violence and Tragedy.* New York, 1969.

Whitmore is a reporter who worked with the police in New York, Chicago and San Francisco. This is his report on "how it was" in the 1960s.

G71 Zemans, Eugene Stanley. *Held without Bail: Physical Aspects of the Police Lockups of the City of Chicago, 1947-48.* Chicago, 1949.

(Public Health, Sanitation and Environmental Control)

See also: F9, 77, 141; H168; J7; L, Social Conditions (medicine)

G72 Alvord, Burdick & Howson. *The Disposal of the Sewage of the Sanitary District of Chicago.* Urbana, 1927.

G73 Alvord, Burdick & Howson. *Report Upon Adequate Water Supply for the Chicago Metropolitan Area 1955-1980.* Chicago, 1955.

A detailed study of the water system in 1955 with some historical analysis as well as a plan for the future.

G74 __________. *Report Upon Adequate Water Supply for the Chicago Metropolitan Area 1969 to 2000.* Chicago, 1969.

An update of the 1955 report.

G75 Anthony, Elliott. *Sanitation and Navigation. Part I. - The History of Legislation in Illinois in Regard to Canals, Including the Present Scheme for a Drainage Ship Canal.* Chicago, 1891.

G76 Bolt, Beranek and Newman, Inc. *Chicago Urban Noise Study. Report No. 1411-1913.* Downers Grove, Ill., 1970.

A study of current levels and methods of control. Bibliography.

G77 Brown, George P. *Drainage Channel and Waterway: A History of the Effort to Secure an Effective and Harmless Method for the Disposal of the Sewage of the City of Chicago, and to Create a Navigable Channel Between Lake Michigan and the Mississippi River.* Chicago, 1894.

A long, detailed description. Bibliography.

G78 Cain, Louis Perkins. "The Sanitary District of Chicago: A Case Study of Water Use and Conservation." N.U. unpub. Ph.D. thesis, 1969.

Cain is the major student of Chicago sanitation. See also his article "Unfouling the Public's Nest: Chicago's Sanitary Diversion of Lake Michigan Water," *Tech. and Culture,* XV, 4 (Summer 1974), 594-613. Northern Illinois University Press has announced publication of his monograph, *Sanitation Strategy for a Lakefront Metropolis: The Case of Chicago,* DeKalb, 1979.

G79 *Chicago Air Pollution Systems Analysis Program Final Report.* Edited by J. J. Roberts. Argonne, Ill., 1971.

A long report with bibliography.

G80 Chicago. Board of Health. *Report of the Board of Health of the City of Chicago . . . 1867-1875.* 3 vol. Chicago, 1871-1876.

Volume 1 includes a sanitary history which is long and detailed; a prime source for early Chicago.

G81 Chicago. Board of Sewerage Commissioners. *Chicago Sewerage.* Chicago, 1858.

Chief Engineer Chesbrough's report on other sewer systems that led to his famous master plan for Chicago.

G82 Chicago. City Engineer. *Report on the Water Supply System of Chicago, Its Past, Present and Future.* Chicago, 1905.

A medium length description with plates, tables and diagrams.

G83 Chicago. Department of Waters and Sewers. *1856-1956: The Chicago Sewer System: 100 Years of Protecting Chicago's Health . . .* Chicago, 1956.

A good short summary with photographs and a map of the major lines in the system.

G84 Chicago. Flood Control Coordinating Committee. *Development of a Flood and Pollution Control Plan for the Chicagoland Area: Summary of Technical Reports.* Chicago, 1972.

G85 Chicago Normal School. Department of Sociology. *The Fight for Life in Chicago: A Sketch of the Sanitary History of the City.* Chicago, 1901.

A short pamphlet, but with useful details compiled from official reports.

G86 Chicago. Sanitary District. *Engineering Works. The Sanitary District of Chicago, August 1928.* Chicago, [1928?]

G87 Cooley, Lyman Edgar. *The Lakes and Gulf Waterway, as Related to the Chicago Sanitary Problem. The General Project of a Waterway from Lake Michigan to the Gulf of Mexico . . . A Preliminary Report with Appendices, Maps and Profiles.* Chicago, 1891.

G88 Croke, E. J. and J. J. Roberts. *Chicago Air Pollution Systems Analysis Program Final Report.* Chicago, 1971.

G89 Davenport, F. Garvin. "The Sanitation Revolution in Illinois, 1870-1900." *JISHS,* LXVI, 3 (Autumn 1973), 306-326.

Not limited to water and waste, it treats milk, toilets, etc.

G90 Decker, Mary Phillips. "Medical Service in the Public and Parochial Elementary Schools in Chicago." U.C. unpub. M.A. thesis, 1935.

A narrative of some aspects of medical care in the schools, including innoculation, exams, dental service and personnel.

G91 DeVise, Pierre. "Chicago's Hospitals - A Disaster." *FOCUS/ Midwest,* VIII, 51 (Dec. 1970), 14-19.

A vigorous criticism of the state and administration of Chicago hospitals.

G92 Diran, Mary. "Medical Care Given to a Group of Clients of the Unemployment Relief Service." U.C. unpub. M.A. thesis, 1935.

A detailed study of post-depression aspects in Roseland.

G93 Flexner, Mirian. "Organized Dental Facilities in Chicago for the Care of the Indigent and Lower Income Groups." U.C. unpub. M.A. thesis, 1934.

A straightforward description, beginning with the laws regulating dentistry.

G94 Frink, Fred Goodrich. "The Garbage Problem in Chicago." U.C. unpub. M.S. thesis, 1902.

Obviously dated, but of value for describing some sanitation problems that no longer exist.

G95 Lyon, Helen Faye. "The History of Public Health Nursing in Chicago, 1883-1920." U.C. unpub. M.A. thesis, 1947.

A straightforward narrative marred only by her failure to consult newspapers.

G96 Maury, Dabney H. *The Water Works System of the City of Chicago.* Chicago, 1911.

G96a Parsons, Ruth E. "The Department of Health of Chicago, 1894-1914." U.C. unpub. M.A. thesis, 1939.

See also G102.

G97 Perry, James C. *Public Health Administration in Chicago, Ill.: A Study of the Organization and Administration of the City Health Department.* Washington, 1915.

G98 Piehl, Frank J. "Chicago's Early Fight to 'Save Our Lake'." *CH,* n.s., V, 4 (Winter 1976-1977), 223-232.

On the reversal of the River.

G99 Randolph, Robert Isham. "The History of Sanitation in Chicago." *J. of the Western Society of Engineers,* XLIV, 5 (Oct. 1939), 227-240.

A history of the sewer and water system by a Chicago engineer.

G100 Schafmayer, A. J. "Chicago Sewer System." *J. of the Western Soc. of Engineers*, XLIX, 4 (Dec. 1944), 300-315.

A good overview.

G101 Schultz, Stanley K. and Clay McShane. "To Engineer the Metropolis: Sewers, Sanitation, and City Planning in Late Nineteenth-Century America." *J. of Am. H.*, LXV, 2 (Sept. 1978), 389-411.

A national study with Chicago references.

G102 Simonson, David F. "The History of the Department of Health of Chicago, 1947-1956." U.C. unpub. Ph.D. thesis, 1962.

A detailed study with some background material.

G103 Steadman, Robert Foster. *Public Health Organization in the Chicago Region*. Chicago, 1930.

A topical description of tuberculosis, milk supply, water and sewage.

G104 United States. Congress. Senate. Committee on Public Works. Subcommittee on Water Resources. *Proposed Chicago Tunnel and Reservoir: Hearing Before the Subcommittee on Water Resources of the Committee on Public Works*. Chicago, 1974.

A central document in this controversial project.

G105 United States. Department of Health, Education and Welfare. *Proceedings of a Conference in the Matter of Pollution of the Waters of the Grand Calumet River, Little Calumet River, Calumet River, Lake Michigan, Wolf Lake and Their Tributaries, Illinois-Indiana*. Chicago, 1965.

G106 United States. Public Health Service. *The Chicago-Cook County Health Survey*. New York, 1949.

An examination of all the health facilities in the metro-Chicago area and an evaluation of them. Included were studies of the water and sanitary systems, water pollution, garbage collection, food processing, eating and drinking establishments, mosquito and rat control, smoke abatement, housing, a long multi-part study of preventive medicine, a long multi-part section on facilities and services for medical care, and recommendations.

G107 __________. *A Summary of the Chicago-Cook County Health Survey*. Chicago, 1947.

A summary of the above (G106).

G108 White, Max Richard. *Water Supply Organization in the Chicago Region.* Chicago, 1934.

Describes water supplies, quality, pollution of Lake Michigan, operation of the water system, finances, with some comparisons to other cities.

G109 Williams, Charles Arch. *The Sanitary District of Chicago: History of Its Growth and Development as Shown by Decisions of the Courts and Work of Its Law Department.* Chicago, 1919.

A series of excerpts from documents strung together by headnotes.

G110 Williams, Elmer Lynn, ed. *That Man Bundesen.* Chicago, 1931.

G111 Wong, Shu Tuck. *Perception of Choice and Factors Affecting Industrial Water Supply Decisions in Northeastern Illinois.* Chicago, 1968.

Metropolitan

(General)

G111a Bailey, John A. *A Proposal for a Regional Transportation Agency for the Chicago Metropolitan Area.* Chicago, 1970.

G112 Banovetz, James M. *Perspectives on the Future of Government in Metropolitan Areas.* Chicago, 1968.

A prediction of what form changes in metropolitan government will take.

G113 Beckman, Ellen Josephine. "The Relationship of the Government of the City of Chicago to Cook County from 1893 to 1916." U.C. unpub. M.A. thesis, 1940.

A sound piece of description.

G114 Illinois. Northeastern Illinois Metropolitan Area Local Governmental Services Commission. *Governmental Problems in the Chicago Metropolitan Area.* Chicago, 1957.

A planning study that sets Chicago's problems in a regional context. Articles on a variety of physical problems: drainage, water supply, sewage disposal, etc.

G115 Lyon, LeVerett S., ed. *Governmental Problems in the Chicago Metropolitan Area.* Chicago, 1957.

G116 Parratt, Spencer D. "The Governments of the Metropolitan Area of Chicago." U.C. unpub. Ph.D. thesis, 1932.

". . . aims to present a panoramic picture of the haphazard political structure serving the population of this area in 1927-1930." Over 200 units of government were studied.

G117 Small, Joseph F. *Governmental Alternatives Facing the Chicago Metropolitan Area*. Chicago, [1966].

Describes the steps being taken to deal with the worst of the problems created by the lack of a metropolitan government.

G118 Steiner, Gilbert Yale. *Metropolitan Government and the Real World: The Case of Chicago*. Chicago, 1966.

An argument that regional government in the Chicago metropolitan area will not work.

(Elections)

G119 Conroy, Edward D. "The Electoral System of Chicago and Cook County." U.C. unpub. Ph.D. thesis, 1951.

A description of the electoral process, organization, and the chief officers dealing with elections.

(Forest Preserves)

G120 Cook County, Ill. Forest Preserve Commissioners. *The Forest Preserves of Cook County*. Chicago, 1918.

G120a Cook County. Forest Preserve District. *The Forest Preserve District of Cook County, Illinois*. Chicago, 1970.

G121 __________. *Land Policy*. River Forest, Ill., 1962.

(Police and Criminal Justice)

G122 Blackiston, Don Topkin. "The Judge, the Defendant, and Criminal Law Administration: A Study of the Administration of Criminal Law in the Cook County Criminal Court." U.C. unpub. Ph.D. thesis, 1952.

Blackiston had access to the material of the Crime Commission. He describes the defendants, the courts, sentences, organization, etc.

G123 Honan, Joseph C. "Cook County Law Enforcement is Fragmented, Mismanaged, and Uncoordinated at Fantastic Prices." *FOCUS/ Midwest,* IX, 60 (1973), 24-26.

G124 International Association of Chiefs of Police. Field Operations Division. *A Survey of the Police Department, Chicago, Illinois.* Chicago, 1970.

A long, detailed description and critical evaluation.

G125 Lepawsky, Albert. *The Judicial System of Metropolitan Chicago.* Chicago, 1932.

A straightforward description of the system.

G126 Oaks, Dallin H. and Warren Lehman. *A Criminal Justice System and the Indigent: A Study of Chicago and Cook County.* Chicago, 1968.

The book is made up of a description of the criminal justice system with special emphasis on the indigent, an examination of the aid to indigents, and a critical analysis.

U. S. Postal Service

G127 Karlen, Harvey M., ed. *Chicago Postal History.* Chicago, 1971.

A series of essays on aspects of Chicago's postal history.

G128 McGee, Henry W. "The Negro in the Chicago Post Office." U.C. unpub. M.A. thesis, 1961.

An account of the efforts by the National Alliance of Postal Employees to open opportunities for promotion to their members.

H
ECONOMICS AND BUSINESS

See also: A23, 25, 26, 28, 29, 31, 38, 49; F, Transportation

General

H1 Abbott, Carl J. "The Divergent Development of Cincinnati, Indianapolis, Chicago and Galena, 1840-1860: Economic Thought and Economic Growth." U.C. unpub. Ph.D. thesis, 1971.

Argues that the divergent development of these cities shows a much more complicated economic life in the west than hitherto believed.

H2 Alexander, Chester S. "The Young Man Employed in the Loop." U.C. unpub. M.A. thesis, 1933.

Alexander used a questionnaire to study a large sample of men in the Loop as to their education, religion, etc.

H3 Andrews, Wayne. *Battle for Chicago*. New York, 1946.

A general survey of major businesses of Chicago set in the context of Chicago history.

H4 Barton, Elmer. *A Business Tour of Chicago, Depicting Fifty Years of Progress*. Chicago, 1887.

A narrative with sketches of some businesses.

H5 Belcher, Wyatt Winton. *The Economic Rivalry Between St. Louis and Chicago, 1850-1880*. New York, 1968 (c1947).

The cities and their advantages are first described, followed by an analysis of the impact of the railroads, the Civil War, and the reconstruction period. His argument about the causes of Chicago's victory are set out in the last chapter.

H6 Breese, Gerald W. *The Daytime Population of the Central Business District of Chicago*. Chicago, 1949.

The study centered on the ". . . daily ebb and flow of population . . ." in the CBD, ". . . to discover its causes, origins, characteristics, and composition." Chicago's CBD was considered the dominant city in a seven state hinterland. This position was strongly reinforced by all kinds of transportation. The principal functions of the CBD were: (1) business; (2) culture and education; (3) "recreation and related activities, particularly commercialized and voluntary association activities;" (4) government; (5) residential, including transients. The full nature of these functions and the nature of the population is fully explored. The study is well documented and there is a comprehensive bibliography.

H7 Bross, William. *History of Chicago. Historical and Commercial Statistics, Sketches, Facts and Figures, Republished from the 'Daily Democratic Press' . . .* Chicago, 1876.

Strong on commercial and railroad facts, mid-1850s.

H8 Chandler, Alfred J. *The Visible Hand: Thc Managerial Revolution in American Business*. Cambridge, 1977.

Chandler uses Chicago firms as models.

H9 Chicago Association of Commerce. *Chicago, the Great Central Market*. Chicago, 1923.

The history is boostering and includes much specific information in the second section.

H10 Chicago. Plan Commission. *Industrial and Commercial Background for Planning Chicago*. Chicago, 1942.

Divided into three parts: I. Historical Review; II. Industrial Trends; III. Commercial Trends. Statistical appendix.

H11 Chicago. University. Center for Urban Studies. *Mid-Chicago Economic Development Study*. 3 vol. Chicago, 1966.

A very detailed survey of economic activity, the potential, etc., of an area between Grand and 79th Street and the Lake and Cicero, excluding the Loop and the S.W. corner south of 50th and west of Racine. Much of the evidence is presented in graphic or tabular form.

H12 Chicago. University. School of Business. *Studies in Business Administration*. Chicago, 1929, 1947.

An important series with many short monographs on Chicago topics.

H13 Clark, Peter B. "The Chicago Big Businessman as a Civic Leader." U.C. unpub. Ph.D. thesis, 1959.

Tends to diminish the influence of the business leader in civic offices.

H14 Currey, Josiah Seymour. *Manufacturing and Wholesale Industries of Chicago*. 3 vol. Chicago, 1918.

Sketches of manv businessmen and businesses.

H15 Draine, Edwin H. *Import Traffic of Chicago and Its Hinterland.* Chicago, 1963.

A sophisticated geographical study of the movement of goods through Chicago, how they moved, their value, their source, etc.

H16 Fellman, Jerome D. "Pre-Building Growth Patterns in Chicago." *Assoc. of Am. Geographers Annals,* XLVII, (Mar. 1954), 59-82.

He describes the factors that influenced the subdivision and sale of land before construction on it. The pattern of subdivision and sale was obviously an important factor in the shaping of the city.

H17 Guyer, Isaac D. *History of Chicago: Its Commercial and Manufacturing Interests . . . with Sketches of Manufacturers and Men Who Have Most Contributed to Its Prosperity . . .* Chicago, 1862.

A useful collection of material on pre-Fire business.

H18 Deleted

H19 *Industrial Chicago.* 6 vol. Chicago, 1891-1896.

A narrative compilation of sundry information on buildings, businesses, lawyers, businessmen, etc. A fundamental reference work.

H20 Larsen, Lawrence H. "Chicago's Midwest Rivals: Cincinnati, St. Louis and Milwaukee." *CH,* n.s., V, 3 (Fall 1976), 141-151.

A short treatment of an important theme in Midwestern history.

H21 Lindsey, David. "Chicago: From Trading Post to Merchandising Metropolis." *Mankind,* IV, 9 (Sept. 1974), 8-17.

H22 McLear, Patrick Edward. "Chicago and the Growth of a Region, 1832 through 1848." U.Mo. unpub. Ph.D. thesis, 1974.

H23 __________. "Speculation, Promotion, and the Panic of 1837 in Chicago." *JISHS,* LXII, 2 (Summer 1969), 135-146.

Describes the speculation prior to the crash in 1837 and the effects that this had on developing new kinds of business in Chicago.

H24 __________. "William Butler Ogden: A Chicago Promoter in the Speculative Era and the Panic of 1837." *JISHS,* LXX, 4 (Nov. 1977), 283-291.

Argues that "As a westerner and Chicagoan, Ogden thought that his financial interests would best be advanced by balanced growth and sound improvements."

H25 Plumbe, George E. *Chicago, the Great Industrial and Commercial Center of the Mississippi Valley*. Chicago, 1912.

Boostering but with important material, particularly the tables about raw materials, various kinds of production, transit, utilities, etc.

H26 Schnell, J. Christopher. "Chicago Versus St. Louis: A Reassessment of the Great Rivalry." *Mo. H. R.*, LXXI, 3 (Ap. 1977), 245-265.

A challenge to Belcher's argument that St. Louis lost to Chicago because "Chicago had a more aggressive entrepreneurial leadership [that] did not hesitate to try new means of transportation, primarily the railroads."

H27 Solomon, Ezra and Zarko G. Bilbija. *Metropolitan Chicago: An Economic Analysis*. Glencoe, Ill., 1960 (c1959).

"This book investigates the economics of the Chicago metropolitan area in terms of the major variables used in modern economic analysis. It presents specially prepared estimates of the size and structure of the area's population, labor forces, employment, output, income, expenditures and saving."

H28 Thorn, W. & Co. *Chicago in 1860: A Glance at Its Business Houses* . . . Chicago, 1860.

Another description of pre-Fire business.

H29 Walker, Louise Drusilla. "The Chicago Association of Commerce: Its History and Policies." U.C. unpub. Ph.D. thesis, 1941.

H30 White, William Alan. "Chicago and Toronto: A Comparative Study in Early Growth." N.U. unpub. Ph.D. thesis, 1974.

An important comparison of the attitude toward growth in the two cities.

H31 Wright, John S. *Chicago: Past, Present, Future* . . . 2nd ed. Chicago, 1870.

An interesting document of economic boostering, with many detailed statistics.

Commerce

(Retail)

General

See also: I4, 137

H32 Berry, Brian J. L. *Commercial Structure and Commercial Blight: Retail Patterns and Processes in the City of Chicago*. Chicago, 1963.

An important piece of geographical analysis ". . . laying out the extent, location, nature and trends of [commercial] blight and deterioration."

H33 Berry, Brian J. L. and Robert J. Tennant. *Chicago Commercial Reference Handbook: Statistical Supplement to "Commercial Structure and Commercial Blight."* Chicago, 1963.

A list of business centers is set out along with a description of the businesses. This is followed by a detailed statistical analysis of each center or ribbon of business activity.

H34 Breen, Leonard Zachary. "A Study of the Decentralization of Retail Trade Relative to Population in the Chicago Area, 1929 to 1948." U.C. unpub. Ph.D. thesis, 1956.

"It was found that within the city, while the Loop from 1935 to 1948 decreased its proportion of the total city expenditures for retail trade, it increased slightly its share of stores. The largest gain in number of stores between 1935 and 1948 was in the retail trade areas of the city outside of the Loop."

H35 Chicago. Sun-Times. *Who Buys What in Chicago Now?* Chicago, 1970-1974.

Market research data on a variety of goods.

H36 Ficks, Alma A. "Comparative Urban Patterns of the Spatial Distribution of Retail Activity." U.C. unpub. M.A. thesis, 1960.

H37 Frueh, Erne Rene. "Retail Merchandising in Chicago, 1833-1848." *JISHS,* XXXII, 2 (June 1939), 149-172.

Describes the nature and merchandise of early Chicago stores.

H38 Kitagawa, Evelyn and DeVer Sholes, ed. *Chicagoland's Retail Market*. Chicago, 1957.

Published to go beyond the census data to provide a detailed economic breakdown by place to aid retailers in planning.

H39 Proudfoot, Malcolm J. "The Major Outlying Business Centers of Chicago." U.C. unpub. Ph.D. thesis, 1936.

A frequently cited, important early work in this field.

H40 Rips, Rae Elizabeth. "An Introductory Study of the Role of the Mail-Order Business in American History, 1872-1914." U.C. unpub. M.A. thesis, 1938.

Mostly a study of Ward's and Sears.

H41 Shideler, Ernest Hugh. "The Chain Store: A Study of the Ecological Organization of a Modern City." U.C. unpub. Ph.D. thesis, 1927.

Biography - Individuals and Firms

(Boston Store)

See: H49, Mollie N. Newbury

(Bowen, George S.)

H42 De Santis, Hugh S. "George S. Bowen and the American Dream." *CH*, n.s., VI, 3 (Fall 1977), 143-154.

(Fair Co.)

H43 Crissey, Forrest. *Since Forty Years Ago: An Account of the Origin and Growth of Chicago and its First Department Store.* Chicago, 1915.

A short, heavily illustrated account of the Fair Store.

(Field, Marshall & Co.)

H44 Hall, Jay Gordon. "A History of the Advertising of Marshall Field and Company, 1918-1940." U.C. unpub. M.A. thesis, 1944.

He argues that honest advertising of quality goods was the basic characteristic of Field's ads.

H45 Tebbel, John William. *The Marshall Fields: A Study in Wealth*. New York, 1947.

A popular account of the men who have borne the name Marshall Field. There is a useful bibliography of popular secondary articles.

H46 Twyman, Robert W. *History of Marshall Field & Co., 1852-1906.* Philadelphia, 1954.

The standard work on Field's in this period. Bibliography.

H47 Wendt, Lloyd and Herman Kogan. *Give the Lady What She Wants.* Chicago, 1952.

A sound, popular history.

(Kroc, Ray)

See: H47a, 48, McDonald's.

(McDonald's)

H47a Boas, Maxwell and Steve Chain. *Big Mac: The Unauthorized Story of McDonald's.* New York, 1976.

A popular history.

H48 Kroc, Ray. *Grinding It Out: The Making of McDonald's.* Chicago, 1977.

The autobiography of Chicagoan Ray Kroc, the founder of the McDonald's chain.

(Newbury, Mollie N.)

H49 Corwin, Margaret. "Mollie Netcher Newbury: The Merchant Princess." *CH,* n.s., VI, 1 (Spring 1977), 34-43.

A powerful business woman who took over the Boston Store after her husband's death, and increased its volume five times.

(Sears, Roebuck & Co.)

H50 Asher, Louis E. and Edith Heal. *Send No Money.* Chicago, 1942.

A life of the founder of Sears, Roebuck, Richard Sears.

H51 Doenecke, Justus D. "General Robert E. Wood: The Evolution of a Conservative." *JISHS,* LXXI, 3 (Aug. 1978), 162-175.

An account of the evolution of his views on national affairs from his support of Roosevelt into the 1950s.

H52 Jeuck, John E. and Boris Emmet. *Catalogues and Counters: A History of Sears, Roebuck & Company.* Chicago, 1950.

A model business history. Bibliography.

H53 Moore, David G. "Managerial Strategies and Organization Dynamics in Sears Retailing." U.C. unpub. Ph.D. thesis, 1954.

The theoretical sociological framework is not as useful as the description of the various parts and divisions of the company.

H54 Weil, Gordon Lee. *Sears, Roebuck, U.S.A.: The Great American Catalog Store and How it Grew.* Briarcliff Manor, N.Y., 1977.

A popular history that drew heavily on the monographic work of earlier scholars.

H55 Werner, Morris R. *Julius Rosenwald: The Life of a Practical Humanitarian.* New York, 1939.

Rosenwald was an important Chicago figure at Sears, Roebuck & Co. and an equally important liberal civic leader. A popular life.

(Speigel, Inc.)

H56 Smalley, Orange A. and Frederick D. Sturdivant. *The Credit Merchants: A History of Spiegel, Inc.* Introduction by Harold F. Williamson. Carbondale, 1973.

(Ward, Montgomery & Co.)

H57 Baker, Nina. *Big Catalogue: The Life of Aaron Montgomery Ward.* New York, 1956.

H58 Boorstin, Daniel J. "A. Montgomery Ward's Mail-Order Business." *CH,* n.s., II, 3 (Spring-Summer 1973), 142-152.

A history of Ward's development to 1919 by a distinguished historian.

H59 Brann, W. L. *The Romance of Montgomery Ward and Company.* New York, 1929.

H60 Herndon, Booton. *Satisfaction Guaranteed: An Unconventional Report to Today's Consumers.* New York, 1972.

A laudatory description of Ward's today.

H61 Hobor, Nancy Allen. "The United States v. Montgomery Ward: A Case Study of Business Opposition to the New Deal 1933-1945." U.C. unpub. Ph.D. thesis, 1973.

A good business history. She argues that Avery was given his head because he produced profits. He in turn fought FDR because he believed that regulations were illegal in that they had not been adopted by Congress. Thus, the conflict was idealogical between individualism and regulation.

H62 Kleiler, Frank M. "The World War II Battles of Montgomery Ward." *CH,* n.s., V, 1 (Spring 1976), 19-27.

An account of the battle between the New Deal and Sewell Avery by the then field examiner of the NLRB.

H63 Deleted

(Wholesale)

H64 Barclay, George. "Chicago - the Lumber Hub." *Southern Lumberman,* CXCIII, 2417 (Dec. 1956), 177-178.

A short description of Chicago's lumber business.

H65 Battin, Charles Thomas. "The Economic Organization and Competitive Status of the Chicago Potato Market." U.C. unpub. Ph.D. thesis, 1937.

An interesting paper with chapters on the impact of chain stores and the motor truck.

H66 Blaine, Louisa Hubbard. "A Problem in the Chicago Milk Market." U.C. unpub. M.A. thesis, 1928.

She set out to study why cooperation among Chicago milk producers had failed but the work is really broader than the topic indicates, giving a considerable history of the business and a description of its organization.

H67 Dizmang, Oscar Kirk. "The Service of Inspection in the Commodity Markets at Chicago." U.C. unpub. M.A. thesis, 1928.

Arranged by type of produce.

H68 Haeger, John D. "The American Fur Company and the Chicago of 1812-1835." *JISHS,* LXI, 2 (Summer 1968), 117-139.

Finds that the Fur Company contributed very little to the future development of Chicago.

H69 Holland, Robert Lee and W. Edward Blackmore. *Chicago Wholesale Food Distribution Facilities*. Washington, D.C., 1967.

H70 Lee, Guy A. "History of the Chicago Grain-Elevator Industry, 1840-1890." Ha.U. unpub. Ph.D. thesis, 1938.

H71 McLear, Patrick E. "Rivalry Between Chicago and Wisconsin Lake Ports for Control of the Grain Trade." *Inland Seas*, XXIV, 3 (Fall 1968), 225-233.

H72 Odle, Thomas D. "The American Grain Trade of the Great Lakes." *Inland Seas*, VIII, 1 (Spring 1952), *passim;* IX, 1 (Spring 1953), *passim*.

Industry

(General)
(except meat packing)

See also: I, Labor; R, Communication; O51

H73 Appleton, John B. *The Iron and Steel Industry of the Calumet District*. Urbana, 1927.

A description of the industry in 1925: production, raw materials, favorable conditions of the area, labor supply and marketing.

H74 Bate, Phyllis A. "The Development of the Iron and Steel Industry of the Chicago Area, 1900-1920." U.C. unpub. Ph.D. thesis, 1948.

A well-organized and thorough paper that argues that it was Chicago's location that caused its iron and steel industry to grow and that this growth was an important cause of the rapid expansion of the city. The location was crucial because it was close to suppliers and to the market.

H75 Bradley, Van Allen. *Music for the Millions: The Kimball Piano and Organ Story*. Chicago, 1957.

A straightforward narrative.

H76 *Central Manufacturing District of Chicago Magazine*. Chicago, 1912- .

There is a great deal of material in the magazine on the economic development of Chicago.

H77 Chicago. Plan Commission. *Chicago Industrial Study: Summary Report*. Chicago, 1952.

An assessment of post-WWII industrial Chicago.

H78 Corplan Associates. *Technological Change, Its Impact on Industry in Metropolitan Chicago: A Report*. Chicago, 1964.

An important series describing technological change and assessing its impact on: electronics, metal working, office industry, primary metals, chemical industries, printing and publishing, with sections on industries of the future, a summary of needs, and a course of suggested action.

H79 Deleted

H80 "Esprit de Corporation." *Am. Heritage,* XXVI, 2 (Feb. 1975), 76-80.

An illustrated popular essay on a set of posters by the Mather Poster Company of Chicago which were designed to increase productivity.

H81 Gutenschwager, Gerald Alfred. "The Scrap Iron and Steel Industry in Metropolitan Chicago." U.C. unpub. M.A. thesis, 1957.

A study in the selection of industrial sites in Chicago. For a short version see his article, "Intra-Metropolitan Industrial Location: The Scrap Industry in Chicago," *Land Econ.,* XL, 2 (1964), 129-139.

H82 Hartnett, Harry Daniel. "A Locational Analysis of Those Manufacturing Firms that Have Located and Relocated within the City of Chicago, 1959-1968." U.I.U. unpub. Ph.D. thesis, 1971.

He concluded that Chicago's industrial areas are more or less alike across the entire city. Thus, there is no special place in the city where a firm with particular needs must locate. Firms that chose to locate or relocated in the city of Chicago did so because of the availability of labor, particularly cheap labor.

H83 *History of the Industrial Club of Chicago: From Its Organization in 1905 to Its Merger with the Commercial Club in 1933*. Chicago, 1934.

Arranged by years with very brief information.

H84 I.I.T. Research Institute. *City of Chicago Industrial Renewal Program*. 4 vol. Chicago, 1963.
"This study, based upon an extensive survey of the physical conditions of Chicago's industrial facilities, is part of

research and action to preserve and strengthen the city's economic basis." The study is divided into: (1) conditions of industrial facilities in Chicago, July 1962; (2) analysis of fifteen selected industrial districts; (3) study appendixes and detailed data tables; (4) summary report.

H85 Deleted

H86 Jucius, Michael James. "Industrial Districts of the Chicago Region and Their Influence on Plant Location." U.C. unpub. M.A. thesis, 1932.

Studies the CMD, Clearing and Kenwood.

H87 Kelly, Alfred H. "A History of the Illinois Manufacturers' Association." U.C. unpub. Ph.D. thesis, 1938.

H88 Kenyon, James B. *The Industrialization of the Skokie Area*. Chicago, 1954.

H89 Ledermann, Robert Charles. "Industrial Functions in Chicago's Near South Area." U.C. unpub. M.A. thesis, 1951.

With Steinhauser (H97), one of two papers studying the South Side between the Loop and the University of Chicago.

H90 Deleted

H91 Mitchell, William Norman. *Trends in Industrial Location in the Chicago Region Since 1920*. Chicago, 1933.

H92 Newell, Howard Francis. "The Measurement of Urban Decentralization with Special Emphasis on the Decentralization of Manufacturing Employment within the Chicago Area, 1890-1930." In.U. unpub. Ph.D. thesis, 1974.

A highly technical economic study which concludes that industrial decentralization came about because of: (1) establishment of a common charge for the Chicago switching area; (2) the belt line; (3) construction of several belt line sponsored manufacturing districts: (4) the motor truck.

H93 Pollina, Ronald Robert. "Industrial Parks in the Chicago Metropolitan Area: Criteria for Successful Development." U.I.U. unpub. Ph.D. thesis, 1974.

H94 Reeder, Leo Glenn. "Industrial Location in the Chicago Metropolitan Area with Special Reference to Population." U.C. unpub. Ph.D. thesis, 1952.

H95 Riley, Elmer. *The Development of Chicago and Vicinity as a Manufacturing Center Prior to 1880*. Chicago, 1911.

A descriptive narrative.

H96 Schroeder, Gertrude G. "The Growth of the Major Basic Steel Companies 1900-1948." J.H.U. unpub. Ph.D. thesis, 1953.

H97 Steinhauser, Fredric Robert. "Dispersed Manufacturing of the South Redevelopment Area." U.C. unpub. M.A. thesis, 1951.

One of two post-WWII theses designed to describe the area between the Loop and the University of Chicago (see H89).

H98 Stetzer, Donald Foster. "Industrial Density in Chicago." U.C. unpub. M.A. thesis, 1966.

A technical study.

H99 Stone, Ursula Batchelder. "The Baking Industry with Special Reference to the Bread Baking Industry in Chicago." U.C. unpub. Ph.D. thesis, 1929.

A thorough description - location, marketing, technology, labor relations, financing, etc. Some of the evidence is presented in tables and graphs.

H100 Weinrott, Lester A. "The Sweet, Sweet Scent of Soap." *CH*, n.s., VI, 1 (Spring 1977), 44-52.

On the soap business in Chicago.

H101 Williamson, Harold Francis, Jr. "An Empirical Analysis of the Movements of Manufacturing Firms in the Chicago Metropolitan Area." Yale U. unpub. Ph.D. thesis, 1969.

A study of the period 1950-1959 and the reason for the relocation of firms in the Chicago SMSA.

H102 Wrigley, Robert L. "Organized Industrial Districts with Special Reference to the Chicago Area." *J. of Land and Public Utility Econ.*, XXIII, 2 (May 1947), 180-198.

(Biography - Individuals and Firms)

Abbott Laboratories

H103 Kogan, Herman. *The Long White Line: The Story of Abbott Laboratories*. New York, 1963.

A friendly, popular history.

Borg, George W.
(Borg-Warner)

H104 Casey, Robert Joseph. *Mr. Clutch, the Story of George William Borg.* Indianapolis, 1948.

A popular life of the founder of Borg-Warner.

Borg-Warner Corp.

See: H104, George W. Borg.

Chicago Bridge and Iron

H104a Imberman, Eli Woodruff. "The Formative Years of Chicago Bridge and Iron Company." U.C. unpub. Ph.D. thesis, 1973.

Basically, a narrative history.

Crane Co.

H104b Crane, R. T. *The Autobiography of Richard Teller Crane.* Chicago, 1927.

This is, in fact, a biography of the firm rather than an autobiography of Richard Teller Crane.

Diversey, Michael

H105 Angle, Paul M. "Michael Diversey and Beer in Chicago." *CH,* VIII, 11 (Spring 1969), 321-326.

Galvin, Paul
(Motorola, Inc.)

H106 Petrakis, Harry Mark. *The Founder's Touch: The Life of Paul Galvin of Motorola.* New York, 1965.

A popular, friendly life.

Gary, Elbert H.
(U.S. Steel)

H107 Olds, Irving Sands. *Judge Elbert H. Gary (1846-1927) His Life and Influence Upon American Industry.* New York, 1947.

A short life of the leader of U.S. Steel taken in large part from the less sympathetic work of Ida Tarbell.

H108 Sevitch, Benjamin. "Elbert H. Gary: Spokesman for Steel." In.U. unpub. Ph.D. thesis, 1972.

International Harvester

See: H109-113, Cyrus and Nettie McCormick, George Perkins; I72

McCormick, Cyrus
(International Harvester)

H109 Casson, H. N. *Cyrus Hall McCormick, His Life and Work.* Chicago, 1909.

An early, short life.

H110 Hutchinson, William T. *Cyrus Hall McCormick.* 2 vol. New York, 1930.

A long, standard biography.

McCormick, Nettie
(International Harvester)

H111 Burgess, Charles O. *Nettie Fowler McCormick: Profile of an American Philanthropist.* Madison, 1962.

This short sketch obviously stresses a different aspect of Mrs. McCormick's life than Roderick's biography (H112).

H112 Roderick, Stella Virginia. *Nettie Fowler McCormick.* Rindge, N.H., 1956.

Mrs. McCormick was a central figure in the McCormick Harvesting Machine Co. and in the formation of International Harvester.

MacDowell, Charles H.

H112a MacDowell, Claire Leavitt. *Two Ears of Corn by Way of the Chemical Kettle: The Life Story of Charles H. MacDowell.* Stonington, Conn., 1954.

Motorola, Inc.

See: H106, Paul Galvin

Perkins, George W.
(International Harvester)

H113 Garraty, John A. *Right-Hand Man: The Life of George W. Perkins.* New York, 1960.

Perkins was a self-made millionaire who was instrumental in the formation of International Harvester. He also was a leading progressive figure. This is the standard life. For a short popular article by Garraty see, *Am. Heritage,* XIII, 2 (Feb. 1962), 41-43.

Pullman, George

See also: O95-99

H114 Harding, Carroll Rede. *George M. Pullman, 1831-1897, and the Pullman Company.* New York, 1951.

H115 Miller, Florence Lowden. "The Pullmans of Prairie Avenue: A Domestic Portrait from Letters and Diaries." *CH,* n.s., I, 3 (Spring 1971), 142-155.

A friendly, domestic account of George M. Pullman by his granddaughter.

U. S. Steel

See: H107, 108, Elbert H. Gary

Wrigley, P. K.

H116 Angle, Paul M. *Philip K. Wrigley: A Memoir of a Modest Man.* Chicago, 1975.

A memoir of a second generation Chicago businessman who expanded the family business in chewing gum and added others such as United Airlines to the family's holdings.

Wrigley, William

H117 Zimmerman, William, Jr. *William Wrigley, Jr., the Man and His Business, 1861-1932.* Chicago, 1935.

A straightforward narrative of the life of the founder of the chewing gum empire.

Meat Packing

(General)

See also: E50; I1, 13, 43, 50, 54, 61, 68, 71, 79, 122, 144; O90-94

H118 Heckler, Edwin L. *The Meat Packing Industry*. Boston, 1944.

A house history.

H119 Herbst, Alma. *The Negro in the Slaughtering and Meat Packing Industry in Chicago*. New York, 1971 (c1932).

A frequently cited standard work.

H120 Hill, Howard C. "The Development of Chicago as a Center of the Meat Packing Industry." *Miss. Valley H. R.*, X, 3 (Dec. 1923), 253-273.

A narrative arguing that "The concentration of the meat packing industry in Chicago is in large measure a story of transportation."

H121 Kujovich, Mary Y. "The Refrigeration Car and the Growth of the American Dressed Beef Industry." *Business H. R.*, XLIV, 4 (Winter 1970), 460-482.

H122 Parkhurst, M. S. *History of the Yards, 1865-1953*. Chicago, 1953.

A short, authorized institutional history.

H123 Perrin, Richard. "The North American Beef and Cattle Trade with Great Britain 1870-1914." *Econ. H. R.*, 2nd ser., XXIV, 3 (Aug. 1971), 430-444.

H124 Scudder, David B. "The Trend of Labor Requirements in Meat Packing." U.C. unpub. M.A. thesis, 1950.

H125 Wade, Louise Carroll. "Something More than Packers." *CH*, n.s., II, 4 (Fall-Winter 1973), 224-231.

An important article that shows how the meat packers expanded the scope of their business by the use of all parts of the animals, control of their employees and by involving their families in the business.

H126 Wallace, Thomas Dudley. "An Analysis of Recent Shifts in the Location of Hog Slaughtering; Special Emphasis on the Corn Belt." U.C. unpub. Ph.D. thesis, 1963.

H127 Walsh, Margaret. "Pork Packing as a Leading Edge of Midwestern Industry, 1835-1875." *Agri. H.*, LI, 4 (Oct. 1977), 702-717.

H128 Whitaker, James W. *Feedlot Empire: Beef Cattle Feeding in Illinois and Iowa, 1840-1900*. Ames, 1975.

A chapter is devoted to Chicago and there are many other references accessible through the index. Bibliography.

(Biography - Individuals and Firms)

Armour, Edward and Family

H129 Davenport, Cora Lillian. "The Rise of the Armours, an American Industrial Family." U.C. unpub. M.A. thesis, 1930.

Chapters on Philip D., the expansion of the firm and the move to Chicago, management, their methods tending towards monoply, and on the role of J. Ogden Armour.

H130 Leech, Harper and John Carroll. *Armour and His Times*. New York, 1938.

A popular life of one of the major Chicago packers.

Cudahy, Edward

H131 Kane, William Terence. *The Education of Edward Cudahy*. Chicago, 1941.

A friendly biography of a major packer.

Swift & Company

H132 Unfer, Louis. "Swift and Company - The Development of the Packing Industry, 1875-1912." U.I.U. unpub. Ph.D. thesis, 1951.

Swift, Gustavus

H133 Neyhart, Louise. *Giant of the Yards*. Boston, 1952.

A simple, popular life of Gustavus Swift, founder of the packing firm.

H134 Swift, Helen. *My Father and My Mother*. Chicago, 1937.

Memoir of Gustavus and Anna Swift.

H135 Swift, Louis Franklin. *The Yankee of the Yards: The Biography of Gustavus Franklin Swift*. Chicago, 1927.

A slightly more sophisticated life, but friendly.

Finance

(General)

H136 Bies, Susan Adair Schmidt. "Commercial Banking in Metropolitan Areas: A Study of the Chicago SMSA [Standard Metropolitan Statistical Area]." N.U. unpub. Ph.D. thesis, 1972.

A highly technical argument which concludes that small banks will be forced out of business because of the movement of their customers to the suburbs.

H137 Boyle, James E. *Speculation and the Chicago Board of Trade*. New York, 1920.

H138 Charlton, Joseph W. "History of Banking in Illinois Since 1863." U.C. unpub. Ph.D. thesis, 1938.

A descriptive narrative.

H139 *Chicago Board of Trade: Origin, Growth, and Usefulness; Its Leading Members, and Representative Businessmen in Other Branches of Trade*. New York, 1885.

A friendly, 19th century account.

H140 Deleted

H141 Chicago Board Options Exchange. *Chicago Board Options Exchange Guide: Chicago Board Options Exchange Directory, Constitution and Rules; Chicago Board Options Exchange Clearing Corporation By-Laws and Rules*. New York, 1973.

A constantly revised set of regulations, descriptions, procedures, etc.

H142 Dailey, Don Marcus. "The Development of Banking in Chicago Before 1890." N.U. unpub. Ph.D. thesis, 1934.

H143 Dies, Edward Jerome. *The Plunger: A Tale of the Wheat Pit*. New York, 1975 (c1929).

A popular study of grain trading.

H144 Fleming, I. A. *Chicago Stock Exchange: An Historical Sketch with Biographies of Its Leading Members*. Chicago, 1894.

A 19th century work useful for reference.

H145 Haeger, John Denis. "Eastern Money and the Urban Frontier: Chicago, 1833-1842." *JISHS*, LXIV, 3 (Autumn 1971), 271-284.

Attempts to establish the influence of early investors in Chicago.

H146 Huston, Francis M. *Financing an Empire: History of Banking in Illinois*. 4 vol. Chicago, 1926.

There is a great deal of Chicago material in this general account.

H147 James, Frank Cyril. *The Growth of Chicago Banks*. 2 vol. New York, 1938.

Mostly a narrative - volume 1 contains material up to 1896, volume 2 to 1938. Both volumes have appendixes listing Chicago banks, important dates in their histories, etc. Bibliography.

H148 Lurie, Jonathan. "The Chicago Board of Trade, 1874-1905, and the Development of Certain Rules and Regulations Governing Its Operation: A Study in the Effectiveness of Internal Regulation." U.W. unpub. Ph.D. thesis, 1970.

The Board of Trade escaped much external regulation because of ". . . the impulse towards effective internal control . . ." See also his article on the same subject in *Am. J. of Legal H.*, XVI, 3 (July 1972), 215-238.

H149 Marquardt, Mary Oona. Sources of Capital of Early Illinois Manufacturers, 1840-1880." U.I.U. unpub. Ph.D. thesis, 1960.

H150 Merrill, Francis Ellsworth. "The Chicago Stock Exchange." U.C. unpub. Ph.D. thesis, 1937.

A sociological description but with many historical chapters.

H151 Palyi, Melchior. *The Chicago Credit Market: Organization and Institutional Structure*. Chicago, [1937].

A full description of the market with supporting statistical material.

H152 Rice, Wallace. *The Chicago Stock Exchange: A History*. Chicago, 1923.

A short official history with a list of officers.

H153 Taylor, Charles H., ed. *History of the Board of Trade of the City of Chicago.* 3 vol. Chicago, 1917.

A long narrative in the first two volumes, and a collection of biographical sketches in the third.

(Biography - Individuals and Firms)

Baker, William Taylor

H154 Baker, Charles Hinkley. *Life and Character of William Taylor Baker, President of the World's Columbian Exposition and of the Chicago Board of Trade.* New York, 1903.

A friendly life by his son.

Binga, Jesse

H155 Osthaus, Carl R. "The Rise and Fall of Jesse Binga, Black Financier." *J. of Negro H.,* LVIII, 1 (Jan. 1973), 39-60.

A key figure in black financial and business life before the depression.

Dawes, Charles G.

H156 Pixton, John Erwin. "The Early Career of Charles G. Dawes." U.C. unpub. Ph.D. thesis, 1952.

H157 Sherman, Richard G. "Charles G. Dawes: An Entrepreneurial Biography, 1865-1951." U.Iowa unpub. Ph.D. thesis, 1960.

A straightforward narrative which deals with areas of Dawes' life other than business.

H158 Timmons, Bascom Nolly. *Portrait of an American: Charles G. Dawes.* New York, 1953.

Dawes was a well-known national figure: Comptroller of the Currency; Director of the Budget, and Vice-President. In Chicago he was a successful lawyer and banker.

Evans, John

H159 Kelsey, Harry E. *Frontier Capitalist: The Life of John Evans.* Denver, c1969.

Evans began life as a physician, made a fortune in Chicago real estate, and helped found Northwestern University.

First National Bank

See also: H161, Gaylord A. Freeman

H160 Morris, Henry Crittenden. *The History of the First National Bank of Chicago . . .* Chicago, 1902.

An official history.

Freeman, Gaylord A. (First National Bank)

H161 Freeman, Gaylord A. *Gaylord Freeman of First Chicago.* 2 vol. Edited by Sidney Hyman. Chicago, 1975.

Essays and speeches; includes a chapter on the First National Bank of Chicago.

Gates, John W.

H162 Wendt, Lloyd. *Bet a Million! The Story of John W. Gates.* Indianapolis, 1948.

Born in Chicago, Gates moved about the U. S. and became a national figure, leading the way to bring capital together for a variety of enterprises. His dealings often involved Chicago.

Supreme Life Insurance Company

H163 Puth, Robert C. "Supreme Life: The History of a Negro Life Insurance Company." N.U. unpub. Ph.D. thesis, 1967.

Walsh, John R.

H164 Tarr, Joel A. "John R. Walsh of Chicago: A Case Study in Banking and Politics, 1881-1905." *Business H. R.*, XL, 4 (Winter 1966), 451-466.

Walsh's banks failed in 1905. Tarr traces his career and involvement with major economic and political leaders.

Agriculture

H165 Duddy, Edward A. *Agriculture in the Chicago Region.* Chicago, 1929.

Little text, mainly a tabular and graphic ordering of statistical data on land use, crops, livestock, farms and people,

H166 Engle, Robert Henry. "The Trends of Agriculture in the Chicago Region." U.C. unpub. Ph.D. thesis, 1941.

A study of the development of agriculture in the Chicago area in the first century of the city's history.

Real Estate

See also: D, City Planning; F95, 123; L, Social Conditions (housing); N44; O, Neighborhoods.

H167 Aschman, Michael Peters. "Three Miles from LA and New York: A Study of Intrametropolitan Office Location Near Chicago-O'Hare International Airport." S.U. unpub. Ph.D. thesis, 1976.

H168 Bednarz, Robert S. *The Effect of Air Pollution on Property Value in Chicago*. Chicago, 1975.

A highly technical study in geography.

H169 Berry, Brian J. L. and Robert S. Bednarz. "A Hedonic Model of Prices and Assessments for Single-Family Homes: Does the Assessor Follow the Market or the Market Follow the Assessor?" *Land Econ.*, LI, 1 (Feb. 1975), 21-40.

H170 Fales, Raymond Lawrence. "Location Theory and the Spatial Structure of the Nineteenth Century City." N.U. unpub. Ph.D. thesis, 1971.

He explores two theories of location in urban areas. He argues that Chicago's pattern shows ". . . that manufacturing was oriented to one means of transport (railroad and vessels), the inter-regional transportation of goods, and that the local population was oriented towards another means (the horse railroad), the intra-urban transportation of people." See also a shorter version by Fales and Leon N. Moses in *Regional Science Assoc. Papers and Proceedings*, XXVIII (1972).

H171 Ferrera, Salvatore Victor. "The Effect of Urban Renewal and Public Housing on Neighboring Property Values and Rents in Chicago." U.C. unpub. Ph.D. thesis, 1969.

H172 Gans, Barbara Gretchen. "Residential Land Use in the Calumet Area of Chicago." U.C. unpub. M.A. thesis, 1954.

H173 Golden, Jay Stewart. *Land Values in Chicago: Before and After Expressway Construction*. Chicago, 1968.

Bibliography.

H174 Helper, Rose. *Racial Policies and Practices of Real Estate Brokers*. Minneapolis, 1969.

See also her 1958 U.C. Ph.D. thesis on the same topic.

H175 Hoyt, Homer. *One Hundred Years of Land Values in Chicago: The Relationship of the Growth of Chicago to the Rise in Its Land Value, 1830-1933*. New York, c1933.

A study of core land sites that give a true market price. This information is then related to general economic periods in Chicago's history. There are valuable appendixes of additional data and a good index. A fundamental work in the field.

H176 Mankin, Wyatt. "Home Ownership and Race." U.C. unpub. Ph.D. thesis, 1971.

A highly technical study in economics.

H177 Monchow, Helen C. *Seventy Years of Real Estate Subdividing in the Region of Chicago*. Chicago, 1939.

In 1928 the Chicago Regional Planning Association collected data on recorded lots in the region of Chicago. Monchow used their information to describe ". . . the underlying forces that have caused or been associated with subdividing activity . . ."

H178 Olcott, George C. and Co. *Olcott's Land Values Blue Book of Chicago*. Chicago, 1900.

A series of maps with estimated land values by block.

H179 Deleted

H180 Putney, Mark H. *Real Estate Values and Historical Notes of Chicago from the Earliest Period to the Present Time*. Chicago, 1900.

A collection of values on some parcels of land in the city.

H181 Schietinger, Egbert F. "Race and Residential Market Values in Chicago." *Land Econ.*, XXX (Nov. 1954), 301-308.

H182 __________. "Racial Succession and Changing Property Values in Residential Chicago." U.C. unpub. Ph.D. thesis, 1953.

H183 Solzman, David M. *Waterway Industrial Sites: A Chicago Case Study*. Chicago, 1966.
Although this is primarily a study in present usage, there are substantial historical sections. He found that "Despite past glory, the presence of the waterway has today little

perceptible impact on property values along its banks . . . the major factor affecting waterfront property values . . . is distance from the city center." Only in the very early stages of the city's growth did the waterway encourage manufacturing development.

H184 Vaughan, Roger J. "The Value of Urban Open Space." U.C. unpub. Ph.D. thesis, 1977.

An exercise in formal economics, Vaughan ". . . presents estimates of the value of urban recreational open space in the city of Chicago." There is valuable information in this piece but it is difficult to extract from the jargon of economics.

H185 Work, Monroe Nathan. "Negro Real Estate Holders of Chicago." U.C. unpub. M.A. thesis, 1903.

H186 Yeates, Maurice H. "Some Factors Affecting the Spatial Distribution of Chicago Land Values, 1910-1960." *Econ. Geography*, XLI, 1 (Jan. 1965), 57-70.

An important article that points to 1930 as the peak for proximity to the urban center as the principal factor in outlying property values. The role of access to public transportation also peaked in 1930.

Utilities

(General)

See also: K19

H187 Kneier, Charles Mayard. *State Regulation of Public Utilities in Illinois*. Urbana, c1927.

A published dissertation.

(Biography - Individuals and Firms)

Commonwealth Edison

H188 Rauber, Earle Leroy. "The Development of the Electric Light and Power Industry in Chicago and Vicinity." U.C. unpub. Ph.D. thesis, 1930.

A close, detailed narrative from the first electric light in Chicago to the development of large holding companies.

Hibbard, Angus Smith
(Illinois Bell)

H189 Hibbard, Angus Smith. *Hello, Goodbye: My Story of Telephone Pioneering.* Chicago, c1941.

The autobiography of the general manager of the Chicago Telephone Co. which became Illinois Bell.

Illinois Bell

See also: H189, Angus Smith Hibbard

H190 Dickerson, William Eugene. "Organization and Control of the Illinois Bell Telephone Company." U.C. unpub. Ph.D. thesis, 1926.

A short overview of the company is followed by a description of the company's policies and its organization, department by department.

H191 Glauber, Robert H. "The Necessary Toy: The Telephone Comes to Chicago." *Ch,* n.s., VII, 2 (Summer 1978), 70-86.

Bell's invention was promoted in Chicago in just over a year after its invention. This is an account of that promotion by Gardiner Hubbard.

H192 Schroeder, Walter Albert. "Determination of the Telephone Hinterland of Metropolitan Chicago." U.C. unpub. M.A. thesis, 1958.

An interesting thesis that shows a correlation with the hinterland identified by Taafe in his study of air traffic (F99).

Insull, Samuel

H193 MacDonald, Forrest. *Insull.* Chicago, 1962.

A scholarly but friendly life of a central figure in the development of Chicago's utilities.

H193a __________. "Samuel Insull and the Movement for State Utility Regulatory Commissions." *Business H. R.,* XXXII, 3 (Autumn 1958), 241-254.

Peoples Gas

H194 Illinois. Bureau of Labor Statistics. *History of the Chicago Gas Companies. Extracts from the Forthcoming Report of the Illinois Bureau of Labor Statistics of George A. Schilling, Secretary of the Bureau of Labor.* [Chicago, 1897?]

Short, but with useful material.

H195 Oates, James Franklin. *The Keepers of the Flame, 1850-1950: 100 Years of Gas Service in Chicago.* New York, 1950.

H196 Ramsay, Marion Livingston. *Pyramids of Power: The Story of Roosevelt, Insull and the Utility Wars.* Indianapolis, c1937.

H197 Rice, Wallace. *75 Years of Gas Service in Chicago . . .* Chicago, 1925.

A short, authorized account favorable to the company.

H198 Smith, Henry Ezmond. "Organization and Administrative Procedure of the Peoples Gas, Light and Coke Company." U.C. unpub. Ph.D. thesis, 1926.

A brief history of the company is followed by a detailed analysis of its departments.

Professions

See also: L, Social Conditions (medicine).

(Law)

General

See also: L7; T46a

H199 Kent, Leonard. "Economic Status of the Legal Profession in Chicago." U.C. unpub. Ph.D. thesis, 1950.

Describes some major groups that lawyers fell into and the variables that were related. Since there were many variables, the study goes beyond simply economic status.

H200 Kogan, Herman. *The First Century: The Chicago Bar Association, 1874-1974.* Chicago, 1974.

A house history.

H201 Lortie, D. C. "The Striving Young Lawyer. A Study of Early Career Differentiation in the Chicago Bar." U.C. unpub. Ph.D. thesis, 1958.

H202 Martin, Edward M. *The Role of the Bar in Electing the Bench in Chicago*. Chicago, 1936.

A long, careful study.

Biography - Individuals and Firms

(Black, William P.)

H203 Kogan, Herman. "William Perkins Black: Haymarket Lawyer." *CH*, n.s., V, 2 (Summer 1976), 85-94.

Black took up the case of the anarchists at great personal cost.

(Bradwell, Myra)

H204 Kogan, Herman. "Myra Bradwell: Crusader at Law." *CH*, n.s., III, 3 (Winter 1974-1975), 132-140.

She sought reform in many areas: law, women's rights, race, etc.

H205 Spector, Robert M. "Women Against the Law: Myra Bradwell's Struggle for Admission to the Illinois Bar." *JISHS*, LXVIII, 3 (June 1975), 228-242.

(Collins, Lorin C.)

H206 Collins, Lorin Cone. *Autobiography*. Chicago, c1934.

Collins was a prominent Chicago lawyer and judge, active in politics in the late 19th and early 20th century.

(Croarkin, Francis E.)

H207 Croarkin, Francis Edward. *Ninety Years, the Autobiography of Francis E. Croarkin*. [Chicago?, 1952].

Croarkin began to practice law in Chicago in 1897.

(Darrow, Clarence)

H208 Darrow, Clarence S. *Attorney for the Damned*. Edited with notes by Arthur Weinberg. New York, 1957.

A collection of his speeches in the courtroom and out.

H209 Darrow, Clarence Seward. *The Story of My Life.* New York, 1932.

Darrow was a national figure but based in Chicago where he did some of his most important work.

H210 Fenberg, Matilda. "I Remember Clarence Darrow." *CH,* n.s., II, 4 (Fall-Winter 1973), 216-223.

A brief sketch of his career.

H211 Ravitz, Abe C. *Clarence Darrow and the American Literary Tradition.* Cleveland, 1962.

Ravitz studies Darrow's writing which included two novels and many essays and argues that it had an impact on American letters.

H212 Stone, Irving. *Clarence Darrow for the Defense.* Garden City, 1941.

A popular life.

(Elting, Victor)

H213 Elting, Victor. *Recollections of a Grandfather.* Chicago, 1940.

A lawyer who knew many well-known Chicagoans. There is a chapter of description on Chicago in the 1890s.

(Gertz, Elmer)

H214 Gertz, Elmer. *A Handful of Clients.* Chicago, 1965.

Gertz was a well-known attorney in the middle third of the 20th century who represented Nathan Leopold in his efforts at parole, in addition to other well-known clients.

H215 __________. *To Life.* New York, 1974.

Autobiography.

(Getty, Gerald W.)

H216 Getty, Gerald W. and James Presley. *Public Defender.* New York, 1974.

(Mayer, Levy)

H217 Masters, Edgar Lee. *Levy Mayer and the New Industrial Era: A Biography*. New Haven, 1927.

A friendly biography.

(Advertising)

Biography - Individuals and Firms

(Burnett, Leo)

H218 Burnett, Leo. *Communications of an Advertising Man. Selections from the Speeches, Articles, Memoranda and Miscellaneous Writings . . .* Chicago, 1961.

Burnett was head of a major Chicago advertising firm from 1935.

(Cone. Fairfax)

H219 Cone, Fairfax. *With All Its Faults: A Candid Account of Forty Years in Advertising*. Boston, 1969.

Cone was a central figure in Chicago advertising and a trustee of the University of Chicago.

(Lasker, Albert D.)

H220 Gunther, John. *Taken at the Flood: The Story of Albert D. Lasker*. New York, 1960.

Albert Lasker was a long-time Chicago resident and "the father of modern advertising."

(Accounting)

Biography - Individuals and Firms

(Andersen, Arthur and Company)

H221 Andersen, Arthur and Company. *The First Fifty Years, 1913-1963*. Chicago, 1963.

An in-house history with a list of the personnel of the organization as of July 1, 1963.

(Young, Arthur)

H222 Young, Arthur. *Arthur Young and the Business He Founded.* Edited by J. C. Burton. New York, 1948.

A short, formal life with some history of the great accounting firm that he founded in Chicago.

(Detectives)

See also: I134.

Biography - Individuals and Firms

(Pinkerton, Allan)

H223 Lavine, Sigmund A. *Allan Pinkerton: America's First Private Eye.* New York, 1963.

A popular, friendly book.

(Pinkerton National Detective Company)

H224 Morn, Frank T. "The Eye That Never Sleeps: A History of the Pinkerton National Detective Agency, 1850-1920." U.C. unpub. Ph.D. thesis, 1975.

A first rate piece of work.

H225 Horan, James D. *The Pinkertons: The Detective Dynasty That Made History.* New York, 1967.

H226 Rowan, Richard Wilmer. *The Pinkertons, a Detective Dynasty.* Boston, 1931.

A popular biography favorable to the Pinkertons.

I
LABOR

Chicago is one of the most important cities in the history of the American labor movement. As such, it appears in most general histories of labor, unionization, and particular national unions. A substantial number of the works that might bear on Chicago were examined, as well as those works which dealt with a specific Chicago topic. Many of these books and articles were rejected, however, because they lacked sufficient material directly related to Chicago. It is fortunate that there are several bibliographies of American labor that organize this mass of material. These have been listed in the section Z, Reference, and readers are urged to consult them for particular topics not found here.

Chicago Labor and Conditions of Work

See also: P36

I1 Abbott, Edith and S. P. Breckenridge. "Women in Industry: The Chicago Stockyards." *J. of Pol. Econ.*, XIX, 8 (Oct. 1911), 632-654.

I2 Abbott, Grace. "The Chicago Employment Agency and the Immigrant Worker." *Am. J. of Soc.*, XIV, 3 (Nov. 1908), 289-305.

A study of the kinds of work offered by private agencies, to whom it was offered, and how much it cost. She concluded that women were exploited less but were offered a narrower list of work than men who were overcharged by the agency for work that was often temporary and far away.

I3 Auten, Nellie M. "Some Phases of the Sweating System in the Garment Trades of Chicago." *Am. J. of Soc.*, VI, 5 (Mar. 1901), 602-645.

An analysis in detail with statistical supporting evidence.

I4 Aydelott, Mary. "Children in Street Trades in Chicago." U.C. unpub. M.A. thesis, 1924.

Street selling was one of the more difficult forms of child labor to regulate. This study extends from 1916 to 1922 and includes statistical and case studies as evidence.

I5 Breen, Leonard. "Separation of Place of Work from Place of Residence in the City of Chicago." U.C. unpub. M.A. thesis, 1950.

Explores the patterns of residence and employment.

I6 Brown, James, IV. "Before the Sunset Fades." *CH,* n.s., I, 2 (Fall 1970), 96-99.

A description of the household labor force of a very rich Chicagoan.

I7 Callahan, Helen C. "Upstairs-Downstairs in Chicago 1870-1907: The Glessner Household." *CH,* n.s., VI, 4 (Winter 1977-1978), 195-209.

How the Glessner's domestic labor force was organized, what they did, etc.

I8 Cassell, Frank H. "Chicago 1960-1970: One Small Step Forward." *Industrial Relations,* IX, 3 (May 1970), 277-293.

A review of the conditions of the black job market between 1960 and 1970.

I9 Cavan, Ruth Shonle. *Business Girls: A Study of Their Interests and Problems.* Chicago, 1929.

Really a study of the interests and problems of WASP women in the 1920s. The case studies and questionnaires were done through the YWCA.

I10 Donovan, Mrs. Frances R. *The Woman Who Waits.* New York, 1974 (c1920).

Donovan was a writer who became a waitress in Chicago for almost a year. The book is a report of what she saw and heard.

I11 Elazar, Daniel J., ed. "Working Conditions in Chicago in the Early 20th Century - Testimony before the Illinois Senatorial Vice Committee, 1913." *Am. Jewish Archives,* XXI, 2 (Nov. 1969), 149-171.

A collection of primary material on sweatshops on the West Side.

I12 Epstein, Joseph. "Blue Collars in Cicero." *Dissent,* XIX, (Winter 1972), 118-127.

An essay in the culture, values and attitudes of working men in Cicero.

I13 Fogel, Walter. *The Negro in the Meat Industry.* Philadelphia, 1970.

Much of the material deals with Chicago. See also his "Blacks in Meatpacking: Another View of the Jungle," *Industrial Relations,* X, 3 (Oct. 1971), 338-353.

I14 Gariss, Jeannette Merk. "A Study of Women Clerical Workers in Chicago." U.C. unpub. M.A. thesis, 1942.

She studied wages, hours, factors in placement and personnel. In general she found that what would now be called a sexist system prevailed.

I15 Gold, Raymond L. "The Chicago Flat Janitor." U.C. unpub. M.A. thesis, 1950.

I16 Hamilton, Mary Townsend. "A Study of Wage Discrimination by Sex: A Sample Survey in the Chicago Area." U.Penn. unpub. Ph.D. thesis, 1969.

The evidence was collected in 1963 for four occupations in the metropolitan Chicago area and demonstrates that then sex was a powerful factor in wage determination.

I17 Deleted

I18 Houghteling, Leila. *The Income and Standard of Living of Unskilled Laborers in Chicago*. Chicago, 1927.

Establishes wage levels and sets standard of living by type of sanitation, lighting, etc.

I19 Humphreys, Elizabeth Jeanne. "Working Women in Chicago Factories and Department Stores, 1870-1895." U.C. unpub. M.A. thesis, 1943.

Women worked because they had to and they worked in bad conditions for less pay than men. Union organization was very slow in coming.

I20 Hymer, Bennett. *The Dynamics of Job Changing: A Case Study of Employment Conditions for Black Workers in the Chicago Labor Market*. Chicago, 1969.

I21 __________. "Racial Dualism in the Chicago Labor Market." N.U. unpub. Ph.D. thesis, 1968.

A long, detailed look at the problem and its manifestation.

I22 Johnson, Borghild Eleanor. "Household Employment in Chicago." U.C. unpub Ph.D. thesis, 1931.

I23 Joray, Paul Albert. "The Temporary Industrial Labor Service Market in the Chicago and St. Louis Metropolitan Areas." U.I.U. unpub. Ph.D. thesis, 1972.

A study of the temporary "help" business.

I24 Kornblum, William. *Blue Collar Community*. Chicago, 1974. Sociological study of the political and communal institutions of Chicago's south side.

I24a Maurer, David J. "Unemployment in Illinois During the Great Depression." *Essays in Illinois History in Honor of Glenn Huron Seymour*. Edited by D. F. Tingley. Carbondale, 1968.

I24b Larson, Margaret Jeanne. "The Movement for Women's Wages and Hours Legislation in Illinois, 1893-1913." U.I.U. unpub. M.A. thesis, 1953.

Much of the evidence is drawn from Chicago.

I25 Myers, Robert J. "The Economic Aspects of the Production of Men's Clothing (with Particular Reference to the Industry in Chicago)." U.C. unpub. Ph.D. thesis, 1937.

A well-documented study with extensive field work in Chicago. In several large parts he discusses the growth of the industry, technical aspects, the organization and finance of the industry, labor aspects, distribution, and the impact of NRA. Much of the evidence, however, is drawn from the period before the depression.

I26 Nelson, Nell (pseud.) *The White Slave Girls of Chicago: Nell Nelson's Startling Disclosure of the Cruelties and Iniquities Practiced in the Workshops and Factories of a Great City*. Chicago, 1888.

I27 Pfeil, Walter F. "Workers' Education in Chicago." U.C. unpub. M.A. thesis, 1935.

A study of labor education for workers 1934-1935. The bibliography is extensive but most of the evidence was in the form of interviews and observations.

I28 Rose, Caroline B. "Workers' Education, the Labor Movement, and the Intellectuals in the United States: 1920-1940." U.C. unpub. Ph.D. thesis, 1943.

Bibliography.

I29 Scott, Estelle Hill. *Occupational Changes Among Negroes in Chicago*. Chicago, 1939.

I30 Seath, William. *The Challenge of the Impossible: The Story of the Chicago Christian Industrial League*. New York, [1967].

I31 Sheldon, Eleanor Harriet. "The Chicago Labor Force, 1910-1940: A Comparative Study of Trends in the Labor Force and in Occupational and Industrial Characteristics." U.C. unpub. Ph.D. thesis, 1949.

I32 Sieder, Violet Marot. "The Wage of Women in the Men's Neckwear Industry in Chicago." U.C. unpub. M.A. thesis, 1936.
A broader study than the topic indicates. In fact, it is a study of the industry and its exploitation of women workers. Some materials on the efforts of labor unions to stop this practice.

I33 Sugeno, Florence T. "The Chicago Labor Force, 1910-1950." U.C. unpub. M.A. thesis, 1955.

A study of trends in various kinds of work. Chicago in the first half of the 20th century tended to follow national demographic patterns, including shifts in kinds of work.

I34 Taylor, David P. and Edwin Berry. *The Unskilled Negro Worker in the Chicago Labor Market.* [Chicago, 1966?].

I35 Wentworth, Edna Louise Clark. "The History of the Controversy Between Labor and Capital in the Slaughtering and Meat Packing Industries in Chicago." U.C. unpub. M.A. thesis, 1922.

Chicago Unions and Unionization

Many, probably most, locals of unions in the Chicago area have published some sort of history of their organization. In general, these have been excluded in favor of selected scholarly references to union organization. See also: P32, 36; R44, 78

I36 Amalgamated Clothing Workers of America. *The Clothing Workers of Chicago 1910-1922.* Chicago, 1922.

A union account of a crucial period of development beginning with the strike of 1910, the union's agreement with Hart, Schaffner & Marx, and the expansion of the union to include most workers in Chicago.

I37 Apel, Paul Herman. "A Study of the Chicago Federation of Musicians, Local No. 10, A. F. of M." U.C. unpub. M.A. thesis, 1933.

A brief history precedes an analysis of the union in 1933.

I38 Barrows, Emily. "Trade Union Organization Among Women in Chicago." U.C. unpub. M.A. thesis, 1927.

Little study had been done on this subject when she wrote. Her paper organizes the subject and gathers the evidence available at the time. She argues, among other things, that not many women had been organized because little effort had been made to do so. This in part reflected a belief by men that women could not be organized.

I39 Beckner, Earl. *A History of Illinois Labor Legislation.* Chicago, 1929.

I40 Behen, David M. "The Chicago Labor Movement, 1874-1896: Its Philosophical Bases." U.C. unpub. Ph.D. thesis, 1953.

I41 Bigham, Truman C. "The Chicago Federation of Labor." U.C. unpub. M.A. thesis, 1925.

An analysis of the Federation in 1924. There is only a brief historical introduction.

I42 Bizjack, Jack E. "The Trade and Labor Assembly of Chicago, Illinois." U.C. unpub. M.A. thesis, 1969.

A narrative of the history of an early attempt at promotion of unionism and certain radical political beliefs in Chicago.

I43 Brody, David. *The Butcher Workmen*. Cambridge, 1964.

The basic text on the subject; a narrative that traces unionization in all areas of the meat trades. Since Chicago was a center of meat packing, it is accorded much space in the study.

I44 Brown, Emily C. *Book and Job Printing in Chicago: A Study of Organizations of Employers and Their Relations with Labor*. Chicago, 1931.

There is a survey of developments in the 19th century but the book deals mostly with post-WWI activity.

I45 Byrnes, Joseph Francis. "Union Development in the Chicago Area Food Distribution Industry, 1900 to 1972." N.U. unpub. Ph.D. thesis, 1974.

Useful chapter on ". . . the bargaining structure development from 1900 to the present of the Chicago meat cutters, the Chicago retail food clerks, and the Chicago teamsters, grocery truck drivers and grocery warehousemen."

I46 Carsel, Wilfred. *A History of the Chicago Ladies Garment Workers' Union*. Chicago, 1940.

A straightforward narrative.

I47 Christenson, C. Lawrence. *Collective Bargaining in Chicago, 1929-1930: A Study of the Economic Significance of the Industrial Location of Trade Unionism*. Chicago, 1933.

Treats construction, building service, metal products, local transportation, amusements, printing industry and wearing apparel.

I48 Commons, John R. "The Teamsters of Chicago." *Trade Unionism and Labor Problems*. Edited by William Z. Ripley. Boston, 190[illegible]

Dated but still one of the most useful works on the early teamsters.

I49 Daly, Kathryn Wilson. "The International Ladies' Garment Workers' Union in Chicago, 1930-1939." U.C. unpub. M.A. thesis, 1939.

She describes the effectiveness of the Union in the different parts of the business: coat and suit; dress; white goods; and miscellaneous crafts and trades. A chapter is added on benefits, as are appendixes of documents.

I50 Douthit, William Evans. "Analysis of the Area of Collective Bargaining in the Meatpacking Industry." U.I.U. unpub. M.A. thesis, 1953.

I51 Fagan, Harrison Bernard. "Industrial Relations in the Chicago Newspaper Industry." U.C. unpub. Ph.D. thesis, 1930.

A narrative of the conditions of work and labor relations since 1873. Some documents are bound in the volume as an appendix. Bibliography.

I52 Handsaker, John Morrison. "The Chicago Cleaning and Dyeing Industry: A Case Study in 'Controlled' Competition." U.C. unpub. Ph.D. thesis, 1939.

A very narrow study which focuses on formal questions of economics. Nevertheless, it includes useful material on labor relations. A separate digest was published.

I53 Deleted

I54 Holcomb, James Rogers. "The Union Policies of Meat Packers, 1929-1943." U.I.U. unpub. M.A. thesis, 1957.

I55 Hutton, Oscar Douglas. "The Negro Worker and the Labor Unions in Chicago." U.C. unpub. M.A. thesis, 1939.

He concluded, somewhat surprisingly given the date, that a large number of blacks were effective members of labor unions in the area.

I56 Jones, Ralph Thomas. "City Employee Unions in New York and Chicago." Ha.U. unpub. Ph.D. thesis, 1972.

I57 Keiser, John H. "Black Strikebreakers and Racism in Illinois, 1865-1900." *JISHS*, LXV, 3 (Autumn 1972), 313-326.

He argues ". . . that racial antagonism in Illinois between 1865 and 1900 stemmed, to a large extent, from the use of black strikebreakers." He deals with statewide examples, including some in Chicago.

I58 Kornblum, William. "Insurgency in the Steel Union." *Dissent,* XXII (Summer 1975), 220-222.

An account of Ed Sadlowski's victory over the old union pols in District 131, the Chicago-Gary-Joliet area.

I59 Kritzberg, Barry. "An Unfinished Chapter in White-Collar Unionism: The Formative Years of the Chicago Newspaper Guild, Local 71, American Newspaper Guild, . . . A.F.L.-C.I.O." *Labor H.,* 3 (Summer 1973), 397-413.

A narrative through Local 71's defeat by Hearst in the early 1940s. The "Unfinished Chapter" refers to the fact that unionization still was incomplete.

I60 Larkin, Rev. William Donald. "Forty-five Years of Collective Bargaining and Arbitration Between Chicago Surface Lines and Its Trainmen." L.U. unpub. M.A. thesis, 1948.

I61 Lewis, Catherine Elizabeth. "Trade Union Policies in Regard to the Negro Worker in the Slaughtering and Meatpacking Industry of Chicago." U.C. unpub. M.A. thesis, 1945.

Treats union racial practices and analyzes the real benefits of unionization for black workers.

I62 McAndrew, Ian Charles. "The Politics of the Public Workers Unions: A Case Study of AFSCME in Illinois." U.I.U. unpub. Ph.D. thesis, 1975.

I63 Deleted

I64 McMurray, Donald L. "Labor Policies of the General Managers' Association of Chicago, 1886-1894." *J. of Econ. H.,* XIII, 2 (Spring 1953), 160-178.

Treats the development of anti-union techniques and organization and notes the ". . . parallel development among national labor associations."

I65 Magee, Mabel Agnes. "The Woman's Clothing Industry of Chicago, with Special Reference to Relations Between the Manufacturers and the Union." U.C. unpub. Ph.D. thesis, 1927.

I66 Mittleman, Edward B. "Chicago Labor in Politics, 1887-1896." *J. of Pol. Econ.,* XXVIII, 5 (May 1920), 407-427.

I67 Montgomery, Royal E. *Industrial Relations in the Chicago Building Trades.* Chicago, 1927.

A narrative and analysis of the union's history. He argues that the rapid growth of population in Chicago is the key to understanding the union and its position. The reason is that the rise of population created a more or less constant demand for building.

I68 Naylor, Samuel J. "The History of Labor Organization in the Slaughtering and Meat Packing Industry." U.I.U. unpub. Ph.D. thesis, 1935.

I69 *Negro Pioneers in the Chicago Labor Movement*. Compiled by Maida Springer Kemp. New York, 1970.

Sketches of some unions that have been important to blacks, with short biographical notes.

I70 Newell, Barbara Warne. *Chicago and the Labor Movement: Metropolitan Unionism in the 1930s*. Urbana, 1961.

A close study of the 1930s in Chicago. One of the best surveys of Chicago union activity. Good bibliography.

I71 Novak, Ralph S. "Collective Bargaining in the Meat Packing Industry." U.Iowa unpub. Ph.D. thesis, 1953.

I72 Ozanne, Robert. *A Century of Labor-Management Relations at McCormick and International Harvester*. Madison, 1967.

A detailed study based on an unusually complete group of records at the State Historical Society of Wisconsin. Good bibliography. See also his article, "Union-Management Relations: McCormick Harvesting Machine Company, 1862-1886," *Labor H.*, IV, 2 (Spring 1963), 132-160.

I73 Purcell, Theodore V. *The Worker Speaks His Mind on Company and Union*. Cambridge, 1953.

A study of the Swift packing plant in Chicago and its workers.

I74 Rosenberg, Bernard. "Torn Apart and Driven Apart: A Portrait of a UAW Local in Chicago." *Dissent*, XIX (Winter 1972), 61-69.

A study of many issues important to the men of Local 6 and International Harvester Company.

I75 Seymour, Helen. "The Organized Unemployed." U.C. unpub. M.A. thesis, 1937.

I76 Stead, William Thomas. *Chicago Today: Or, the Labour War in America*. New York, 1969 (c1894).

I77 Stein, Jack M. "History of Unionization in the Steel Industry in the Chicago Area." U.C. unpub. M.A. thesis, 1948.

I78 Terkel, Studs. "A Steelworker Speaks." *Dissent,* XIX, (Winter 1972), 9-20.

I79 Tuttle, William M., Jr. "Labor Conflict and Racial Violence: The Black Worker in Chicago 1894-1919." *Labor H.,* X, 3 (Summer 1969), 408-432.

Describes the growth of black-white tension growing out of the use of blacks as strikebreakers.

I80 __________. "Some Strikebreakers' Observations of Industrial Warfare." *Labor H.,* VII, 2 (Spring 1966), 193-196.

A brief note and documents on strikebreaking in the Chicago meat industry.

I81 Deleted

I82 Weber, Arnold R. "Paradise Lost: Or, Whatever Happened to the Chicago Social Workers?" *Industrial and Labor Relations R.,* XXII, 3 (Ap. 1969), 323-338.

I83 Wolman, Leo, *et.al. The Clothing Workers of Chicago, 1910-1922.* Chicago, 1922.

Major Chicago Strikes

The fundamental work for labor disputes in Chicago is:

I84 Myers, Howard Barton. "The Policing of Labor Disputes in Chicago: A Case Study." U.C. unpub. Ph.D. thesis, 1929.

A massive, frequently cited study of important labor disputes through 1925, *viz.:* railroad riots of 1877; McCormick lockouts, 1886 and the Haymarket riot; the stockyard stoppages, 1886; Pullman strike, 1894; building trades lockout, 1900-1901; packing house teamsters strike, 1902; freight handlers' strike, 1902; the street railway strike of 1908; Kellogg Switchboard strike, 1903; press feeders' stoppage, 1903; the International Typographical Union strike, 1905; stockyards strike, 1904; the Teamsters strike, 1905; men's clothing strike, 1910; newspaper stoppage, 1912; waitresses' (Henrici) strike, 1914; men's clothing strike, 1915; dress and waist industry strikes, 1917; stockyards strike, 1921; dress and waist industry strike, 1924; and the International Tailoring Company strike of 1925. The focus of his inquiry was ". . . various methods for maintaining order or punishing violations of law in industrial disputes." Complete documentation includes over 300 interviews.

(Haymarket Riot/McCormick Strike)

See also: H203.

I85 *The Accused and the Accusers: The Famous Speeches of the Eight Chicago Anarchists in Court.* Introduction by Leon Stein and Philip Taft. New York, 1970.

A good, scholarly reprint of an important labor document.

I86 Altgeld, John P. *Reasons for Pardoning Fielden, Neebe and Schwab.* [Springfield, 1893].

The text of Altgeld's pardon of three of the convicted anarchists.

I87 Busch, Francis X. "The Haymarket Riot and the Trial of the Anarchists." *JISHS,* XLVIII, 3 (Autumn 1955), 247-270.

A review of the trial that is not friendly to the anarchists. There are differences in questions of fact between Busch's account and that of Wish cited below (I100).

I88 Carter, Everett. "The Haymarket Affair in Literature." *Am. Q.,* II, 3 (Fall 1950), 270-278.

A short discussion of fiction that dealt with the Haymarket riot.

I89 *The Chicago Martyrs.* London, 1912.

A short, radical pamphlet on Haymarket.

I90 David, Henry. *The History of the Haymarket Affair: A Study in the American Social-Revolutionary and Labor Movements.* Rev. ed. New York, 1963.

The second edition of the standard account of the affair.

I91 Foner, Philip Sheldon, ed. *The Autobiographies of the Haymarket Martyrs.* New York, 1969.

Another standard document.

I92 Kebabian, John S., ed. *The Haymarket Affair and the Trial of the Chicago Anarchists, 1886. Original Manuscripts, Letters, Articles, and Printed Material of the Anarchists and of the State Prosecutor, Julius S. Grinnell (Grinnell's Own Collection).* New York, 1970.

A reprint of an early important collection.

I93 Kogan, Bernard, ed. *The Chicago Haymarket Riot: Anarchy on Trial*. Boston, 1959.

A standard collection of primary and secondary material.

I94 Lum, Dyer Daniel. *The Great Trial of the Chicago Anarchists*. New York, 1969 (c1886).

A reprint of an early account.

I95 McLean, George N. *The Rise and Fall of Anarchy in America . . .* New York, 1972 (c1888).

Hostile to the rioters.

I96 Pasteris, Joseph M. "The Haymarket Riot of 1886: An Analysis of the Popular Press." N.I.U. unpub. M.A. thesis, 1966.

I97 Schaack, Michael. *Anarchy and Anarchists . . . The Chicago Haymarket Conspiracy . . .* Chicago, 1889.

An early account hostile to the accused.

I98 Werstein, Irving. *Strangled Voices: The Story of the Haymarket Affair*. New York, 1969.

A short, popular account.

I99 Wheelock, Lewis F. "Urban Protestant Reactions to the Chicago Haymarket Affair, 1886-1893." U.Iowa unpub. Ph.D. thesis, 1956.

I100 Wish, Harvey. "Governor Altgeld Pardons the Anarchists." *JISHS*, XXXI, 4 (Dec. 1938), 424-448.

A brief summary of the events is followed by a narrative of the movement to pardon the living anarchists and Altgeld's response.

I101 Zeisler, Ernest Bloomfield. *The Haymarket Riot*. Chicago, 1956

I102 Zeisler, Sigmund. *Reminiscences of the Anarchist Case*. Chicago, 1927.

Zeisler was an attorney for the defense.

(Pullman Strike)

I102a Cobb, Stephen. "William H. Carwardine and the Pullman Strike." N.U. unpub. Ph.D. thesis, 1970.

Cobb argues that Carwardine responded to the strike as he did because of a fundamental shift in values in American society.

I103 Eggert, Gerald G. "The Great Pullman Strike." *Am. H. Illus.*, VI, 1 (Ap. 1971), 32-39.

A popular account.

I104 Jebsen, Harry, Jr. "The Role of Blue Island in the Pullman Strike of 1894." *JISHS,* LXVII, 3 (June 1974), 275-293.

Blue Island was involved in the strike in an important way because the Rock Island Line freight yards were there. Also, Everett St. John, Chairman of the General Managers' Association was an important officer of the Rock Island Line.

I105 Lindsey, Almont. *The Pullman Strike: The Story of a Unique Experiment and of a Great Labor Upheaval.* Chicago, 1964 (c1942).

The standard account. The book grew out of an earlier study of the town. Lindsey treats the national implication of the strike but focuses on Chicago. Bibliography.

I106 Manning, Thomas G., ed. *The Chicago Strike of 1894: Industrial Labor in the Late Nineteenth Century.* New York, 1960.

A selection of readings about the Pullman Strike drawn from original sources.

I107 Stein, Leon, ed. *The Pullman Strike.* New York, 1969.

It reprints the following publications: William H. Carwardine, *The Pullman Strike,* c1894; Grover Cleveland, *The Government in the Chicago Strike 1894,* 1913; George M. Pullman, *Statements on the Strike at Pullman,* 1894; Eugene V. Debs, *Liberty,* 1895. All of these are important documents of the strike. Carwardine was the minister of the church in Pullman.

I108 United States. Strike Commission, 1894. *Report on the Chicago Strike of June-July 1894.* Washington, 1894.

A narrative summary with some data in tabular form and recommendations.

I109 Warne, Colston Estey, ed. *The Pullman Boycott of 1894: The Problem of Federal Intervention.* Boston, 1955.

Another collection of readings on the strike, with a long bibliography.

I110 Wish, Harvey. "The Pullman Strike: A Study in Industrial Warfare." *JISHS,* XXXII, 3 (Sept. 1939), 288-312.

A narrative of the course of the strike with a minimum of analysis and background.

(Memorial Day Massacre)

I111 Citizens Joint Commission of Inquiry on South Chicago Memorial Day Incident. *Report of Citizens Joint Commission of Inquiry on South Chicago Memorial Day Incident.* Chicago, 1937.

A short, official report.

I112 Leab, Daniel. "The Memorial Day Massacre." *Midcontinent Am. Studies J.*, VIII, 1 (Fall 1967), 3-17.

A serious new evaluation of the evidence. He argues that the incident brought about a significant change in labor's tactics.

I113 Sofchalk, Donald G. "The Chicago Memorial Day Incident: An Episode of Mass Action." *Labor H.*, VI, 1 (Winter 1965), 3-43.

A careful examination of one of the bloodiest events in Chicago labor history.

I114 United States. Congress. Senate. Committee on Education and Labor. *The Chicago Memorial Day Incident: Hearings June 30, July 1 and 2, 1937. La Follette Committee Report on the Chicago Memorial Day Incident.* New York, 1971 (c1937).

National Strikes Bearing on Chicago

I115 Brody, David. *Labor in Crisis: The Steel Strike of 1919.* Philadelphia, 1965.

The standard account of a national strike that involved Chicago.

I116 Bruce, Robert V. *1877: Year of Violence.* Indianapolis, 1959.

A well-written account of the nationwide strike of railway workers in which Chicago labor was much involved.

I117 Eggert, Gerald G. *Railroad Labor Disputes: The Beginnings of Federal Strike Policy.* Ann Arbor, 1967.

There are chapters on the major Chicago strikes and references throughout the book.

I118 Foner, Philip S. *The Great Labor Uprising of 1877.* New York, 1977.

I119 McMurry, Donald L. *The Great Burlington Strike of 1888*. Cambridge, 1956.

Chicago references run throughout the book. Useful bibliography.

I120 Pinkerton, Allan. *Strikers, Communists, Tramps and Detectives: Railroad Strike of 1877*. New York, 1969 (c1878).

I121 Sigmund, Elwin W. "Federal Laws Concerning Railroad Labor Disputes: A Legislative and Legal History, 1877-1934." U.I.U. unpub. Ph.D. thesis, 1961.

I122 Sklar, David. "Some Aspects of the 1948 Strike in the Meatpacking Industry." U.C. unpub. M.A. thesis, 1949.

Sets out the background, analyzes the causes of the strike and the factors that determined the outcome. Sklar knew many of the principals on the labor side and much of his evidence is drawn from personal interviews.

I123 Taft, Philip. "The Limits of Labor Unity: The Chicago Newspaper Strike of 1912." *Labor H.*, XIX, 1 (Winter 1978), 100-129.

Describes the problem created by the rival claims of the various unions in the newspaper business.

I124 Warne, Colston E., ed. *The Steel Strike of 1919*. Boston, 1963.

I125 Women's Trade Union League of Chicago. *Official Report of the Strike Committee: Chicago Garment Worker's Strike, October 29, 1910-February 18, 1911*. Chicago, 1911.

National Studies

Works included here have a broader scope than Chicago but deal with the city in a substantial way. Many times the best-known work of a national subject is excluded because it does not treat Chicago in sufficient detail for this list.

I126 Brody, David. *Steelworkers in America: The Nonunion Era*. Cambridge, 1960.

A fundamental book on the steelworker which, though national in scope, is important to understanding the industry in Chicago.

I127 Christie, Robert A. *Empire in Wood: A History of the Carpenters Union*. Ithaca, 1956.

I128 Conlin, Joseph R. *Bread and Roses Too: Studies of the Wobblies*. Westport, 1969.

I129 Davis, Allen F. "The Women's Trade Union League: Origins and Organizations." *Labor H.*, V, 1 (Winter 1964), 3-17.

A study of the origins of the group in which Margaret Dreir Robins led the Chicago chapter with great distinction.

I130 Dubofsky, Melvyn. *We Shall Be All: A History of the Industrial Workers of the World*. Chicago, 1969.

The IWW was a national, not a Chicago, organization; yet much that involved the Wobblies involved or occurred in Chicago.

I131 Foner, Philip S. *Organized Labor and the Black Worker, 1619-1973*. New York, 1974.

I132 __________. "United States of America vs. Wm. D. Haywood, *et.al.:* The I.W.W. Indictment." *Labor H.*, XI, 4 (Fall 1970), 500-530.

Prints the Chicago indictment of the IWW.

I133 Greenstone, J. David. *Labor in American Politics*. New introduction. Chicago, 1977 (c1969).

A chapter on Chicago argues the theme of the book - that the organized labor movement is so closely identified with the Democratic Party that it often seems only to be its chief organization. See also his 1963 U.C. unpub. Ph.D. thesis, "Labor Politics in Three Cities: Political Action in Detroit, Chicago, and Los Angeles, 1963."

I134 Hogg, J. Bernard. "Public Reaction to Pinkertonism and the Labor Question." U.C. unpub. Ph.D. thesis, 1943.

Describes the Pinkerton organization, shows why it was disliked; concentrates on the company's supplying guards. A summary article from his thesis is under the same title in *Penn. H.*, (1944), 171-199.

I135 Jacobson, Julius, ed. *The Negro and the American Labor Movement*. Garden City, 1968.

See in particular "The Negro Worker in the Chicago Labor Market," by Bennett Hymer and Hal Baron.

I136 Josephson, Matthew. *Union House, Union Bar: The History of the Hotel and Restaurant Employees and Bartenders International Union, AFL-CIO*. New York, 1956.

I137 Kirstein, George G. *Stores and Unions: A Study of the Growth of Unionism in Dry Goods and Department Stores.* New York, 1950.

I138 Larrowe, Charles P. *Maritime Labor Relations on the Great Lakes.* East Lansing, 1959.

Deals with the whole area of the Great Lakes but it is of obvious importance for Chicago.

I139 Lightner, David L. *Labor on the Illinois Central Railroad, 1852-1900: The Evaluation of an Industrial Environment.* New York, 1977 (c1970).

An ". . . investigation of the wages, hours, and working conditions of railroaders; of the attitude of railroad managers toward their work force; and of the methods by which employers endeavored to recruit, train, discipline, and provide for the safety and welfare of their employees."

I140 Meltzer, Milton. *Bread and Roses: The Struggle of American Labor, 1865-1915.* New York, 1967.

I141 Nelli, Humbert S. "The Italian Padrone System in the United States." *Labor H.*, V, 2 (Spring 1964), 153-167.

A careful study of a labor institution that was important to Chicago's Italian population both as a reality and as a source of misconception about them as an ethnic group.

I142 Nelson, Daniel. "'While Waiting for the Government': The Needle Trades Unemployment Insurance Plans, 1919-28." *Labor H.*, XI, 4 (Fall 1970), 482-499.

The Chicago needle trades were the first to develop unemployment insurance. This article describes this and some of its implications.

I143 Nestor, Agnes. *Brief History of the International Glove Workers Union of America.* Milwaukee, 1942.

An account of a national union by an important Chicago figure.

I144 Orear, Leslie F. and Stephan H. Diamond. *Out of the Jungle.* Chicago, 1968.

A photographic history of the packinghouse workers with some graphic Chicago pictures.

I145 Renshaw, Patrick. *The Wobblies: The Story of Syndicalism in the United States.* London, 1967.

I146 Rosko, Thomas A. "The Illinois State Federation of Labor 1929-1941." U.I.U. unpub. M.A. thesis, 1954.

I147 Segal, Martin. *The Rise of the United Association: National Unionism in the Pipe Trades, 1884-1924.* Cambridge, 1970.

I148 Spero, Sterling D. and Abram L. Harris. *The Black Worker: The Negro and the Labor Movement.* New York, 1931.

One of the first important studies on blacks in the labor force. While it is a national survey, there is much material on Chicago, particularly the Pullman (coach) and stockyard workers. Bibliography.

I149 Staley, Eugene. *History of the Illinois State Federation of Labor.* Chicago, 1930.

I150 Taft, Philip. "Federal Trials of the IWW." *Labor H.*, III, 1 (Winter 1962), 57-91.

One of the three major trials was in Chicago. See also: Richard Brazier, "The Mass I.W.W. Trial of 1918: A Retrospect," *ibid.*, 178-192.

I151 U. S. Department of Labor. *Important Events in American Labor History, 1778-1971.* Washington, 1976.

Biography

(Bisno, Abraham)

I152 *Abraham Bisno: Union Pioneer . . .* Foreword by Joel Seidman. Madison, 1967.

Autobiographical fragments of a leading figure in Chicago's labor history (garment workers).

(Debs, Eugene V.)

I153 Ginger, Ray. *The Bending Cross: A Biography of Eugene Victor Debs.* New Brunswick, 1949.

A long, documented biography of a national labor figure who was involved in Chicago labor affairs.

(Germer, Adolph)

I154 Cary, Lorin Lee. "Adolph Germer: From Labor Agitator to Labor Professional." U.W. unpub. Ph.D. thesis, 1968.

See also his article in *JISHS*, LXVIII, 4 (Sept. 1975), 337-343.

(Hagerty, Thomas J.)

I155 Doherty, Robert E. "Thomas J. Hagerty, the Church and Socialism." *Labor H.*, III, 1 (Winter 1962), 39-56.

Hagerty was an important figure in the Chicago convention that formed the IWW.

(Hillman, Sidney)

I156 Josephson, Matthew. *Sidney Hillman, Statesman of American Labor*. Garden City, 1952.

Hillman is listed because of his early work in the Chicago clothing trades rather than his work as a national labor spokesman.

(Morgan, Elizabeth)

I157 Scharnau, Ralph. "Elizabeth Morgan, Crusader for Labor Reform." *Labor H.*, XIV, 3 (Summer 1973), 340-351.

(Morgan, Thomas J.)

I158 __________. "Thomas J. Morgan and the United Labor Party of Chicago." *JISHS*, LXVI, 1 (Spring 1973), 41-61.

A narrative of the rise and fall of the party in the 1880s. For a wider scope see his "Thomas J. Morgan and the Chicago Socialist Movement, 1876-1901," N.I.U. unpub. Ph.D. thesis, 1969.

(Nestor, Agnes)

I159 Nestor, Agnes. *Woman's Labor Leader: An Autobiography*. Rockford, 1954.

A famous woman leader of the labor movement in Chicago. She was head of the Chicago Women's Trade Union and the Women's Eight-Hour-Day Law campaign in Illinois.

(Parsons, Albert R.)

I160 Calmer, Alan. *Labor Agitator: The Story of Albert R. Parsons*. New York, 1937.

A very favorable study of Parsons.

I161 Johnson, Michael R. "Albert R. Parsons: An American Architect of Syndicalism." *Midwest Q.*, IX, 2 (Winter 1968), 195-206.

I162 Parsons, Lucy E. *Life of Albert R. Parsons, with Brief History of the Labor Movement in America*. Chicago, 1903.

This is a fundamental source for the Haymarket Riot and aftermath.

(Randolph, A. Philip)

I163 Anderson, Jervis. *A. Philip Randolph: A Biographical Portrait*. New York, 1973.

Uneven. Better on Randolph the man than as a detailed biography of a labor leader.

(Robins, Margaret D.)

I164 Dreier, Mary E. *Margaret Dreier Robins: Her Life, Letters and Work*. New York, 1950.

An important woman leader of union activity.

I165 Estes, Barbara Ann. "Margaret Dreier Robins: Social Reformer and Labor Organizer." B.S.U. unpub. Ph.D. thesis, 1977.

She argues that Robins was a model progressive, save for her advocacy of power for the working class.

J
SOCIAL STATISTICS

The various decennial U. S. census reports form the basic source for social statistics of Chicago. One must bear in mind the distinction between the census schedules, which are the lists made by the enumerators, and the tabulations of the census schedules. The schedules are a list of people, the tabulations the sum of those people. The extant census schedules 1790-1900 have been microfilmed and are available at the National Archives or one of its regional centers and at some research libraries. Census schedules after 1900 are still considered confidential documents and access is limited.

The decennial census began to be more than a head count about the time that Chicago became a city (1837). The Fifth Census ". . . presents data for each State and Territory by minor civil divisions showing number of free white persons, slaves, and free colored persons by sex and age, as well as the number of white persons and slaves and colored who were deaf and dumb, and blind, and the number of white aliens by age." (Dubester)

The questions asked in the census became more detailed and the data was divided by ward in large cities. By the 13th Census the number and distribution of inhabitants, their color, race, nativity, parentage, sex, age, marital status, state or country of birth, mother tongue, year of immigration, voting age, naturalization, education, illiteracy, ability to speak English, material on dwellings and families, and ownership of homes were given.

In 1910 the census returns of eight large cities were divided into very small geographic units called tracts. "Census tracts are small areas, having a population usually between 3,000 and 6,000, into which certain large cities (and sometimes their adjacent areas) have been subdivided for statistical and local administrative purposes . . ." The Bureau of the Census, however, did not publish these until the 1940 census. The unpublished data for 1920 (J1), 1930 (J2), and 1934 (J3) were published for Chicago by members of the faculty of the University of Chicago. Some of the data for 1910 appear in the 1920 volume.

Published reports of census tabulations through the census of 1900 will be found in most libraries under United States, Census Office. The 1910 census tabulations and all subsequent tabulations appear under United States, Bureau of the Census. A list of official census publications may be found in:

> Dubester, Henry J. *Catalog of United States Census Publications 1790-1945.* Washington, 1950.

While census publications are too numerous to list here, some other useful collections follow below.

See also: A10, 24; H7, 33; L6, 11, 12, 18, 34-36; M6; N6, 47, 51, 55, 76, 89, 114, 146, 147, 166; P5, 17, 20

J1 *Census Data of the City of Chicago, 1920.* Edited by Ernest W. Burgess and Charles Newcomb. Chicago, 1931.

J2 *Census Data of the City of Chicago, 1930.* Edited by Ernest W. Burgess and Charles Newcomb. Chicago, 1933.

J3 *Census Data of the City of Chicago, 1934.* Edited by Charles S. Newcomb and Richard O. Lang. Chicago, 1934.

A very useful, detailed compilation of census material taken from published and manuscript sources. The 1934 data were taken from a special census. A wide variety of questions were asked and the data arranged by question and geographical unit. The geographical units are small and comparable from year to year. Groups of tracts may be used with later local community fact books (J26-29).

J4 Chicago Association of Commerce and Industry Research and Statistics Division. *Community Area Data Book for the City of Chicago: 1970 Census Data by 75 Community Areas.* [Chicago, c1972].

There is no 1970 Local Community Fact Book. This and the Welfare Council publication can be used to help fill the gap.

J5 Chicago Community Renewal Program. *An Atlas of Chicago's People, Jobs and Homes.* Chicago, 1963.

"The maps in this collection are intended to describe the distribution of metropolitan Chicago's people, jobs and homes as shown in relation to Chicago's major land uses . . . all of the maps are based on data from the Census of Population and Housing for 1960 and 1950, and from the Census of Manufacturers and Business for 1958." There is a useful superimposition of census tract areas over the 75 designated local communities.

J6 Chicago. Department of Development and Planning. *Chicago Statistical Abstract.* 6 vol. Chicago, 1973.

A detailed report that presents detailed data from the 1970 census in six geographical divisions: I. 1970 Census - Community Area Summary Tables; II. 1970 Census - Census Tract Tables; III. 1970 Census - Community Area Profiles; IV. 1970 Census - Ward Summary Tables; V. City and Community Area Profiles; VI. City and Ward Profiles.

J7 Chicago. Department of Health. *Chronological Summary of Chicago Mortality 1843-1902.* Chicago, 1903.

Lists by month the number of deaths from 26 leading causes. An important document.

J8 Chicago Health Statistics Survey. Works Progress Administration. *Health Data Book for the 75 Local Community Areas of the City of Chicago*. Chicago, 1939.

An examination of a variety of indexes for the established communities.

J9 Chicago. Plan Commission. *Population Facts for Planning Chicago*. Chicago, 1942.

An analysis of the data at hand in 1941 and some of the historical comparisons back to the city's origin.

J10 Chicago. University. Chicago Community Inventory. *[Releases] 1-9*. Chicago, n.d.

A series of releases that summarize statistical findings about the city in the period after WWII.

J11 __________. *Demographic and Socio-Economic Characteristics of the Population of the City of Chicago and of the Suburbs and Urban Fringe: 1950. A Report . . . to the Chicago Plan Commission and the Office of the Housing and Redevelopment Coordinator*. Chicago, 1954.

Drawn from the 1950 census, the data describe: population mobility, years of education, marital status, family status, employment status, major occupation group, and personal income.

J12 __________. *Estimates and Projections Series*. Chicago, 1957-

Under this series title and others a number of important analyses of Chicago's population have been published.

J13 __________. *Index of Sources of Data for the Chicago Metropolitan Area*. Chicago, 1954.

J14 Chicago. University. Local Community Research Committee. *Social Base Map of Chicago Showing Industrial Areas, Parks, Transportation, and Language Groups*. Chicago, 1926.

Exactly what it says it is, but good copies are difficult to locate.

J15 Council of Social Agencies of Chicago. *Census Data of the City of Chicago. Community Areas: 1930*. Chicago, 1930.

J16 DeVise, Pierre. *Chicago's People, Jobs and Homes: The Human Geography of the City and Metro Area*. Chicago, 1964.

J17 Dollar, Melvin. *1934 Chicago Census Data: Supplementary Tables, Family Statistics . . .* 2 vol. Chicago, 1942.

A massive refinement of the statistical data of the 1934 census.

J18 Dollar, Melvin. *Vital Statistics for Cook County and Chicago.* Chicago, 1942.

A very detailed multi-volume compilation, 1919-1936.

J19 Edwards, Richard. *Chicago Census Report and Statistical Review, Embracing a Complete Directory of the City . . . Compiled from Actual Canvass, at the Request of the Mayor, City Council, Business Firms and Capitalists of Chicago.* Chicago, 1871.

Chicago citizens believed the Federal census to be wrong and had a special census taken. The information is arranged in the 1871 directory by name. Very little of the data is in tabular form.

J20 Hauser, Philip Morris. "Differential Fertility, Mortality, and Net Reproduction in Chicago, 1930." U.C. unpub. Ph.D. thesis, 1938.

J21 Illinois. Commission on Human Relations. *Non-White Population Changes in Chicago's Suburbs.* Rev. ed. Chicago, 1962.

1950-1960 saw a greater percentage increase in non-white population in the suburbs than in Chicago. The report is a statistical breakdown by county and parts of counties.

J22 Jeter, Helen Rankin. *Trends of Population in the Region of Chicago.* Chicago, 1927.

An important statistical study of nine counties in Illinois, three counties in Indiana, and three in Wisconsin that make up Chicago and its immediate hinterland. Detailed tables of population for the area and for various civil jurisdictions with some projections to 1950.

J23 Johnson, Carl Everett. "A Study of Age at Marriage in Chicago, Illinois." U.C. unpub. M.A. thesis, 1948.

J24 Langum, John K. "New Definition of Chicago Metropolitan Area: Census Bureau Adds Two Counties to Former Six." *Commerce,* LVI, 7 (Aug. 1959), 14-16.

A short explanation of what is now included.

J25 *District Fact Book for 75 Chicago Local Communities.* Edited by Edward L. Burchard and Martin J. Arvin. Chicago, 1935.

The beginning of a series. See the entry for Wirth (J26).

J26 *Local Community Fact Book 1938.* Edited by Louis Wirth and Margaret Furez. Chicago, 1938.

A refinement of the District Fact Book of 1935. The material compares the years 1930 and 1934. A brief history of each community is given, drawn from standard sources. It describes the built environment, lists points of interest, schools, churches, recreational facilities, registered voters, morbidity rates by disease, social agencies, and civic organizations. The statistical data was drawn from the Chicago census volumes and other sources. The population is analyzed by age, nativity, marital condition, nationalities of foreign birth, citizenship, literacy, occupation, vital statistics, insanity, family size, education and kind of dwelling.

J27 *Local Community Fact Book of Chicago.* Edited by Louis Wirth and Eleanor H. Bernet. Chicago, 1949.

The 1940 census analyzed. The short narrative was dropped to accommodate the greatly expanded scope of the 1940 census. Data on age, occupation and employment is more sophisticated and detailed. New material on wages, salaries, and other economics was added at the expense of rates of insanity, illegitimacy, infant death, and morbidity tables.

J28 *Local Community Fact Book for Chicago, 1950.* Edited by Philip M. Hauser and Evelyn M. Kitagawa. Chicago, 1953.

The major changes in comparison to the 1930 book were the restoration of the community histories in a more comprehensive form, the inclusion of maps that show non-residential land use, more complete statistical data that shows total family income and data on retail trade and certain unpublished census data.

J29 *Local Community Fact Book: Chicago Metropolitan Area, 1960.* Edited by Evelyn M. Kitagawa and Karl E. Taeuber. Chicago, 1963.

The major changes in this edition of the fact book were: 1. the inclusion of the Chicago-Northwestern Indiana Standard Consolidated Area, and the Gary-Hammond-East Chicago SMSA; 2. rewritten histories of the communities adding accounts of 24 suburbs; 3. inclusion of non-census data, e.g., components of population change 1950-1960; data relating to unemployment compensation beneficiaries; public assistance recipients; mental patients; juvenile delinquency; data on parks and recreational personnel; and data about selected institutions; 4. an organizational change that presented part of the information by topic as well as by area.

J30 Mayer, Albert Joseph. "Differentials in Length of Life, City of Chicago: 1880-1940." U.C. unpub. Ph.D. thesis, 1950.

There was an increase in Chicago of 24 years for men and 26 years for women in life expectancy. The chief cause was a decline in infant mortality. Women and the young increased more than other groups. Whites were shown to live longer than blacks, the better-off longer than the poor, but the poors' life expectancy increased faster, as did that of non-whites. Urban (Chicago) life expectancy was rapidly growing closer to that of rural society. Some implications of these changes are then drawn, e.g., fewer orphans, more widows, an older population, more importance attached to pension plans, etc. See also his article, "Life Expectancy in the City of Chicago, 1880-1950," *Human Biology*, XXVII, 3 (Sept. 1955), 202-210.

J31 Pullen, Paul Pike. "Population Movements in the Chicago Metropolitan Area from 1900 to the Present." N.U. unpub. M.A. thesis, 1942.

J32 Skogan, Wesley G. *Chicago Since 1840: A Time-Series Data Handbook*. Urbana, 1976.

Probably the most generally useful collection of data for novice students of Chicago.

J33 Stuart, Johannes. "Study of Divorce in Cook County." U.C. unpub. M.A. thesis, 1931.

J34 Taeuber, Alma F. *Comparability of Census Tracts, 1950 and 1960 Censuses of Population and Housing, Chicago, Illinois*. Chicago, 1963.

The census tracts of 1930-1950 were changed in the 1960 census. This article explains how to compare the two sets of data.

J35 Welfare Council of Metropolitan Chicago. Research Department. *1970 Census Data: Report Number One, General Population and Housing Characteristics, Chicago SMSA*. Chicago, 1971.

The first of a series, containing ". . . a total of 62 tables on basic population and housing statistics gathered in the 1970 U. S. Census of the Chicago . . ." SMSA. The tables are general and do not provide as detailed data as are found in the *Community Data Book*. Report Two gives general data for *General Population and Housing Characteristics Chicago Community Areas*, which, again, are less useful than the *Community Data Book*. Also general in its statistical treatment of a smaller area is Report Three, *General Population and Housing Characteristics - Chicago Model Cities Target Areas*.

J36 Westmoreland, Guy T. *Urban Statistics: A Selected Guide to Reference Sources*. Evanston, 1974.

A very useful guide for those seeking more detail. Particularly useful for current statistics.

K
SOCIAL LIFE AND CUSTOMS

General

See also: E6, 142; I6, 7; M11; J23, 33

K1 Angle, Paul M. *Chicago History.*

A series of brief articles in both the old and new series of *Chicago History* that describe social life and customs.

K2 Banks, Nancy. "The World's Most Beautiful Ballrooms." *CH,* n.s., II, 4 (Fall-Winter 1973), 206-215.

On Chicago's big-band ballrooms in the inter-war period.

K3 Barlow, Irene Smith. "Leisure-Time Activities of Two Hundred High-School Girls in Chicago." U.C. unpub. M.S. thesis, 1934.

Two different income groups' behavior on weekends was studied. Much of the data is compiled in a series of useful tables.

K4 Bushnell, George D. "When Chicago was Wheel Crazy." *CH,* n.s., IV, 3 (Fall 1975), 167-175.

A description of the bicycle craze.

K5 Carson, Gerald. "In Chicago: Cruelty and Kindness to Animals." *CH,* n.s., III, 3 (Winter 1974-1975), 151-158.

A short account of the Illinois Anti-Cruelty Act.

K6 Chicago Recreation Commission. W.P.A. *The Chicago Recreation Survey, 1937-1940.* 5 vol. Chicago, 1937-1940.

An important large-scale study of organized recreation in Chicago in the 1930s. The study is divided into: I. Public Recreation; II. Commercial Recreation; III. Private Recreation; IV. Recreation by Community Areas; V. Recommendations.

K7 Duis, Perry R. "The Saloon and the Public City: Chicago and Boston, 1880-1920." U.C. unpub. Ph.D. thesis, 1975.

Duis treats the saloon as a public institution with both public functions and public influences. The study thus treats many aspects of Chicago history in this forty-year period. The bibliography of primary material is particularly noteworthy. See also his article, "The Saloon in a Changing Chicago," *CH,* n.s., IV, 4 (Winter 1975-1976), 214-224.

K8 Fagin, Sophia. "Public Forums in Chicago." U.C. unpub Ph.D. thesis, 1939.

An interesting study of the evolution of various public forums (e.g., a lecture hall) in Chicago.

K9 Griffin, Al. "The Ups and Downs of Riverview Park." *CH*, n.s., IV, 1 (Spring 1975), 14-22.

An account of one of Chicago's most famous amusement parks which closed in 1967 after more than 60 years of operation.

K10 Griffin, Dick. "Opium Addiction in Chicago: 'The Noblest and the Best Brought Low'." *CH*, n.s., VI, 2 (Summer 1977), 107-116.

An account of widespread drug addiction in all classes before Federal regulation.

K11 Halsey, Elizabeth. *The Development of Public Recreation in Metropolitan Chicago*. [Chicago], 1940.

A history of public recreation in Chicago and the surrounding area. She deals with parks, waterfront areas, recreational areas, schools, etc.

K12 Jachimowicz, Elizabeth. *Eight Chicago Women and Their Fashions 1860-1929*. Chicago, 1978.

A view of the fashion of prominent women and their lives beyond fashion.

K13 Lopata, Helena Znaniecki. "Social Relations of Black and White Widowed Women in a Northern Metropolis." *Am. J. of Soc.*, LXXVIII, 4 (Jan. 1973), 1003-1010.

K14 Moore, Joan Willard. "Stability and Instability in the Metropolitan Upper Class." U.C. unpub. Ph.D. thesis, 1959.

A study of the ruling elite of St. Luke's and Presbyterian hospitals.

K15 Page, Eleanor. "The Passavant Cotillion and Others." *CH*, n.s., II, 2 (Fall 1972), 68-77.

An account of an important Chicago social tradition.

K16 Pederson, Lee. "Chicago Words: The Regional Vocabulary." *Am. Speech*, XLVI, 3/4 (Fall 1971), 163-192.

K17 Quenzel, Carrol Hunter. "Society in New York and Chicago 1888-1900." U.W. unpub. Ph.D. thesis, 1938.

A study of the rich and their life: houses, social functions, sports, marriage and children, dress and manners, culture and patronage of the fine arts, religion and philanthropy, and politics and public service.

K18 Riley, Thomas James. *The Higher Life of Chicago.* Chicago, 1905.

A survey of the improving bodies of Chicago, *viz*: schools, libraries, museums, civic clubs, settlements, unions, charities, art and music societies, and religious institutions. Very useful sketches.

K19 Rosher, Anne Allyn. "Residential Telephone Usage Among the Chicago Civic-Minded, 1895-1905." U.C. unpub. Ph.D. thesis, 1968.

K20 Russell, Daniel. "The Road House: A Study of Commercialized Amusements in the Environs of Chicago." U.C. unpub. M.A. thesis, 1931.

Argues that the road house is wholly a product of the automobile era. The patrons, regular and "passerby", are described as well as the types of road houses: prostitution, gambling, dance, saloon, eating etc.

K21 Shikoh, Jane Allen. "The 'Higher Life' in the American City of the 1890's: A Study of Its Leaders and Their Activities in New York, Chicago, Philadelphia, St. Louis, Boston, and Buffalo." N.Y.U. unpub. Ph.D. thesis, 1972.

K22 Uskup, Frances Land. "Social Markers of Urban Speech: A Study of Elites in Chicago." I.I.T. unpub. Ph.D. thesis, 1974.

K23 Weinrott, Lester A. "Play That Player Piano." *CH,* n.s., IV, 2 (Summer 1975), 78-86.

Player pianos were in vogue in the first part of this century and Chicago was a leading center of the industry.

K24 Wind, Herbert Warren. "Golfing in and Around Chicago." *CH,* n.s., IV, 4 (Winter 1975-1976), 244-251.

K25 Wood, Morrison. "A Half Century of the Culinary Arts in Chicago." *CH,* n.s., II, 1 (Spring 1972), 18-25.

K26 Deleted

Clubs

See also: H83; M22; N69, 78, 79, 87

K27 Beadle, Muriel. *Fortnightly of Chicago: The City and Its Women: 1873-1973*. Chicago, 1973.

K28 Cerza, Alphonse. *A History of the Ancient Accepted Scottish Rite in Illinois 1846-1965*. Bloomington, 1966.

A narrative and lists.

K29 *Chicago Clubs Illustrated*. Chicago, 1888.

A brief sketch and illustration of these clubs: Calumet, Chicago, Douglas, Farragut, Illinois, Indiana, Logan, Kenwood, Lakeside, LaSalle, Oakland, Oaks, Park, Standard, Union League, Union, University, and Washington Park.

K30 Cookman, Aubrey O. "Chicago's Exclusive Playground: The South Shore Country Club." *CH*, V, 2 (Summer 1976), 66-75.

K31 Cram, Norman L. "The Caxton Club of Chicago: Three Generations of Bibliophiles." *Book Club of California Q. News Letter*, XXI, 2 (Spring 1955), 35-44.

K32 Dedmon, Emmett. *A History of the Chicago Club*. Chicago, 1960.

A narrative which includes a reprint of the first history of the Club by Edward T. Blair.

K33 Frank, Henriette Greenbaum and Amalie Hofer Jerome, comp. *Annals of the Chicago Woman's Club for the First Forty Years of Its Organization, 1876-1916*. Chicago, 1916.

Detailed account with many excerpts from the records.

K34 Hill, Edward T. "The Cliff Dwellers of Chicago." DeP.U. unpub. M.A. thesis, 1953.

K35 Potter, Dalton. "Some Aspects of the Social Organization of the Elite of Chicago." U.C. unpub. M.A. thesis, 1949.

An attempt to define the elite is followed by an interesting survey of some of the important Chicago clubs.

K36 Powers, Dorothy Edwards. "The Chicago Woman's Club." U.C. unpub. Ph.D. thesis, 1939.

An account of the activities of the Club, the membership and its link with the women's movement.

K37 Reedy, June. *It's Fun to Remember: A Story of the Woman's Board of the Chicago Horticultural Society and Other Kindred Events.* [Chicago], 1974.

K38 *Rotary? A University Group Looks at the Rotary Club of Chicago.* Chicago, 1934.

A scholarly examination of the Rotary Club by a team from the University of Chicago. Traces the rise of the Club and its nature in the 1930s.

K39 The Standard Club of Chicago. *The Standard Club's First Hundred Years.* Chicago, 1969.

The premier Jewish club in Chicago.

K40 *University Club of Chicago: Floor Plans, Illustrative Sketches and Brief Description of the New Building of the Club.* Chicago, 1908.

K41 Van Mell, Richard and Wendy, ed. *The First Hundred Years: A History of the Chicago Yacht Club, 1875-1975.* Chicago, 1975.

K42 Wild, Payson Sibley. *The Chicago Literary Club: Its History from the Season of 1924-1925 to the Season of 1945-1946.* Chicago, 1947.

Popular Attitudes

See also: L, Social Conditions; M, Public and Private Social Reform and Welfare; N122; R, Communication (newspapers); S21; T89

K43 Abbott, Carl. "Civic Pride in Chicago, 1844-1860." *JISHS*, LXIII, 4 (Winter 1970), 399-421.

On the growth of civic pride before the Civil War.

K44 Block, Richard and Lauren Langman. "Youth and Work: The Diffusion of 'Countercultural' Values." *Youth and Society*, V, 4 (June 1974), 411-432.

A statistical analysis of attitudes of Loyola University students.

K45 Bogue, Donald Joseph and Richard McKinley. *Militancy for and Against Civil Rights and Integration in Chicago, Summer 1967.* Chicago, 1967.

A detailed questionnaire was used to elicit responses from whites and blacks to find what the bulk of each group believed about race. The book is a report of the results.

K46 Cook, Lester Harold. "Anti-Slavery Sentiment in the Culture of Chicago, 1844-1858." U.C. unpub. Ph.D. thesis, 1952.

Shows how slavery became transformed from a moral position with little vocal support into the symbol of the differences between the new Northwest and the South. Good list of primary readings.

K47 Dillon, Merton L. "The Anti-Slavery Movement in Illinois, 1809-1844." U.Mich. unpub. Ph.D. thesis, 1951.

The key work on the origins of the movement in Illinois.

K48 Ehrensaft, Kenneth B. "Attitudes of Residents in a Chicago Area Toward Local Institutions." DeP.U. unpub. M.A. thesis, 1970.

K49 Grant, Catherine M. "Public Opinion in Chicago During the Civil War." DeP.U. unpub. M.A. thesis, 1937.

K50 Jones, Stanley L. "John Wentworth and Anti-Slavery in Chicago to 1856." *Mid-America*, XXXVI, 3 (July 1954), 147-160.

K51 Lujack, Larry. *Superjock: The Loud, Frantic, Nonstop World of a Rock Radio DJ*. Chicago, 1975.

A popular life of a pop disc-jockey.

K52 Deleted

K53 May, Henry F. *The End of American Innocence: A Study of the First Years of Our Own Time, 1912-1917*. New York, 1959.

A study of the changes in American attitudes and customs before World War I. Much evidence is drawn from Chicago.

K54 Palmore, James A. "The Chicago Snowball: A Study of the Flow and Diffusion of Family Planning Information." U.C. unpub. Ph.D. thesis, 1966.

K55 Starr, Joyce R. and Donald E. Carns. "Singles in the City." *Society*, IX, 4 (Feb. 1972), 43-48.

K56 Zimmerman, James Allen. "Chicago and the Imperial Question: A Study in Public Attitudes toward National Expansion, 1897-1900." U.I.U. unpub. Ph.D. thesis, 1972.

Studies Chicago's "opinion leaders" on the question of imperialism. He found that they were split, the anti's tending to have a desire to reform conditions at home and to be influenced by example.

Sports

The books and articles listed below are popular with the exception of Riess' thesis, which is recommended. Special attention ought to be paid to the memoirs of Farrell and Veeck. See also: H116, 117

K57 Ahrens, Arthur R. "Chicago's City Series: Cubs Versus White Sox." *CH,* n.s., V, 4 (Winter 1976-1977), 243-252.

K58 __________. "How the Cubs Got Their Name." *CH,* n.s., V, 1 (Spring 1976), 39-44.

K59 Angle, Paul M. "Mr. Wrigley's Cubs." *CH,* n.s., V, 2 (Summer 1976), 105-115.

K60 Asinof, Eliot. *Eight Men Out: The Black Sox and the 1919 World Series.* New York, 1963.

K61 Brown, Warren. *The Chicago White Sox.* New York, 1952.

K62 Condon, Dave. *The Go-Go Chicago White Sox.* Foreword by Bill Veeck. New York, 1900.

K63 Enright, Jim. *Chicago Cubs.* New York, 1975.

K64 Farrell, James T. *My Baseball Diary.* New York, 1957.

K65 Federal Writers' Project. Illinois. *Baseball in Old Chicago, Compiled and Written by the Federal Writers' Project (Illinois) Work Project Administration; Sponsored by the Forest Park Baseball Museum, Inc.* Chicago, 1939.

K66 Fischler, Stan. *Chicago's Black Hawks.* Englewood Cliffs, c1972.

K67 Grange, Harold Edward. *The Red Grange Story: The Autobiography of Red Grange, As Told to Ira Morton.* New York, 1953.

K68 Leonard, Will. "Tinker to Evers to Chance." *CH,* n.s., I, 2 (Fall 1970), 69-79.

K69 Logan, Bob. *The Bulls and Chicago: A Stormy Affair.* Chicago, 1975.

K70 Luhrs, Victor. *The Great Baseball Mystery: The 1919 World Series.* South Brunswick, NJ, 1966.

K71 Magnuson, Keith and Robert Bradford. *None Against: [Hockey].* New York, 1973.

K72 Morris, Jeannie. *Brian Piccolo: A Short Season.* Chicago, 1971.

K73 Riess, Steven Allen. "Professional Baseball and American Culture in the Progressive Era: Myths and Realities, with Special Emphasis on Atlanta, Chicago, and New York." U.C. unpub. Ph.D. thesis, 1974.

K74 Roberts, Howard. *The Chicago Bears*. New York, 1947.

K75 Schoor, Gene. *Red Grange, Football's Greatest Halfback*. New York, 1952.

K76 Schwab, Rick. *Stuck on the Cubs*. Evanston, 1977.

K77 Smith, Dean. "The Black Sox Scandal." *Am. H. Illus.*, XI, 9 (Jan. 1977), 16-24.

K78 Sterling, Chandler W. *The Icehouse Gang: My Year with the Black Hawks*. New York, 1972.

K79 Vass, George. *The Chicago Black Hawks Story*. Chicago, 1970.

K80 __________. *George Halas and the Chicago Bears*. Chicago, 1971.

K81 Veeck, Bill and Ed Linn. *Veeck - As in Wreck: The Autobiography of Bill Veeck*. New York, 1962.

K82 __________. *The Hustler's Handbook*. New York, 1965.

K83 Ward, Archie. *The New Chicago White Sox*. Chicago, 1951.

L
SOCIAL CONDITIONS

General

See also: I, Labor (conditions of work); J, Social Statistics; N, Religious, Racial and Ethnic Groups; O, Neighborhoods; P67, 85.

L1 Bogue, Donald J. and Ernest W. Burgess, ed. *Contributions to Urban Sociology*. Chicago, 1964.

A collection of essays, many of which are excerpts or summaries of key articles and books on social and economic conditions in Chicago.

L2 Bremner, Robert. *From the Depths: The Discovery of Poverty in the United States*. New York, 1956.

A study of poverty and changing attitudes towards poverty from the mid-19th century to the 1920s. Chicago's reformers were important advocates of newer ideas about poverty and the book is useful in their study. A long bibliography lists many works by the reformers as well as a wealth of secondary material.

L3 Buettinger, Craig. "Economic Inequality in Early Chicago 1840-1850." *J. of Social H.*, XI, 3 (Spring 1978), 413-418.

He argues that marked economic inequality was present in Chicago early, at least by 1850. Many members of the rich had vast fortunes that rivaled those of the East. He advances the argument that the rich got to Chicago early, before 1839, with capital and were then in a position to exploit the city's rapid growth.

L4 Cavan, Ruth S. *The Family and the Depression: A Study of One Hundred Chicago Families*. New York, 1971 (c1938).

A frequently cited study but based on limited research.

L5 *Chicago: An Experiment in Social Science Research*. Edited by Thomas V. Smith and Leonard D. White. Chicago, [1929].

Essays by Park, Burgess, Gosnell, Lasswell, *et.al.*, on their research in Chicago.

L6 Chicago. Department of Development and Planning. *Chicago's Elderly Population: Progress and Goals*. [Chicago], 1974.

A summary document describing the situation of the aged in regard to: economics, health, housing, transportation, public facilities, community and social service. A brief description of general population characterisitcs is also given.

L7 Cook County, Illinois. Department of Public Aid. *An Exploratory Study of the Legal Needs of the Poor.* [Chicago, 1968?]

L8 Elazar, Daniel Judah. *Some Social Problems in the Northeastern Illinois Metropolitan Region.* Urbana, 1961.

A pamphlet-length overview of conditions and problems at the beginning of the 1960s.

L9 Freund, Roger Henry. "Begging in Chicago." U.C. unpub. Ph.D. thesis, 1925.

The only survey but the author was biased against a "vicious" practice.

L10 Heise, Kenan, ed. *They Speak for Themselves: Interviews with the Destitute in Chicago.* Chicago, 1965.

Twenty-eight very short interviews.

L11 Lang, Richard O. "The Relation of Educational Status to Economic Status in the City of Chicago, by Census Tracts, 1934." U.C. unpub. Ph.D. thesis, 1936.

L12 Monroe, Day. *Chicago Families: A Study of Unpublished Census Data.* Chicago, 1932.

Monroe was one of the first to make use of census data that were not in the printed schedules. His study resulted in a detailed description of the nature of families: details of the average household; composition of families, dependent children, the number of breadwinners in the average family; and how these conditions varied among families of different status.

L13 Park, Robert E., Ernest Burgess and Roderick D. McKenzie. *The City.* Chicago, 1967 (c1925).

Essays in urban sociology, which, though dated, draw on Chicago evidence. A long bibliographical essay surveys literature on the city in 1925; some of it bears on Chicago.

L14 *The People vs. the System: A Dialogue in Urban Conflict. Proceedings of the Community Service Workshop . . . Held at the University of Chicago, October 1966-June 1967.* Edited by Sol Tax. Chicago, 1968.

A great mass of material on social and political conditions in Chicago.

L15 Sennett, Richard. *Families Against the City: Middle Class Homes of Industrial Chicago, 1872-1890*. New York, 1974 (c1970).

Discusses middle-class families in the last third of the 19th century. The book has received strong criticism; see Perry R. Duis' review in *American Journal of Sociology*, March 1971, 956-959.

L16 Short, James A., ed. *The Social Fabric of the Metropolis: Contributions of the Chicago School of Urban Sociology*. Chicago, 1971.

A collection of essays by some of the figures in the Chicago School of Sociology.

L17 Suttles, Gerald D. *The Social Order of the Slum: Ethnicity and Territory in the Inner City*. Preface by Morris Janowitz. Chicago, 1968.

A study of the Near West Side of Chicago. Suttles argues that the morality of the world is, to a real degree, replaced by the values of the community, hence, a "social order of the slum."

L18 U. S. Bureau of Labor. *The Slums of Baltimore, Chicago, New York, and Philadelphia*. Edited by Carroll D. Wright. New York, 1970 (c1892).

The product of a Congressional investigation into slum conditions in major cities. By far the largest part of the document is a series of detailed statistical tables which cover a wide variety of subjects.

L19 Welfare Council of Metropolitan Chicago. *Community Services for Older People: The Chicago Plan*. Chicago, 1952.

One of the first studies of the needs of the aged population in an American city.

Homeless Men

L20 Anderson, Nels. *The Hobo: The Sociology of the Homeless Man*. Chicago, 1961 (c1923).

A full description of the hobo and his environment based mainly on Chicago evidence, including extensive field study.

L21 Beasley, Robert M. *Man in the Crucible: A Report of the Clearing House for Men Operated under the Authority of the Illinois Relief Commission*. Chicago, 1932.
See also his U.C. thesis of the same title which has appendixes of additional documentary material. Again, there is much Chicago evidence.

L22 Booth, Mary. "Homeless Men: Occupational Mobility and Related Background Factors." U.C. unpub. M.A. thesis, 1962.

A retabulation of the data of the Homeless Men Project of the late 1950s. She offers a strong argument against the contemporary views of homeless men as all downwardly mobile "skidders."

L23 National Opinion Research Center. *The Homeless Man on Skid Row: A Research Report on Housing and Home Finance Agency Demonstration Project Number III.D-1*. Chicago, 1961.

The study supports urban renewal of the 1950s' kind and argues that skid row can be cleaned up in Chicago as well as the need for it if certain obvious steps are taken. There is a full description of conditions in the 1950s. A bibliography has a good selection of material about the problem in other cities.

L24 Sutherland, Edwin Hardin. *Twenty Thousand Homeless Men: A Study of Unemployed Men in the Chicago Shelters*. New York, 1971 (c1936).

A large group was formed in the mid-1930s to study men on public relief. Case studies and interviews were used more than quantitative method. The book seeks to explain the life experiences and attitudes of the shelter men and their reactions to the relief policies which were being used.

Housing

See also: D12, 17; H168-186; M29; T87

L25 Abbott, Edith. *The Tenements of Chicago, 1908-1935*. New York, 1970 (c1936).

An important study by one of the members of the Chicago School. It is an analysis and summary of 25 years of research by the School of Social Service Administration. The development of tenements and tenement legislation is surveyed in the 19th century. The bulk of the book is given over to a detailed study of tenements in the first third of the 20th century. The discussion has wide significance, e.g., for ethnic, legal, architectural history, etc., as well as for social conditions. She argues basically that housing was bad and is bad and that it won't get better until there is a stronger housing code with more officers to enforce it.

Crime

See also: G, Government (police and criminal justice); K10, 20; M35; N116; T58; U, Civil Disorders

(Popular Histories)

L56 Allsop, Kenneth. *The Bootleggers: The Story of Chicago's Prohibition Era.* New Rochelle, 1968.

L56a Asbury, Herbert. *The Great Illusion: An Informal History of Prohibition.* New York, 1968 (c1950).

L57 Baruch, Hugo. *Carrying a Gun for Al Capone: The Intimate Experiences of a Gangster in the Bodyguard of Al Capone.* New York, 1932.

L58 Boettiger, John. *Jake Lingle.* New York, 1931.

L59 Burns, Walter N. *The One Way Ride: The Red Trail of Chicago Gangland from Prohibition to Jake Lingle.* Garden City, 1931.

L60 *Chicago Murders.* New York, 1945.

L61 Coffey, Thomas M. *The Long Thirst: Prohibition in America, 1920-1933.* New York, 1975.

L62 Cromie, Robert. *Dillinger: A Short and Violent Life.* New York, 1962.

L63 Demaris, Ovid. *Captive City.* New York, 1969.

L64 Ellis, John. *The Social History of the Machine Gun.* New York, 1975.

L65 Franke, David. *The Torture Doctor [H. H. Holmes].* New York, 1975.

L66 Halper, Albert. *The Chicago Crime Book.* Cleveland, 1967.

L67 Higdon, Hal. *The Crime of the Century.* New York, 1975.

L68 Hynd, Alan. *The Giant Killers.* New York, 1945.

L69 Kidner, John. *Crimaldi, Contract Killer: A True Story.* Washington, c1976.

L70 Kobler, John. *Ardent Spirits: The Rise and Fall of Prohibition.* New York, 1973.

L71 __________. *Capone.* New York, 1971.

L72 Lee, Henry W. *How Dry We Were: Prohibition Revisited.* Englewood Cliffs, 1963.

M
PUBLIC AND PRIVATE WELFARE AND REFORM

General

See also: A31; E154; G, Government; H13, 204; I82; K46, 47, 50, 56; L25, 52, 118; N49, 69, 87, 170; R25; S19, 24; T11, 25, 30, 32, 37, 40-45, 47, 52, 60, 87, 135, 149

M1 Abbott, Edith. *Social Service Review*. XXIV, 3/4 (Sept./Dec. 1950), *passim*; XXVI, 3 (Sept. 1952), 334-338.

Articles on Hull House and on her sister, Grace.

M2 Amberg, Mary Agnes. *Madonna Center: Pioneer Catholic Social Settlement*. Chicago, 1976.

A history of the first Catholic social settlement in Chicago which was located on the West Side and served the Italian community. Mary Agnes Amberg is the daughter of the founder.

M3 Belles, A. Gilbert. "The Julius Rosenwald Fund: Efforts in Race Relations, 1928-1948." Nash.U. unpub. Ph.D. thesis, 1972.

M4 Bicknell, Ernest Perry. "Problems of Philanthropy in Chicago." *Annals of the Am. Academy of Pol. and Social Science*, XXI (May 1903), 379-388.

M4a Bosch, Allan Whitworth. "Public Outdoor Poor Relief in Chicago, 1907-1914." U.C. unpub. M.A. thesis, 1950.

Not as mature as his Ph.D. thesis (M5), it is, however, a useful treatment of charity.

M5 __________. "The Salvation Army in Chicago, 1885-1914." U.C. unpub. Ph.D. thesis, 1965.

A careful, sound study.

M6 Brandenburg, Clorinne McCulloch. "Chicago Relief and Service Statistics, 1928-1931." U.C. unpub. M.A. thesis, 1932.

She was very much influenced by the U.C. School of Sociology but the evidence is sound.

M7 Breckinridge, Sophonisba P. *The Illinois Poor Law and Its Administration*. Chicago, 1939.

M8 Brookter, Marie. *Chicago's War on Poverty*. Jericho, NY, 1970.

M9 Brown, James. *The History of Public Assistance in Chicago, 1833 to 1893*. Chicago, 1941.

Surveys ". . . county and municipal services concerned with the relief of destitution," public health, and voluntary charities.

M9a Buroker, Robert Lesley. "From Voluntary Association to Welfare State: Social Welfare Reform in Illinois, 1890-1920." U.C. unpub. Ph.D. thesis, 1973.

There is much Chicago material in this detailed account.

M10 __________. "From Voluntary Association to Welfare State: The Illinois Immigrants' Protective League, 1908-1926." *J. of Am. H.*, LVIII, 3 (Dec. 1971), 643-660.

A brief account.

M11 Carbaugh, Harvey C. *Human Welfare Work in Chicago*. Chicago, 1917.

Short descriptions of "Art in Chicago," "City's Public Schools," etc.

M12 Carson, Gerald. "In Chicago: Cruelty and Kindness to Animals." *CH*, n.s., III, 3 (Summer 1974-1975), 151-158.

A short account of the SPCA, the Illinois Anti-Cruelty to Animals Act, and the movement to protect animals.

M13 Chambers, Clarke. *Seedtime of Reform: American Social Service and Social Action, 1918-1933*. Minneapolis, 1963.

An account of the efforts of researchers and reformers in the 1920s to describe and treat social ills. The similarity of the Progressives and the New Dealers is shown. There is material that bears on Chicago, but the omission of the Chicago School of Sociology is curious. Bibliography.

M14 Chicago. Commission on Human Relations. *Community Organizations in Chicago*. Chicago, 1967- .

M15 Cole, Dwayne Charles. "The Relief Crisis in Illinois During the Depression, 1930-1940." S.L.U. unpub. Ph.D. thesis, 1973.

The crisis was the failure of the state to develop an adequate system to fund relief needs, This affected Chicago, which was an area hard hit by the depression.

N
RELIGIOUS, RACIAL AND ETHNIC GROUPS

General

See also: I2; J, Social Statistics; L25; M37; O, Neighborhoods; S19; T2, 16, 22-24, 80, 136.

N1 Beijbom, Ulf. "Scandinavians in Chicago 1850-1860." *Swedish Pioneer H. Q.*, XIV, 4 (Oct. 1963), 163-174.

A useful statistical analysis of Scandinavians in Chicago with particular attention to neighborhood patterns, age groups, and occupations.

N2 Buck, Carl Darling. *A Sketch of the Linguistic Conditions of Chicago*. Chicago, 1903.

A short essay and a list of languages spoken in Chicago with the number of speakers.

N3 Chicago. Commission on Human Relations. Migration Services Committee. *Institute on Cultural Patterns of Newcomers: Selected Papers*. Chicago, 1958.

N4 Deleted

N5 Chicago. Department of Development and Planning. *Historic City: The Settlement of Chicago*. Chicago, 1976.

A survey of the settlement and growth of the city with emphasis on the ethnic groups that made the city. A good starting place for the study of any group. Excellent maps. Bibliography, but beware - some items do not exist.

N6 __________. *The People of Chicago: Who We Are and Who We Have Been. Census Data on Foreign Stock and Race, 1837-1970. Mother Tongue Addendum, 1910-1970*. [Chicago], 1976.

N7 Chicago. Public Library. Omnibus Project. Works Progress Administration. *The Chicago Foreign Language Press Survey: A General Description of Its Contents*. Chicago, 1942.

A description of this valuable resource that translated and classified many of Chicago's ethnic foreign language newspapers. A vital source which is easily available on microfilm.

N8 Cressey, Paul Frederick. "The Succession of Cultural Groups in the City of Chicago." U.C. unpub. Ph.D. thesis, 1930.

One of the most important works on ethnics. Frequently cited. Fundamental.

N9 Curtis, Mildred. "Statistics of Arrests in Chicago in Relation to Race and Nativity." U.C. unpub. M.A. thesis, 1926.

N10 DeVise, Pierre and Ruth Ramirez. *Shifts in Chicago's Ethnic Communities, 1960-1970*. Chicago, 1973.

N11 __________. "The Wasting of Chicago." *Focus Midwest,* IX, 58 (1973), 7-9.

A discussion of middle-class flight and the consequent loss of business and industry.

N12 Fisher, Irving Nuttall. *The Impact of Migration on the Chicago Metropolitan Population*. Santa Monica, 1973.

N13 Freedman, Ronald. *Recent Migration to Chicago*. Chicago, 1950.

Studies the difference between migrants from the U.S. and their predecessors, the immigrants. He describes a "migrant zone" of settlement and patterns of association between the migrants. Many tables and maps.

N14 Galford, Justin B. "The Foreign Born and Urban Growth in the Great Lakes, 1850-1950: A Study of Chicago, Cleveland, Detroit, and Milwaukee," N.Y.U. unpub. Ph.D. thesis, 1957.

The chapters on Chicago are a summary of the census data and describe the numerical change in various ethnic groups.

N15 Holli, Melvin G. and Peter d'A. Jones, ed. *The Ethnic Frontier: Essays in the History of Group Survival in Chicago and the Midwest*. Grand Rapids, 1977.

An important collection of essays dealing with Chicago's multi-ethnic background, housing, ethnic leaders, Jews, Poles, Blacks, and Mexicans.

N16 *Hull-House Maps and Papers: By Residents of Hull-House*. New York, 1970 (c1895).

A study of the area to the east of Hull House. Maps and graphs show the ethnic composition and income level of families in the area. The maps do not show exact statistical data; these are found in the U. S. Department of Labor report (L18). Essays by residents treat the sweat shop, child labor, Bohemians, Italians, charities, etc.

N17 Kiang, Ying-Cheng. "Distribution of the Ethnic Groups in Chicago." *Am. J. of Soc.*, LXIV, 34 (Nov. 1968), 292-296.

Covers the two decades 1940-1960.

N18 Lennon, John Joseph. "A Comparative Study of the Patterns of Acculturation of Selected Puerto Rican, Protestant and Roman Catholic Families in an Urban Metropolitan Area." U.N.D. unpub. Ph.D. thesis, 1963.

N19 Lieberson, Stanley. "Comparative Segregation and Assimilation of Ethnic Groups." U.C. unpub. Ph.D. thesis, 1960.

N19a Miller, Randall and Thomas D. Marzik, ed. *Immigrants and Religion in Urban America*. Philadelphia, 1977.

There is much Chicago material.

N20 Moore, Maurice and James McKeown. *A Study of Integrated Living in Chicago*. Chicago, 1969.

N21 Parot, Joseph. "Ethnic Versus Black Metropolis: The Origins of Polish-Black Housing Tensions in Chicago." *Polish Am. Studies*, XXIX, 1/2 (Spring/Autumn 1972), 5-33.

Traces the historical origins of conflict between Chicago's blacks and the city's Polish Americans, a conflict brought about by competition for good housing. See also: Vecoli, Rudolph J., "'Ethnic Versus Black Metropolis': A Comment," *ibid.*, 34-39; and Parot's "Racial Dilemma in Chicago's Polish Neighborhoods, 1920-1970," *ibid.*, XXXII, 2 (Autumn 1975), 27-37.

N22 Pierce, Bessie Louise. "The Fabric of Chicago's Early Society." *Essays in Honor of William E. Dodd*. Chicago, c1935.

A description of the sorts of people who made up the "social fabric" of early Chicago.

N23 Price, Daniel O. "Rural to Urban Migration of Mexican Americans, Negroes and Anglos." *Internat. Migration R.*, V, 3 (Fall 1971), 281-291.

N24 Radzialowski, Thaddeus. "The Competition for Jobs and Racial Stereotypes: Poles and Blacks in Chicago." *Polish Am. Studies*, XXXIII, 2 (Autumn 1976), 5-18.

N25 Ringo, Miriam. *Adjustment of In-Migrant Spanish-Speaking and Southern White Workers to Jobs and Life in the Chicago Area*. Evanston, 1971.

N26 Roberts, Robert E. T. *Chicago's Ethnic Groups*. Chicago, 1965.

The best short survey of the major groups in the city.

N27 Simons, William M. "Ethnic America: A College Curriculum." C-M.U. unpub. Ph.D. thesis, 1977.

N28 Welfare Council of Metropolitan Chicago. *Selected Papers. Institute on Cultural Patterns of Newcomers.* Chicago, 1957.

Deals with Mexicans, Puerto Ricans, Blacks, Southern Mountain Whites.

N29 Votaw, Albert N. "Sixteen Tongues [Foreign Language Radio in Chicago]." *Chicago,* III, 2 (Ap. 1956), 37-39.

Individual Groups

(Arabs)

N30 Haddād, Safīyah Fahmī. "Socialization and Cultural Change Among Syrian-Americans in Chicago." U.C. unpub. Ph.D. thesis, 1964.

Short chapters on the background and emigration are followed by descriptions of changing family relationships.

N31 Oschinsky, Lawrence. "Islam in Chicago, Being a Study of the Acculturation of a Muslim Palestinian Community in That City." U.C. unpub. M.A. thesis, 1947.

N32 Tahir, Abdul Jalil al. "The Arab Community in the Chicago Area: A Comparative Study of the Christian-Syrians and the Muslim-Palestinians." U.C. unpub. Ph.D. thesis, 1952.

A study of three waves of Arab immigration to Chicago, the last 1933-1951. The distinction between the two main bodies - Muslim-Palestinian and Christian-Syrian - is clearly made. Chapters then treat the locations, nature and compactness of the settlements, social institutions, and the degree of assimilation. The persistence of customs is a theme throughout the work. Statistical information is presented in a series of tables.

(Bielarusians)

N33 Romuk, Vera. *The Bielarusian Community of Chicago.* Chicago, 1975.

A short narrative written for *Historic City* (N5).

(Bohemians)

See: N64-72, Czechs/Slovaks/Bohemians

N50 "The Negro in Illinois History." *JISHS,* LVI, 3 (Autumn 1963).

An entire issue devoted to blacks in Illinois history. Articles on chronology of black history, du Sable, black laws, free blacks, churches, press and civil liberties.

N51 Rather, Ernest R. *Chicago Negro Almanac and Reference Book.* Chicago, 1972.

Black "firsts," biographies, lists of blacks in various occupations, offices, schools, churches, etc.

N52 Robb, Frederic H., ed. *The Negro in Chicago, 1779-1929.* 2 vol. Chicago, 1927-1929.

". . . A survey of the Negroes educational, athletic, civic and commerical life . . . Who's Who in Chicago . . .", etc.

N53 Ross, Wesley E. "Chicago Negroes and the New Deal: A Study of Social Crisis and Local Power Politics." N.I.U. unpub. M.A. thesis, 1966.

N54 Spear, Allan. *Black Chicago: The Making of a Negro Ghetto, 1890-1920.* Chicago, 1967.

The book traces the development of the ghetto: "It attempts to show how, in a thirty-year period, a relatively fluid pattern of race relations gave way to a rigid pattern of discrimination and segregation." Bibliography.

N55 U. S. Work Projects Administration. Illinois. *The Chicago Negro Community, a Statistical Description.* Chicago, 1939.

An important statistical source that was produced on a WPA grant by Mary Elaine Ogden.

N56 Wilson, James Q. "Negro Leaders in Chicago." U.C. unpub. Ph.D. thesis, 1959.

Wilson is a major student of blacks in Chicago.

N57 Wood, Junius B. *The Negro in Chicago.* Chicago, 1916.

Reprints a series of articles in the *Daily News* that supplied an historical background and context of blacks in Chicago.

(Bulgarians)

N58 Abbott, Grace. "The Bulgarians of Chicago." *Charities,* XXI (Jan. 1909), 653-660.

(Catholics)

See: S, Religion

(Chinese)

N59 Chinese American Civic Council of Chicago. *Chinese American Progress*. [An annual volume].

N60 Fan, Ting-Chiu. "Chinese Residents in Chicago." U.C. unpub. M.A. thesis, 1926.

Short history of Chinese immigration to the U.S. and Chicago is followed by essays on demography, economics, and social life. Useful tables. No bibliography.

N61 Deleted

N62 Liang, Yuan. "The Chinese Family in Chicago." U.C. unpub. M.A. thesis, 1951.

A study of acculturation of Chinese and Chinese-Americans to Chicago. The description is based primarily on statistical evidence arranged in tabular form.

N63 Wilson, Margaret Gibbons. "Concentration and Dispersal of the Chinese Population of Chicago, 1870 to the Present." U.C. unpub. M.A. thesis, 1969.

A more general narrative than its title indicates.

(Czechs/Slovaks/Bohemians)

N64 Bicha, Karel D. "The Survival of the Village in Urban America: A Note on Czech Immigrants in Chicago to 1914." *Internat. Migration R.*, V, 1 (Spring 1971), 72-74.

Argues that Czechs retained close-knit communities in America much like the Italians described by Vecoli (N121).

N65 Droba, Daniel. *Czech and Slovak Leaders in Metropolitan Chicago*. Chicago, 1934.

Subtitle, "A Biographical Study of 300 Prominent Men and Women of Czech and Slovak Descent." Arranged by occupation.

N66 Goldsborough, Robert. "The Bohemians." *Chicago*, VI, 1 (Spring 1969), 46-52.

A short survey of the group in Chicago.

(Italians)

See also: L110; S23; T13, 43

N113 Chicago. Board of Education. "Italian Americans." *Ethnic Studies Process*. Chicago, 1972.

N114 Chicago. Department of Development and Planning. *Chicago's Italian Population: Selected Statistics*. Chicago, 1976.

"This report gives a general description of the characteristics of the Italian foreign-born population in 1970 . . . Data in the report come from two sources - published census data and a sample of 1970 census data on computer tape."

N115 Graham, Jory. "The Italians." *Chicago*, VI, 4 (Winter 1969), 72-78.

A short, illustrated overview.

N116 Nelli, Humbert S. *Italians in Chicago, 1880-1930*. New York, 1970.

Covers a broader span of time than Vecoli (N121) and includes sections on politics and crime in addition to other economic and social topics. Nelli argues that the Italians in Chicago were a highly mobile people, not confined in particular "villages."

N117 *Perspectives in Italian Immigration and Ethnicity: Proceedings of the Symposium Held as Casa Italiana, Columbia University, May 21, 23, 1976*. Edited by S. M. Tomasi. New York, 1977.

A review of current Italian American ethnic studies.

N118 Quaintance, Esther Crockett. "Rents and Housing Conditions in the Italian District of the Lower North Side of Chicago, 1924." U.C. unpub. M.A. thesis, 1925.

Part of a series of such studies done at U.C. during this time.

N119 Sager, Gertrude E. "Immigration: Based Upon a Study of the Italian Women and Girls of Chicago." U.C. unpub. M.A. thesis, 1914.

Useful mostly for the primary data that she presents.

N120 Schiavo, Giovanni E. *The Italians in Chicago: A Study in Americanization*. Chicago, 1928.

A short narrative of Italian immigration into Chicago, with many lists, statistics, biographical sketches, and accounts of institutions. Written to improve the image of Italians.

N121 Vecoli, Rudolph John. "Chicago's Italians Prior to World War I: A Study of Their Social and Economic Adjustment." U.W. unpub. Ph.D. thesis, 1962.

A survey of Italian immigration before 1880 in Chapter One. The other chapters are devoted to social and economic history, touching on the influx of peasants past 1870, settlement in the River wards and suburbs, the padrone system, work on the railroads and in industry, and the Italians as the "Chinese of Europe." Vecoli argues that the Italians were badly treated because they were unable to form a coherent national group. They came from villages in Italy and they formed villages in the U.S. Bibliography has a useful section on printed primary sources.

N121a Whyte, William Foote. *Street Corner Society: The Social Structure of an Italian Slum.* Enlarged ed. Chicago, 1955.

Chicago evidence, based on a University of Chicago thesis.

N122 Zaloha, Anna. "A Study of the Persistence of Italian Customs among 143 Families of Italian Descent, Members of Social Clubs at Chicago Commons." N.U. unpub. M.A. thesis, 1937.

A fairly long thesis based on a series of interviews.

(Japanese)

N123 Caudill, William A. and George DeVos. "Achievement, Culture and Personality: The Case of the Japanese Americans." *Am. Anthropologist,* LVIII, 6 (Dec. 1956), 1102-1126.

Studies the Japanese response to resettlement in Chicago, 1943-1946.

N124 Jacobson, Alan and P. L. Rainwater. "A Study of Evaluations of Nisei as Workers by Caucasian Employment Agency Managers and Employers of Nisei." U.C. unpub. M.A. thesis, 1951.

A study of limited scope strangely influenced by the attitudes of post-WWII America.

N125 Nagata, Kiyoshi. "A Statistical Approach to the Study of Acculturation of an Ethnic Group Based on Communication Oriented Variables: The Case of Japanese-Americans in Chicago." U.I.U. unpub. Ph.D. thesis, 1969.

N126 [Nakane, Kenji]. *History of the Japanese in Chicago.* Chicago, 1968.

The best work, but in Japanese.

N127 Nishi, Setsuko Matsunaga. "Japanese American Achievement in Chicago: A Cultural Response to Degradation." U.C. unpub. Ph.D. thesis, 1963.

He treats the response of Japanese-Americans to their forced removal to Chicago in the 1940s.

N128 Okada, Dave M. "A Study of Male Nisei Workers in Two Chicago Industrial Plants under Wartime Conditions." U.C. unpub. M.A. thesis, 1947.

Like other studies, it is strongly influenced by WWII.

N129 Uyeki, Eugene Shigemi. "Process and Patterns of Nisei Adjustment in Chicago." U.C. unpub. Ph.D. thesis, 1953.

She describes Nisei adjustment to Chicago, their relation to other ethnic groups, and how the Nisei changed over ten years.

(Jews)

See also: K39; M30; R53; T94

N130 American Jewish Congress. *A Guide to Jewish Chicago.* Chicago, 1974.

A guide to Jewish institutions.

N131 Berkow, Ira. *Maxwell Street: Survival in a Bazaar.* Garden City, 1977.

Personal history of the Maxwell Street area of the West Side which was for many decades the principal Jewish market.

N132 Bernheimer, Charles, ed. *The Russian Jew in the United States.* Philadelphia, 1905.

Deals with Russian-Jewish life in Chicago, Philadelphia and New York.

N133 Bregstone, Philip P. *Chicago and Its Jews: A Cultural History.* Chicago, 1933.

A description of Jewish life from c1887 to c1930. No notes.

N134 Chicago Hebrew Mission. *Twenty-Five Years of Blessing. Historical Sketch of . . .* Chicago, 1912.

A Christian effort to convert Jews.

N135 *Faith and Form. An Exhibition Organized by the Maurice Spertus Museum of Judaica.* Chicago, 1976.

A narrative history of the Jews in Chicago by Morris A. Gutstein is included.

N136 Felsenthal, Emma. *Bernard Felsenthal: Teacher in Israel.* New York, 1924.

Some material on Felsenthal when he was an important figure in Chicago Judaism in the late 19th and early 20th century.

N137 Gutstein, Morris Aaron. *A Priceless Heritage: The Epic Growth of Nineteenth Century Chicago Jewry.* Chicago, 1953.

A detailed account of the development of Chicago's Jewish community in the 19th century. Bibliography.

N138 Horwich, Bernard. *My First Eighty Years.* Chicago, 1939.

Particularly useful for Jewish life and Zionism in Chicago.

N139 Korey, Harold. "The History of Jewish Education in Chicago." U.C. unpub. M.A. thesis, 1942.

A long narrative, particularly useful for its exploitation of WPA newspaper clippings.

N140 Kraus, Adolf. *Reminiscences and Comments.* Chicago, 1925.

Kraus came to Chicago in the 1870s as a Jewish refugee from Austria-Hungary. He found work, studied law and became active in civic and religious affairs.

N141 Krug, Mark M. "History of the Yiddish Schools in Chicago (1912-53)." *Jewish Education,* XXV, 2 (Fall 1956), 67-73.

N142 Mayo, Louise A. "The Ambivalent Image: The Perception of the Jew in Nineteenth Century America." C.U.N.Y. unpub. Ph.D. thesis, 1977.

She argues that there was considerable anti-Semitism before the 1890s.

N143 Meites, Hyman, ed. *History of the Jews of Chicago.* Chicago, 1924.

Divided into three main sections. The first is a narrative account of the growth of the Jewish community from the beginning to 1923. The second is a section on accomplishments in the arts, professions, politics, labor, finance, industry, and athletics. The third part treats major Jewish organizations and institutions. All sections have biographical sketches interspersed.

N162 Blegen, T. C. *Norwegian Migration to America: The American Transition*. Northfield, Minn., 1940.

Deals with Chicago as a place of settlement and as a distribution center.

N163 Strand, Algot E., comp. *A History of the Norwegians of Illinois*. Chicago, c1905.

A long narrative of Norwegian settlement in Illinois includes scattered references to Chicago. In addition, there is a short section on Chicago. Other essays treat Norwegian churches, organizations, industry, and leading citizens.

(Poles)

See also: T7, 13, 14, 16, 78

N164 Andrea, M. "The Societies of St. Stanislaw Kosta Parish, Chicago." *Polish Am. Studies*, IX, 1/2 (Jan./June 1952), 27-37

N165 Deleted

N166 Chicago. Department of Development and Planning. *Chicago's Polish Population: Selected Statistics*. Chicago, 1976.

See N114

N167 Emmons, Charles Frank. "Economic and Political Leadership in Chicago's Polonia: Some Sources of Ethnic Persistence and Mobility." U.I.C. unpub. Ph.D. thesis, 1971.

He argues that certain ethnic roles may be used to go beyond the larger ethnic community.

N168 Greene, Victor. *For God and Country: The Rise of Polish and Lithuanian Ethnic Consciousness in America, 1860-1910*. Madison, 1975.

Greene argues that Poles and Lithuanians came to the U.S. with little ethnic consciousness. Identification with a national group came about because of the domination of parish life by aliens. Bibliography.

N169 Inviolata Ficht, Sister M. "Noble Street in Chicago: Socio-Cultural Study of Polish Residents within Ten Blocks." DeP.U. unpub. M.A. thesis, 1952.

N170 Ireland, Pat. "Factors in the Americanization of a Second Generation People: A Settlement House and Its Polish Young People with a Study of Adjustments between an Immigrant Colony and Its Adopted City." Unpub. ms. [Chicago], 1932.

In the possession of the author.

N171 Lopata, Helena Znaniecki. "The Function of Voluntary Associations in an Ethnic Community: 'Polonia'." *Contributions to Urban Sociology*. Edited by Ernest W. Burgess and Donald J. Bogue. Chicago, 1964.

N172 Magierski, Louis. "Polish American Activities in Chicago 1919-1939." U.I.U. unpub. M.A. thesis, 1940.

N173 Michalski, Diane Marie. "The Family in a Polish-American Community in Chicago." U.I.C. unpub. M.A. thesis, 1973.

N174 Nowosielski, Janina Eugenia. "The Changes in the Residential Pattern of the Polish Population in Chicago, Illinois, as a Measure of Acculturation." N.E.I.S.C. unpub. M.A. thesis, 1971.

N175 Ozog, Julius John. "A Study of Polish Home Ownership in Chicago." U.C. unpub. M.A. thesis, 1942.

Describes ownership patterns in Poland, acquisition of a home in America, the extent of ownership in Chicago and the relationship between ownership and assimilation.

N176 Parot, Joseph John. "The American Faith and the Persistence of Chicago Polonia, 1870-1920." N.I.U. unpub. Ph.D. thesis, 1971.

The longest sustained narrative of the Chicago Polish community in general to 1920. Parot lays stress on the role of the Catholic Church.

N177 Pawlowski, Eugene Joseph. "The Polish American Element in the Politics of Chicago." N.U. unpub. M.A. thesis, 1970.

N178 *Poles in America: Their Contribution to a Century of Progress*. Chicago, 1933.

Much material in scattered references.

N179 *Poles of Chicago, 1837-1937: A History of One Century of Polish Contribution to the City of Chicago, Illinois.* Chicago, 1937.

Brief essays on various topics, e.g., "Poles in Chicago," "Polish Stage in Chicago," etc. Sections on Polish organizations, national holidays. Biographical sketches.

N180 Slowiak, Walter J. "A Comparative Study of the Social Organization of the Family in Poland and the Polish Immigrant Family in Chicago." L.U. unpub. M.A. thesis, 1950.

N181 Zaranga, Ronald. *Teacher's Guide for Using Oral History Materials on the Immigrant Experience: Prepared by Ronald Zaranga for the Oral History Archives of Chicago Polonia.* Chicago, 1977.

See also the *Oral History Archives of Chicago Polonia. Master Index* and the *Oral History Archives of Chicago Polonia. Passages,* Chicago, 1977. The tapes are housed in CHS.

Roumanians

N182 Galitzi, Christine A. *A Study of Assimilation Among the Roumanians in the United States.* New York, 1929.

Much material on Chicago.

N183 Trutza, Peter George. "The Religious Factor in Acculturation, a Study of the Assimilation and Acculturation of the Roumanian Group in Chicago." U.C. unpub. Ph.D. thesis, 1956.

Trutza uses over 300 tables to present his quantitative evidence of acculturation in the mid-1950s.

Russians

N184 Hall, Thomas Randolph. "The Russian Community of Chicago." *Papers in Ill. H.,* XLIV, (1937), 102-108.

A summary of the Russian community 1887-1924.

N185 __________. ["Russians in Chicago"]. Unpub. ms., U.C. Pierce Papers, Regenstein Library.

The most comprehensive study available.

O
NEIGHBORHOODS

The history of Chicago's neighborhoods is still mostly in the primary sources. More of them have been listed in this chapter than in any other for that reason.

Much material is contained in works listed in other chapters, particularly J, Social Statistics, L, Social Conditions (housing), and in M, Ethnic Groups.

Three works listed elsewhere need to be singled out: the *Local Community Fact Books* (J25-29); the Chicago Plan Commission's *Housing in Chicago Communities* (L32); and *Historic City* (N5) published by the City.

Finally, much material is to be found in general studies. Readers are reminded that many Chicago neighborhoods were once independent towns or neighborhoods in an independent town. Thus, county and town histories must be consulted for the period before annexation.

See also: D6, 12; H11, 32-34, 39, 84, 86, 172; J4, 25, 28, 29; L32, 33; N10

General

O1 Bennett, Charles Ernest. "Residential Segregation of Occupational Groups: Chicago Metropolitan District, 1950 and 1960, Considered by Color and Sex." U.C. unpub. Ph.D. thesis, 1975.

An interesting study based on statistical research. He argues that "spatial segregation of occupation groups is highly correlated, in a U shaped curve to their rank order of socio-economic status."

O2 Bull, Alfred. *The Township of Jefferson, Ill. and "Dinner-Pail Avenue," from Mastodon to Man Whether Red, White, Black or Piebald*. Irving Park, Ill., 1911.

Part history, part reminiscences, with material on the villages of the township: Albany Park, Avondale, Bandow, Bowmanville, Cragin, Dunning, Elsmere, Forest Glen, Galewood, Grayland, Humboldt Park, Irving Park, Jefferson Village, Maplewood, Mont Clare, Montrose (Mayfair), Penrock, Ravenswood Manor, Wicker Park, Whisky Point.

O3 Chamberlin, Everett. *Chicago and Its Suburbs*. New York, 1974 (c1874).

The last quarter is given over to short narratives of subdivisions and suburbs that were outside the city in 1874. Many of these, obviously, are now in the city.

O4 Chicago. Community Renewal Program. *Aspects of Environmental Design: A Section of a Report on the Chicago Experience in Community Change.* Chicago, 1963.

O5 Chicago Historical Society. Chicago Communities Clipping File.

Since the 1930s the Historical Society has clipped from various newspapers selected articles about all seventy-six communities. This is probably the largest ordered collection of material, other than statistics, on Chicago communities. It should be stressed, however, that it is a primary source.

O6 Chicago Historical Society. *Documents. History of . . . Communit[ies], Chicago.* Research under the direction of Vivien M. Palmer. 6 vol. Typescript. Chicago, 1925-1930.

Contents: vol. 1. Rogers Park, West Rogers Park (West Ridge); vol. 2. Uptown, Ravenswood; vol. 3. North Center, Hamlin Park, Lake View, Lower North Side (Near North Side); vol. 4. Near South Side, Armour Square, Douglas, Oakland; vol. 5. Grand Boulevard, Washington Park, Woodlawn, Grand Crossing; vol. 6. West Englewood, Bridgeport, Canaryville (Fuller Park), Riverdale, East Side.

The documents consist of oral histories, excerpts from newspapers, pamphlets, scrapbooks, etc. The information found in these is frequently unique but, like the CHS clipping file, it is raw data, not verified.

O7 Chicago. Metropolitan Housing and Planning Council. *People and Neighborhood Renewal: Report of the Center for Neighborhood Renewal . . .* [Chicago, 1972].

O8 Chicago Plan Commission. *Forty-Four Cities in the City of Chicago.* Chicago, 1942.

Actually, a short narrative history of each of the 75 communities outlined by Burchard in 1935 (J25). They were written under the supervision of Homer Hoyt and first published in the magazine *Real Estate*, 1941-1942.

O9 Clark, Stephen Bedell. *The Lake View Saga.* Chicago, 1974.

First published as a series of 29 articles in the *Lerner Booster Skyline* newspapers. Includes material on Uptown, Lincoln Square, North Center, Lake View and Lincoln Park.

O10 Drury, John. "Old Chicago Neighborhoods." *Landlord's Guide,* XXXVIII, 3 (Ap. 1947); XLI, 8 (Aug. 1950).

A series of brief articles on some of Chicago's neighborhoods: Hyde Park, Lake View, Englewood, Near West Side, South Chicago,

Jefferson Park, Grand Crossing, Kenwood, Norwood Park, Morgan Park, Near South Side, Near North Side, Logan Square, Austin, Ravenswood, Rogers Park, Beverly, Pullman, North Center, South Shore, Lawndale, Irving Park, Woodlawn, Uptown, Roseland, Chicago Lawn, Bridgeport, Edison Park, Oakland, East Side, and Albany Park.

O11 *Fifteen Areas in Chicago and the People Who Live in Them.* Prepared for the City of Chicago, Dept. of Development and Planning, by Leo J. Shapiro & Associates, Inc., 1968.

O11a Holt, Glen E. and Dominic A. Pacyga. *Chicago: A Historical Guide to the Neighborhoods.* Chicago, 1979.

Now the standard introduction.

O12 Hunter, Albert. *Symbolic Communities: The Persistence and Change of Chicago's Local Communities.* Chicago, 1974.

A re-examination of some of the communities defined by Burchard and the Chicago School. He explores those things that have remained constant and those that have changed, such as the trend towards less segregation by ethnic group and more by race.

O13 __________. "Community Change: A Stochastic Analysis of Chicago's Local Communities, 1930-60." *Am. J. of Soc.*, LXXIX, 4 (Jan. 1974), 923-947.

O14 __________. "The Ecology of Chicago: Persistence and Change, 1930-1960." *Am. J. of Soc.*, LXXVII, 3 (Nov. 1971), 425-444.

Hunter finds a remarkable stability in Chicago's human ecology. Important changes are the decline in the importance of the family as an element in fixing the ecology, and the rise in importance of race, ethnicity and age as factors in segregation.

O15 Hunter, Edith Marie. "The Evolution of Chicago's South Side within the Last Fifty Years." N.U. unpub. M.A. thesis, 1942.

O16 Lake. *Journal. Golden Jubilee Edition.* Chicago, 1939.

Some material on the communities in the old town of Lake.

O17 *Our Suburbs . . .* Reprinted from the *Chicago Times.* Chicago, [1873].

Many of these suburbs became part of the City of Chicago.

O18 Palmer, Vivien Marie. "The Primary Settlement as a Unit of Urban Growth and Organization." U.C. unpub. Ph.D. thesis, 1932.

O19 __________. *Social Backgrounds of Chicago's Local Communities*. Chicago, 1930.

O19a Posadas, Barbara M. "Community Structures of Chicago's Northwest Side: The Transition from Rural to Urban, 1830-1889." N.U. unpub. Ph.D. thesis, 1976.

The single most important work on the area.

O19b __________. "A Home in the Country: Suburbanization in Jefferson Township, 1870-1889." *CH*, n.s., VII, 3 (Fall 1978), 134-149.

An account of suburban growth of the villages in the Township and the reasons for their growth. The failure of these villages to provide adequate services, thus bringing annexation, is also explored.

O20 Spray, John Campbell. *Chicago's Great South Shore*. Chicago, c1930.

Boostering, but fairly long.

O21 Suttles, Gerald D. *The Social Construction of Communities*. Chicago, 1972.

Draws heavily on his research into Chicago's history.

O22 White, Marian. *Book of the North Shore: Homes, Gardens, Lands, Highways and Byways, Past and Present*. Chicago, 1910.

Fairly long but mostly pictures of houses in the northside and northern suburbs.

Neighborhood Organizations

See also: P10, 44

O23 Alinsky, Saul. "Citizen Participation and Community Organization in Planning and Urban Renewal." Paper presented to the Chicago Chapter of the National Association of Housing and Redevelopment Officials, Chicago, January 29, 1962.

O24 __________. *Reveille for Radicals*. Chicago, 1946.

The longest statement of this Chicago radical.

O25 Bailey, Robert. *Radicals in Urban Politics: The Alinsky Approach*. Chicago, 1974.

Really an account of the Organization for a Better Austin which was an example of Alinsky's methods. Based on his N.U. thesis.

O26 Brazier, Arthur M. *Black Self-Determination: The Story of The Woodlawn Organization*. Grand Rapids, 1969.

A short study of the most important South Side black neighborhood group.

O27 Fish, John, *et.al*. *The Edge of the Ghetto: A Study of Church Involvement in Community Organization*. New York, 1968 (c1966).

O28 __________. *Black Power/White Control: The Struggle of The Woodlawn Organization in Chicago*. Princeton, 1973.

TWO, The Woodlawn Organization, was founded in 1961 to stop the decline of the neighborhood. In particular the book centers on the experimental schools project, model cities project and a youth project that included the Blackstone Rangers. Bibliography.

O29 Hoehn, Richard A. "Model Cities and Community Organizations in Chicago: A Study in Social Ethics." U.C. unpub. Ph.D. thesis, 1972.

A paper done in the Divinity School; it includes much useful material about Model Cities in Chicago.

O30 Jennings, Russell Wayne. "A Community-Action Group's Definition of Urban Tension: A Situational Analysis through Public Address in Cicero, Illinois in 1967-1968." S.I.U. unpub. Ph.D. thesis, 1968.

O31 Mikva, Zorita Wise. "The Neighborhood Improvement Association: A Counter-Force to the Expansion of Chicago's Negro Population." U.C. unpub. M.A. thesis, 1951.

A description of 97 such groups organized to block black expansion into white housing and the effect on the groups of a court ruling against restrictive covenants.

O32 Piaskowski, Ralph E. *A Survey of Community Organization in West Town, Chicago, Illinois*. Chicago, 1948.

O33 Sanders, Marion K. *The Professional Radical: Conversations with Saul Alinsky*. New York, 1970.

Alinsky talks about his life and his work in this short transcription of interviews.

O34 Sarchet, Bettie. *Block Groups and Community Change: An Evaluation of the Block Program of the Hyde Park-Kenwood Community Conference*. Chicago, 1955.

A detailed study.

O35 Southside Community Committee, Chicago. *Bright Shadows in Bronzetown: The Story of the Southside Community Committee*. Chicago, c1949.

A history and an evaluation of a local group formed to combat social decay.

O36 Spergel, Irving. *Youth Manpower: What Happened in Woodlawn*. Chicago, 1969.

O37 **Deleted**

Individual Neighborhoods

The names given to communities in the *Local Community Fact Books* (J25-29) have gained general currency. Some exceptions have been cross-referenced to the "official name." When a book or article treats more than one community, however, no cross reference has been made. Always check contiguous communities for additional material.

Since most of the articles and books cited are very short and lacking in documentation, no annotation was made. The articles and books that are exceptions to this do have annotations.

Albany Park

O38 Meltzer, (Jack) Associates. *Albany Park-North Park Area: A Planning Report to the Community*. Chicago, 1962.

O39 North Mayfair Improvement Association. *A Historical Account of North Mayfair*. Chicago, 1976.

Andersonville

See: O108-115, Uptown.

Archer Heights

O40 Chicago. Kelly High School. *The Kelly Community*. Chicago, 1938.

Includes information on Archer Heights, Brighton Park and Garfield Ridge.

Argyle Park

See: O108-115, Uptown.

Armour Square

O41 Conroy, John. "The Dark Side of Chinatown." *Chicago,* XXVII, 5 (May 1978), 112-119.

The growing problems in Chinatown are reported.

O42 Drury, John. "A Night in Chinatown." *Chicago Visitor,* IV, 5 (May 1932), 14-15.

Auburn-Gresham

O43 Barlow, Carrie Mae. "Auburn-Gresham: The Survey of a Local Community." U.C. unpub. M.A. thesis, 1934.

A short historical and sociological survey with maps locating community institutions such as churches and taverns.

Austin

O44 Danegger, Anne N. *Early Austin from its Beginnings Until the Time of Annexation to the City of Chicago, 1899.* Chicago, 1944.

O45 McKinlay, Richard and Ethyl Chanas. *Austin: Civil Rights and Integration in a Chicago Community.* Chicago, 1969.

Back of the Yards

See: O90-94, New City.

Beverly

O46 Heinemann, Cora De Graff. *A History of Beverly Hills.* Chicago, 1926.

Reprinted in the Ridge Historical Society *Bulletin,* No. 3, 1973.

O47 Deleted

Bridgeport

048 Fanning, Charles F., Jr. "Mr. Dooley's Bridgeport Chronicle." *CH,* n.s., II, 1 (Spring 1972), 47-57.

Brighton Park

049 Hamzik, Joseph. *Gleanings of Archer Road.* Typescript. Chicago, 1961.

Longer than most such informal accounts. On file at CHS.

Canaryville

See: 054, Fuller Park.

Chinatown

See: 041-42, Armour Square

Death Corner

See: 078-84, Near North Side.

East Garfield Park

050 Ullrich, Polly. "Start Small, Conquer the World." *Chicago,* XXV, 8 (Aug. 1976), 82-87.

East Side

051 Brosch, David. *The Historical Development of Three Chicago Millgates: South Chicago, East Side, South Deering.* [Chicago?, 1972].

A documented narrative, written under an NEH grant. Longer and much more useful than most neighborhood histories.

Edgewater

See: 0108-115, Uptown.

Edison Park

052 Scholl, Edward Thomas. *Seven Miles of Ideal Living.* Berwyn, Ill., 1957.
A 134 page, chatty narrative of Edison Park and Norwood Park.

Englewood

053 Sullivan, Gerald E. *Story of Englewood, 1835-1923.* Chicago, c1924.

A 224 page boostering account of the community, its institutions, leading citizens, etc.

Fishtown

See: 078-84, Near North Side.

Fuller Park

054 *St. Gabriel's Church Diamond Jubilee Book.* Chicago, 1955.

The narrative centers on the church, but there is also much material on the neigborhood.

Forest Glen

055 Edgebrook Community Association, Chicago. *Edgebrook, from Billy Caldwell to 1973.* Chicago, 1973.

A few notes and a short bibliography.

Gold Coast

See: 078-84, Near North Side.

Grand Crossing

056 Johnson, Phillip A. *Call Me Neighbor, Call Me Friend: The Case History of the Integration of a Neighborhood on Chicago's South Side.* Garden City, 1965.

An account by a participant from the origin of the problem in 1949.

Greektown

See: 087, 88, Near West Side

Hermosa

057 Skeris, Peter and Maria T. Armendariz. *Hermosa: A Study of a Community in Transition.* Chicago, 1971.

Written in six weeks by two Loyola graduate students, it is a good compilation of material from standard sources.

Humboldt Park

058 Chicago. Community Renewal Program. *Facts: East Humboldt Park, Near Northwest Community.* 2 vol. Chicago, 1964-65.

Deals mostly with the situation in the early 1960s but some of the material can be used to trace historical development.

059 Illinois. University. Department of Architecture. *East Humboldt Park, a Study of a Gray Area Neighborhood.* n.p., 1965.

060 Marciniak, Ed. *Reviving an Inner City Community: The Drama of Urban Change in East Humboldt Park in Chicago.* Chicago, c1977.

Hyde Park

See also: E140; H86; P, Education (University of Chicago); S33

061 Abrahamson, Julia. *A Neighborhood Finds Itself.* New York, 1959.

A detailed, but undocumented history of the effort to save Hyde Park-Kenwood, written by a participant.

062 Annis, Barbara, ed. *Our Hyde Park.* Chicago, 1976.

063 Beadle, Muriel. *The Hyde Park-Kenwood Urban Renewal Years.* n.p., 1967.

A useful account of the effort from 1949 to make Hyde Park-Kenwood a successful, integrated community.

064 Craig and Messervey, Chicago, Publishers. *Picturesque Kenwood, Hyde Park, Illinois: Its Artistic Homes, Boulevards, Drives, Scenery and Surroundings . . .* Chicago, [1880?].

065 Harper, Lucretia S. *Hyde Park.* 3 vol. Typescript. Chicago, 1938-1939.

Detailed, but organized oddly. Prepared for the Writers Project, Illinois.

066 *Hyde Park Now and Then.* Chicago, 1929.

Useful materials on early Hyde Park, particularly in the 1920s.

067 Rossi, Peter H. and Robert A. Dentler. *The Politics of Urban Renewal: The Chicago Findings.* New York, 1961.

A detailed study of how Hyde Park was successfully "renewed." An interesting comparison with Morningside Heights in New York City tentatively suggests that the Hyde Park example shows the necessity of citizen involvement in planning.

Lakeview

068 Chicago. Commission on Chicago Historical and Architectural Landmarks. *Alta Vista Terrace Landmark District. Summary of Information.* 2 vol. Chicago, 1970.

A full architectural description of townhouses erected by developer S. E. Gross at the turn of the century.

069 Lakeview Citizens Council, Chicago. *A Profile of Lakeview: Its Problems and Opportunities.* [Chicago?, c1961].

A survey of many aspects such as transportation, churches, shopping, etc.

Lawndale

070 Rosenthal, Erich. "This Was North Lawndale: The Transplantation of a Jewish Community." *Jewish Social Studies,* XXII, 2 (Ap. 1960), 67-82.

Lincoln Park

071 Angle, Paula, ed. *City in a Garden: Homes in the Lincoln Park Community.* Chicago, 1963.

072 Chicago. Commission on Chicago Historical and Architectural Landmarks. *Draft: Summary of Information on Mid-North Landmark District.* Chicago, 1971.

A good historical narrative with excellent descriptions of building types, specific buildings, and other physical features. Mid-North is the triangle formed by Lincoln, Clark and Fullerton. Excellent drawings.

072a Chicago. Commission on Chicago Historical and Architectural Landmarks. *Mid-North District. A Discussion of the History and Architectural Features of This Distinctive Area of Chicago*. Chicago, 1975.

A useful, short account.

O73 Healy, John J. *A Little Bit of the Old North Side*. Chicago, 1947.

O74 Molotch, Harvey Luskin. *Managed Integration: Dilemmas of Doing Good in the City*. Berkeley, c1972.

O75 Paolini, A. Rod. *Lincoln Park Conservation Association: The Politics of a Community Organization*. Chicago, 1970.

A sociological analysis of the group which also touches on many of the changes in the area in the 1950s and 1960s.

O76 Reiger, Howard Melvin. "Redeveloping Chicago's Lincoln Park Area." S.I.U. unpub. Ph.D. thesis, 1970.

Little Hell

See: O78-84, Near North Side

Little Italy

See: O87, 88, Near West Side

Little Sicily

See: O78-84, Near North Side

Loop

See also: H2, 6; S42

O77 Johnson, Earl Shepard. "The Natural History of the Central Business District with Particular Reference to Chicago." U.C. unpub. Ph.D. thesis, 1941.

A narrative analysis of the changing function of the Loop area.

Near North Side

See also: N118

O78 Broomell, Kenneth F. and Harlow M. Church. "Streeterville Saga." *JISHS*, XXXIII, 2 (June 1940), 153-165.
An undocumented narrative.

079 Bronté, Patricia. *Vittles and Vice: An Extraordinary Guide to What's Cooking on Chicago's Near North Side*. Chicago, 1952.

A very light treatment of a variety of subjects connected with the Near North Side.

080 Chicago. Commission on Chicago Historical and Architectural Landmarks. *Astor Street District*. Chicago, 1976.

081 Palmer, Vivien M. "Study of the Development of Chicago's Northside." Typescript. Chicago, 1932.

An important study of the development of the Near North Side and Lincoln Park. On file at CHS.

082 Rubloff, Arthur & Company, Chicago. *Proposal for the Redevelopment of the Chicago Land Clearance Commission North-La Salle Project. Carl Sandburg Center, a Joint Venture*. Chicago, 1962.

Many floor plans, drawings of the buildings, photographs of the area before redevelopment.

083 Tessendorf, K. C. "Captain Streeter's District of Lake Michigan." *CH*, n.s., V, 3 (Fall 1976), 152-160.

A short, illustrated narrative stressing Streeter.

084 Zorbaugh, Harvey Warren. *Gold Coast and Slum: A Sociological Study of Chicago's Near North Side*. Chicago, 1929.

A careful sociological study of the Near North Side. He describes a variety of groups in the community and argues that it is a geographical designation rather than an integrated community of people.

Near South Side

See also: I24

085 Deleted

086 Pruter, Robert. "The Prairie Avenue Section of Chicago: The History and Examination of Its Decline." U.C. unpub. M.A. thesis, 1976.

Covers the period 1880s to the 1970s. Attempts " . . . to show chronologically and in detail the social and physical transformation of Prairie Avenue."

Near West Side

O87 Orphan, Constantine D. "Goodbye Greektown." *Inland,* 38 (Spring 1963), 20-23.

O88 Selz, Thalia Cheronis. "Switchboard: A Lament for the Passing of the Old Greek Community." *Chicago,* XXV, 10 (Oct. 1976), 128-131.

O89 Sorrentino, Anthony. *Autobiography.* Typescript, 1953.

New City

O90 Blythe, June. "'Back of the Yards' Reverses the Flight to Suburbia." *Commerce,* LII, 12 (Dec. 1956), 20-25.

O91 Bushnell, Charles J. *The Social Problem at the Chicago Stock Yards.* Chicago, 1902.

Describes the industry, the community and the relationship between them. Some early photographs are printed.

O92 Pacyga, Dominic A. "Crisis and Community: The Back of the Yards 1921." *CH,* n.s., VI, 3 (Fall 1977), 167-176.

Describes the community during the 1921 meat cutters' strike.

O93 Skillin, Edward. "Back of the Stockyards." Reprinted from *The Commonweal.* New York, 1940.

O94 University of Chicago Settlement. *A Study of Chicago's Stockyards Community.* 3 vol. Chicago, [1912-1914].

Old Town

See: O71-76, Lincoln Park

Pilsen

See: O87-89, Near West Side

Pullman

See also: L26

O95 Adelman, William. *Touring Pullman, a Study in Company Paternalism: A Walking Guide to the Pullman Community in Chicago.* Chicago, 1972.

A good, brief description with a pro-labor bias.

096 Bach, Ira J. "Pullman: A Town Reborn." *CH*, n.s., IV, 1 (Spring 1975), 44-53.

The most useful short account.

097 Buder, Stanley. *Pullman: An Experiment* . . . New York, 1967.

Buder argues that the town was an expression of Pullman's desire to apply his "system" to a town as well as to his factory. Pullman wanted to do this to show that industrialization need not lead to social disintegration. In addition to the origins and development of the town, Buder treats the impact of the strike on the town and its gradual integration into the city (to 1930). Bibliography.

098 Chicago. Commission on Chicago Historical and Architectural Landmarks. *A Summary of Information on the South Pullman District*. Chicago, 1972.

A good physical description, photographs, and some copies of original drawings.

099 Doty, Duane (Mrs.). *Town of Pullman, Illinois*. Pullman, 1893.

A detailed account of Pullman before the strike.

Rogers Park

0100 "75th Anniversary, Township of Rogers Park Annexation to the City of Chicago. 1893-1968 Diamond Jubilee. Historical Supplement." *Lerner Home Newspapers*. Chicago, April 3, 1968.

0100a Sequeira, Paul. "Rainbow in Rogers Park." *Chicago*, XXIV, 8 (Aug. 1975), 104-109.

An account of change in this ethnically mixed area.

Roseland

0100b Eenigenburg, Harry. *The Calumet Region and Its Early Settlers*. Chicago, c1935.

0101 "One Hundred Years of Roseland's History, in Picture and Story." *Calumet Index*. Pullman, June 20, 1949.

The Sands

See: 078-84, Near North Side

Sauganash

See: O55, Forest Glen

South Chicago

See also: I24; L26

O102 Conroy, John. "Mill Town: South Chicago is Home to Some of the World's Largest Steel Mills . . . It is the Political Base of Ed Vrdolyak and Ed Sadlowski . . ." *Chicago*, XXV, 11 (Nov. 1976), 164-182.

O103 Dyett, E. *Study of the Development of the South Chicago Community*. n.p., 1924.

O104 Gillette, John Morris. *Culture Agencies of a Typical Manufacturing Group: South Chicago*. Chicago, 1901.

Really a general survey of the community.

O105 Immaculate Conception B.V.M. Parish. *Diamond Jubilee*. Chicago, 1957.

Obviously centers on the church, but a great deal of material about South Chicago is included.

O106 Kijewski, Marcia. *The Historical Development of Three Chicago Millgates: South Chicago, East Side, South Deering*. [Chicago?, 1972].

See annotation for O51.

South Deering

See also: L26

O107 Bulanda, Robert. *The Historical Development of Three Chicago Millgates: South Chicago, East Side, South Deering*. [Chicago?, 1972].

See annotation for O51

South Shore

O107a Molotch, Harvey Luskin. *Managed Integration: Dilemmas of Doing Good in the City*. Berkeley, c1972.

O107b South Shore Commission. *This is South Shore*. [Chicago, 1961].

Streeterville

See: 078-84, Near North Side

Towertown

See: 078-84, Near North Side

Uptown

0108 Adler, Jody. *Decent Housing Through Community Involvement.* Chicago, 1978.

0109 Amidei, Neal. "The Agony of Uptown." *Omnibus Chicagoland,* V, 9 (July 1968), 35-39.

0110 Chicago. Commission on Human Relations. *The Uptown Community Area and the Southern White Immigrant.* Chicago, 1957.

An interesting early study of the area in Uptown east of Racine Avenue.

0111 Ganong, W. B. "The Business Structure of the Uptown Area of Chicago." U.C. unpub. M.S. thesis, 1965.

Another product of Berry and Mayer's Central Place Research Project. It is ". . . a survey of the business structure, as it existed in June, 1960, of an area of approximately three square miles surrounding the Uptown business center - one of the major outlying business centers of Chicago."

0112 Gitlin, Todd and Nanci Hollander. *Uptown: Poor Whites in Chicago.* New York, 1970.

A series of interviews with poor southern whites in Uptown in the 1960s.

0113 Johnson, Flora. "In Order to Save It." *Chicago,* XXV, 12 (Dec. 1976), 164-186.

0114 Ratcliffe, Jane E. *A Community in Transition: The Edgewater Community in Chicago.* Chicago, 1978.

A good description of the area and the changes that it has recently undergone. Edgewater is in the N.E. corner of Uptown.

0115 Uptown Hull House Gallery. *More than Stone . . . A Nostalgic View of Uptown Architecture.* Chicago, 1975.

Catalog for an exhibition. Description has much detail about specific places and buildings in Uptown. Bibliography.

The Valley

See: 087-89, Near West Side

West Pullman

0116 West Pullman Land Association. *West Pullman and Stewart Ridge, Chicago, Illinois, 1892-1900.* Chicago, 1900.

A boostering photographic essay.

Wolf Point

See: 078-84, Near North Side

Woodlawn

0117 Bragdon, Marion L. *Early History of Woodlawn.* Chicago, 1941.

0118 Deleted

0119 Lindstrom, Frederick Burgess. "The Negro Invasion of the Washington Park Subdivision." U.C. unpub. M.A. thesis, 1941.

Studies three stages of Washington Park: white flight, black settlement, and the effect of the change.

0120 Moore, Winston, Charles P. Livermore and George F. Galland, Jr. "Woodlawn: The Zone of Destruction." *Public Interest,* 30 (Winter 1973), 41-59.

A study of the decline of Woodlawn, 1931-1971.

0121 Spray, John Campbell. *The Book of Woodlawn.* Chicago, c1920.

0122 Spergel, Irving A. and Richard E. Mundy. *A Community Study, East Woodlawn: Problems, Programs, Proposals.* Mimeograph. Chicago, 1963.

P

EDUCATION

See also: I27, 28; R129

Chicago Public Schools

See also: E155; N48, 84, 139

P1 Beck, John Matthew. "Chicago Newspapers and the Public Schools, 1890-1920." U.C. unpub. Ph.D. thesis, 1953.

P2 Bell, John Wesley. *The Development of the Public High School in Chicago.* Chicago, 1939.

The material is arranged topically and the discussion is influenced by then current educational theory, but much useful material can still be extracted.

P3 Campbell, Jack K. *Colonel Francis W. Parker, the Children's Crusader.* New York, 1967.

This is a well-researched life of the famous progressive educator who did most of his work in Chicago.

P4 Candeloro, Dominic. "The Chicago School Board Crisis of 1907." *JISHS,* LXVIII, 5 (Nov. 1975), 396-406.

A study of the interaction between "progressive education" and Chicago politics.

P5 Chicago. Board of Education. *Chicago and the Chicago Public Schools: Maps and Charts Showing Racial Composition and Selected Data [1950-1966].* Chicago, 1966.

A basic document on the racial composition of the public school population. The material is presented entirely in graphic form, *i.e.,* tables and graphs; there is no text.

P6 __________. *Historical Sketches of the Public School System of the City of Chicago.* By Shepherd Johnston. Chicago, 1880.

Detached from the 25th annual report of the Board of Education of the City of Chicago. Some details not found elsewhere.

P7 Chicago. Board of Education. *High School Education in the Chicago Public Schools.* Chicago, 1880.

P8 Chicago. Public Schools. Department of Operations Analysis. *Racial/Ethnic Survey: Staff as of October 29, 1976.* Chicago, 1977.

P9 "The Chicago Free Kindergarten Association." *Kindergarten Mag.*, V, 10 (June 1893), 734-738.

P10 Cibulka, James. "Administrators as Representatives: The Role of Local Communities in an Urban School System." U.C. unpub. Ph.D. thesis, 1973.

An investigation into how much administrators in Chicago represented local communities. See also, "School Decentralization in Chicago," *Education and Urban Society*, VII, 4 (Aug. 1975), 412-438.

P10a Cierpik, Ann Felicia. "History of the Development of Music Education in the Chicago Public Schools." DeP.U. unpub. M.A. thesis, 1941.

P11 Clark, Hannah B. *The Public Schools of Chicago, a Sociologica Study*. Chicago, 1897.

A topical history and an analysis of the organization in 1897. Many details for that period.

P12 Counts, George Sylvester. *School and Society in Chicago*. New York, 1971 (c1928).

An important work in the history of progressive education.

P13 "Evolution of the Kindergarten Idea in Chicago, Mrs. Alice H. Putnam and the Froebl Association." *Kindergarten Mag.*, V, 10 (June 1893), 729-733.

P14 Gardner, Frank William. "The History, Role and Operation of the Board of Examiners, Chicago Public Schools, 1917-1974." N.U. unpub. Ph.D. thesis, 1975.

A study of how Chicago came to have its own power to certify its teachers and how that power has been used.

P15 Gilpatric, Clarence Edward. "Urban Federalism in Educational Policy." U.C. unpub. Ph.D. thesis, 1977.

A Chicago study.

P16 Haggard, William Wade. "The Legal Basis of the Organization and Administration of the Public Schools of Illinois." U.C. unpub. Ph.D. thesis, 1937.
This, obviously applies to Chicago as well as the state.

P17 Havighurst, Robert James. *The Public Schools of Chicago: A Survey for the Board of Education of the City of Chicago*. Chicago, 1964.
A detailed examination of all aspects of the city's schools in the early '60s, from elementary school to college and adult education, including special programs such as those for gifted students.

P18 Hazlett, James Stephen. "Crisis in School Government: An Administrative History of the Chicago Public Schools, 1933-1947." U.C. unpub. Ph.D. thesis, 1968.

P19 Heffron, Ida C. *Francis Wayland Parker*. Los Angeles, 1934.

A friendly biography by one who knew him well.

P20 Herrick, Mary J. *The Chicago Schools: A Social and Political History*. Beverly Hills, 1971.

The standard work. The bibliography lists most of the theses and dissertations that relate to Chicago education as well as a long list of official reports.

P21 Hirsh, Elizabeth Francis. "A Study of the Chicago and Cook County School for Boys." U.C. unpub. M.A. thesis, 1926.

P22 Homel, Michael W. "The Politics of Public Education in Black Chicago, 1910-1941." *J. of Negro Education*, XLV, 2 (Spring 1976), 179-191.

A narrative of increasing dissatisfaction and action. For a more detailed and broader view see also, "Negroes in the Chicago Public Schools 1910-1941," U.C. unpub. Ph.D. thesis, 1972.

P23 Hug, Clarissa H. *A Study of the Home Instruction Program of the Chicago Public Schools from Its Inception to 1963*. Evanston, c1966.

P24 Jones, Alan. *Students! Do Not Push Your Teacher Down the Stairs on Friday*. [New York, c1972].

The story of a new teacher at DuSable Upper Grade School in Chicago's black ghetto.

P25 Kamin, Kay Hodes. "A History of the Hunt Administration of the Chicago Public Schools, 1947-1953." U.C. unpub. Ph.D. thesis, 1970.

P26 Koerner, Thomas F. "Benjamin C. Willis and the Chicago Press." N.U. unpub. Ph.D. thesis, 1968.

Koerner studied the press during Willis' tenure as Superintendent of Schools, 1953-1966. He found that the press failed to provide adequate coverage of school issues and that all of the daily newspapers tended to slant their news coverage in favor of their editorial position, except the *American*. Willis failed to deal frankly and openly with the press and in this contributed to the problem.

P26a Lawson, Charlotte M. "The Development of Radio Education in the Chicago Public Schools." DeP.U. unpub M.A. thesis, 1942.

P27 Lloyd, Neil Ellsworth. "The Decision-Making Process and the Chicago Board of Education: The Busing Decision." L.U. unpub. Ph.D. thesis, 1974.

A description of the first limited efforts to bus.

P28 London, Stephen David. "Business and the Chicago Public School System." U.C. unpub. Ph.D. thesis, 1969.

P29 Miller, Mary Jean. "Account of the Chicago Kindergarten Club." *Kindergarten Mag.*, X, 3 (Nov. 1897), 203-207.

P30 Orfield, Gary. "Chicago: Failure in the North." *The Reconstruction of Southern Education: The Schools and the 1964 Civil Rights Act*. New York, 1969.

P31 Parker, Franklin. "Francis W. Parker and Public Education in Chicago." *Chicago Schools J.*, XLII, 7 (Ap. 1961), 305-312.

An attempt to sketch Parker's contribution to modern education (Franklin Parker is not related to Francis W. Parker).

P32 Peterson, Paul Elliott. *School Politics, Chicago Style*. Chicago, 1976.

Studied the question of desegregation, collective bargaining and decentralization in an attempt to define the influence of the machine, the reformers and racial change on policy. He found that there were important factors but that they worked in the context of the School Board policy objectives and the limits of the Board's bureaucracy.

P33 Deleted

P34 Pois, Joseph. *The School Board Crisis: A Chicago Case Study*. Chicago, 1964.

Pois served on the Board for five years.

P35 Raymond, Joan Marie Duck. "The Evolution of the Chicago Public School Superintendency." N.U. unpub. Ph.D. thesis, 1967.

A narrative in which she attempts to define those historical factors that caused the position to assume a different shape in four distinct periods. She argues that these were 1853-189 1898-1929, 1929-1946, and 1946-1966.

P36 Reid, Robert Louis. "The Professionalization of Public School Teachers: The Chicago Experience, 1895-1920." N.U. unpub. Ph.D. thesis, 1968.

Argues that the forces of industrialism and urbanization caused teachers to seek to "professionalize." Bibliography.

P37 Rosenbaum, Judy Jolley. "Black Education in Three Northern Cities in the Early Twentieth Century." U.I.U. unpub. Ph.D. thesis, 1974.

Studies of Chicago, Indianapolis and Philadelphia. She found that in Chicago transfers and district boundaries were used to create separate all-white and all-black schools. The all-black schools tended to receive inferior treatment.

P38 Saumier, Andre. "Social Climate in a Chicago High School." U.C. unpub. M.A. thesis, 1960.

P39 Stone, Marie Kirchner, ed. *Between Home and Community: Chronicle of the Francis W. Parker School 1901-1976.* Chicago, 1976.

A house history with many illustrations.

P39a Suloway, Orwin J. "Chicago's High School Curriculums, 1856-1956: A Centennial Survey." *Chicago Schools J.*, XXXVIII, 3/4 (Nov./Dec. 1956), 93-98.

P40 Tostberg, Robert Eugene. "Educational Ferment in Chicago, 1883-1904." U.W. unpub. Ph.D. thesis, 1960.

A study of the influence of Francis Parker and John Dewey on Chicago schools either directly or through the work of Ella Flagg Young. There is also a section on the U.C. lab school.

P41 Vandewalker, Nina C. "The Kindergarten in the Chicago School System. *Kindergarten Mag.*, IX, 9 (May 1897), 679-686.

P42 Vieg, John Albert. *The Government of Education in Metropolitan Chicago*. Chicago, 1939.

". . . describes the major developments of the last quarter-century [1915-1939] and indicates some of the ways that are open for the solution of basic problems that have emerged."

P43 Vrame, William Anton. "A History of School Desegregation in Chicago Since 1954." U.W. unpub. Ph.D. thesis, 1970.

He studied the busing plan in Austin in particular. The conclusions of the study as a whole are not surprising - that Chicago's school system resisted efforts to end *de facto* segregation, that this was aided by the attitude of the machine, etc. Good bibliography.

P44 Weeres, Joseph G. "School Politics in Thirty-Three of the Local Community Areas within the City of Chicago." U.C. unpub. Ph.D. thesis, 1971.

P45 Wrigley, Julia. "The Politics of Education in Chicago: Social Conflicts and the Public Schools." U.W. unpub. Ph.D thesis, 1977.

Catholic Education

There are many works on particular schools, teachers, etc. These have not been included. They are listed in depth in Montay (P49) and Sanders (P53). See also: S10.

P45a DePaul University. *DePaul in Chicago: The First Fifty Years*. Chicago, 1948.

P46 Kucera, Daniel. *Church-State Relationships in Education in Illinois*. Washington, 1955.

Chicago is obviously a major concern of Kurcera's book. Bibliography.

P47 Larkin, Helen M. "Catholic Education in Illinois." *Ill. Catholic H. R.*, IV, 4 (Ap. 1922), 339-354.

A short survey.

P48 McCarthy, Joseph J. "History of Black Catholic Education in Chicago: 1871-1971." L.U. unpub. Ph.D. thesis, 1973.

A topical narrative.

P49 Montay, Mary I. *A History of Catholic Secondary Education in the Archdiocese of Chicago*. Washington, 1953.

A detailed narrative written as a Ph.D. thesis at Catholic University. The bibliography is long with many primary materials: articles, books, theses, etc., for individual schools and they have not been reproduced here.

P50 Deleted

P51 Paul, Norma A. *Religious Orders and Their Schools in Illinois, 1834-1939*. [Chicago], 1970.

A fact-filled sketch of schools in Illinois in the period; e.g., attendance by year where known.

P52 Riordan, D. J. "The University of St. Mary of the Lake." *Ill. Catholic H. R.*, II, 2 (Oct. 1919), 135-160.

An overview with a partial list of students.

P53 Sanders, James W. *The Education of an Urban Minority: Catholics in Chicago, 1833-1965*. New York, 1977.

Centers on the parochial school system in Chicago. He argues that the parochial system became the largest Catholic system because it was able to accommodate diversity better than the public schools. See his 1970 U.C. dissertation for a full bibliography.

P54 Walch, Timothy George. "Catholic Education in Chicago and Milwaukee, 1840-1890." N.U. unpub. Ph.D. thesis, 1975.

He argues that the experience of the founders of Catholic schools in the Midwest was different from the experience in the East. Chicago was a new city and its citizens welcomed Catholic institutions as additions to the community. Even as the community grew and Catholics became a "minority" they retained influence in the affairs of the city, including education. There was no monolithic Catholic church but a diversity of ethnic groups. The schools were, like the public system, an Americanizing force. Long, useful bibliography. Parts of his paper are summarized in articles in *CH*, n.s., VII, 2 (Summer 1978), 87-98, and *Ill. Catholic H. R.*, LXIV, 1 (Jan. 1978), 16-32.

University of Chicago

(General)

See also: L61-63, 65; T32.

P55 Arnold, Charles Harvey. *Near the Edge of Battle: A Short History of the Divinity Schools and the Chicago School of Theology, 1866-1966*. Chicago, c1966.

P56 Beadle, Muriel. *Where Has All the Ivy Gone? A Memoir of University Life*. Garden City, 1972.

An account of her life as the wife of the president of the University of Chicago, 1961-1968.

P57 Blake, Lincoln C. "The Concept and Development of Science at the University of Chicago 1890-1905." U.C. unpub. Ph.D. thesis, 1966.

A narrative.

P58 Boucher, Chauncey Samuel. *The Chicago College Plan*. Chicago, 1935.

In the 1930s U.C. made important changes in undergraduate education. This is the plan that was used.

P59 Boycheff, Kooman. "Intercollegiate Athletics and Physical Education at the University of Chicago, 1892-1952." U.Mich. unpub. Ph.D. thesis, 1954.

P60 Carey, James T. *Sociology and Public Affairs: The Chicago School*. Beverly Hills, c1975.

Treats recruitment, training, organization, policy, civic involvements, the paradigm of social disorganization, the local sponsors of the work, and the Chicago sociologists as an intellectual community. Long, useful bibliography.

P61 Cremin, Lawrence A. *The Transformation of the School: Progressivism in American Education, 1876-1957.* New York, 1961.

Deals with Dewey's work in education in a national context.

P62 Curti, Merle and Roderick Nash. *Philanthropy in the Shaping of American Higher Education.* New Brunswick, 1965.

Sets U.C. in the context of national philanthropy.

P63 De Pencier, Ida B. *The History of the Laboratory Schools, the University of Chicago, 1896-1965.* Chicago, 1967.

A sound narrative, but without notes or bibliography.

P64 *Dreams in Stone.* Edited by D. J. R. Bruckner and Irene Macauley. Chicago, 1976.

A visual history of building at U.C.

P65 Ellsworth, Frank L. *Law on the Midway: The Founding of the University of Chicago Law School.* Chicago, c1977.

Very careful research with full documentation. Bibliography.

P66 Engle, Gale W. "William Rainey Harper's Conception of the Structuring of the Functions Performed by Educational Institutions." Stanford U. unpub. Ph.D. thesis, 1954.

P67 Faris, Robert E. L. *Chicago Sociology, 1920-1932.* San Francisco, 1967.

An account of how the U.C. sociology department rose to national dominance in the first third of the 20th century.

P68 Fay, Maureen Anne. "Origins and Early Development of the University of Chicago Extension Division, 1892-1911." U.C. unpub. Ph.D. thesis, 1976.

Long chapters of introductory material on the role of early extension schools and the Chautauqua on U.C.'s program, a survey of U.C.'s extension program and an evaluation of its impact.

P69 Flint, Nott. *The University of Chicago.* Chicago, 1905.

P70 Goodspeed, Thomas Wakefield. *A History of the University of Chicago, Founded by John D. Rockefeller: The First Quarter Century.* Chicago, 1916.
Concentrates on the beginnings of the University when

Goodspeed had personal knowledge as Secretary to the Board of Trustees and as a principal fund raiser.

P71 Gould, Joseph E. *The Chautauqua Movement: An Episode in the Continuing American Revolution.* New York, 1961.

William Rainey Harper was a leader in the Chautauqua movement in America and based much of his design for U.C.'s extension service on it.

P72 Gunther, John. *Chicago Revisited.* Chicago, 1967.

Gunther was invited by the University to return and describe his impressions many years after he was an undergraduate.

P73 Gustafson, David. "The Origin and Establishment of the University High School of the University of Chicago." U.C. unpub. M.A. thesis, 1927.

P74 Haggerty, William James. "The Purpose of the University of Chicago." U.C. unpub. Ph.D. thesis, 1943.

A topical survey.

P75 Hofstadter, Richard and Walter P. Metzger. *The Development of Academic Freedom in the United States.* New York, 1955.

Touches on the Bemis case at U.C.

P76 Humphreys, Joseph Anthony. "Changes in Certain Aspects of the College of the University of Chicago Following the Inauguration of the New Plan (1931)." U.C. unpub. Ph.D. thesis, 1934.

Measures student response to the "New Plan" and compares it with the old.

P77 Hutchins, Robert Maynard. *The State of the University, 1929-1949: A Report by Robert M. Hutchins Covering the Twenty Years of His Administration.* Chicago, 1949.

P78 *The Idea and Practice of General Education: An Account of the College of the University of Chicago, by Present and Former Members of the Faculty.* Chicago, 1950.

A series of essays with "Reading Lists" for each chapter which are interesting.

P79 *The Idea of the University of Chicago: Selections from the Papers of the First Eight Chief Executives of the University of Chicago from 1891 to 1975.* Edited by D. J. R. Bruckner and William Michael Murphy. Chicago, 1976.

A useful collection.

P80 Levi, Edward Hirsch. *An Adventure in Discovery*. Chicago, 1972

P81 Matthews, Fred H. *Quest for an American Sociology: Robert E. Park and the Chicago School*. Montreal, 1977.

P81a Mayhew, Katherine. *The Dewey School: The Laboratory School of the University of Chicago, 1896-1903*. New York, 1966.

A friendly, detailed account.

P82 Nichols, Terry. "Student Dissent at the University of Chicago." U.C. unpub. Ph.D. thesis, 1974.

More a study of attitudes than of events or particular dissenters. See also, William Stern Aron "Political Radicalism - Ideology and Behavior Among Students at the University of Chicago," U.C. unpub. Ph.D. thesis, 1972, which is also a study of attitudes rather than events.

P83 Patterson, Robert Meddin. "The Development of Academic Sociology at the University of Chicago, 1892-1920." V.U. unpub. Ph.D. thesis, 1973.

P84 Ryan, W. Carson. *Studies in Early Graduate Education*. Carnegie Foundation for the Advancement of Teaching, Bull. No. 31. New York, 1939.

Compares the programs at Johns Hopkins, Clark and U.C.

P85 Short, James F., ed. *The Social Fabric of the Metropolis: Contributions of the Chicago School of Urban Sociology*. Chicago, [1971].

P86 Selk, Merry. "Styles of Handling Student Demonstrations." *Bull. of the Atomic Scientists*, XXV, 6 (June 1969), 36-38.

Study of massive protest at U.C. over a faculty decision.

P87 Storr, Richard. *Harper's University: The Beginnings*. Chicago, 1966.

A careful, detailed study of the early years of U.C. The best book for the period that it covers. A long, annotated bibliography.

P88 Stumpf, Wippert. "A Comparative Study of Certain Aspects of the Old and the New Plan at the University of Chicago." U.C. unpub. Ph.D. thesis, 1941.

P89 Tannler, Albert M. *One in Spirit*. Chicago, 1973.

P90 Veblen, Thorstein. *The Higher Learning in America: A Memorandum on the Conduct of Universities by Business Men*. New York, 1918.

An important book for American education in general, but

of special importance to U.C. because of Veblen's involvement with the University.

P91 Veith, Ilza. *The University of Chicago Clinics and Clinical Departments, 1927-1952: A Brief Outline of the Origins, the Formative Years, and the Present State of Medicine at the University of Chicago*. Chicago, 1952.

A short narrative on the history and various departments and clinics at U.C.

P92 Veysey, Laurence R. *The Emergence of the American University*. Chicago, 1965.

A general account of American higher education which sets U.C. in the context of the country.

P93 White, Woodie T. "The Study of Education at the University of Chicago, 1892-1958." U.C. unpub. Ph.D. thesis, 1977.

(Biography)

P94 Goodspeed, Thomas Wakefield. *The University of Chicago Biographical Sketches*. Chicago, 1922.

Accounts of the lives of donors to U.C. A useful collective biography.

Ames, Edward S.

P95 Ames, Edward Scribner. *Beyond Theology: The Autobiography of Edward Scribner Ames*. Chicago, 1959.

Barker, Lewellys F.

P96 Barker, Lewellys F. *Time and the Physician: The Autobiography of Lewellys F. Barker*. New York, 1942.

Barker, one of the leading forces in 20th century medicine, devotes one chapter to his career at U.C.

Breasted, James H.

P97 Breasted, Charles. *Pioneer to the Past: The Story of James Henry Breasted, Archaeologist*. New York, 1943.

Breasted was a great U.C. archaeologist from 1894-1935.

Coulter, John M.

P98 Rodgers, Andrew D., III. *John Merle Coulter, Missionary in Science*. Princeton, 1944.

A figure in the botany department.

Cuppy, Will J.

P99 Cuppy, Will J. *Maroon Tales: University of Chicago Stories*. Chicago, 1910.

Based on his experiences at U.C.

Dewey, John

P100 Boydston, Jo Ann. *The Early Works of John Dewey*. 5 vol. Carbondale, 1969-1972.

P101 __________. *The Middle Works of John Dewey*. I- . Carbondale, 1976- .

P102 Dykhuizen, George. *The Life and Mind of John Dewey*. Carbondale, 1973.

P103 McCaul, Robert. "Dewey and the University of Chicago." *School and Society*, LXXXIX, 2189-2191 (Mar./Ap. 1961), 152-157.

P104 Wirth, Arthur G. *John Dewey as Educator: His Design for Work in Education 1894-1904*. New York, 1966.

Eckersall, Walter H.

P105 Peterson, James Andrew. *Eckersall of Chicago*. Chicago, 1957.

An early football player at U.C.

Goodspeed, Edgar J.

P106 Cobb, James Harrell and Louis B. Jennings. *A Biography and Bibliography of Edgar Johnson Goodspeed*. Chicago, 1948.

P107 Goodspeed, Edgar J. *As I Remember*. New York, 1953.

Goodspeed was a member of the University of Chicago faculty from 1898 to 1937. He was best known for his translation of the Bible. This autobiography also sheds much light on the role of his father in founding the University.

Goodspeed, Thomas W.

P108 Goodspeed, Charles Ten Broeke. *Thomas Wakefield Goodspeed.* Chicago, 1932.

A study of his father.

Harper, William R.

P109 Goodspeed, Thomas Wakefield. *William Rainey Harper.* Chicago, 1928.

A life of U.C.'s founder by one of his closest associates.

Herrick, Robert

See also: Q78, 79

P110 Herrick, Robert. *Chimes.* New York, 1926.

Herrick was a long-time U.C. English faculty member and this novel about the founding of Eureka U. is clearly based on his participation in founding U.C.

Hutchins, Robert M.

P111 Hutchins, Robert Maynard. *No Friendly Voice.* Chicago, 1936.

Hutchins served as U.C.'s president for many years.

Laughlin, J. L.

P112 Bornemann, Alfred. *J. Laurence Laughlin: Chapters in the Career of an Economist.* Washington, D.C., 1940.

Laughlin was a member of the economics faculty and editor of the *J. of Pol. Econ.*

Lovett, Robert M.

P113 Lovett, Robert Morss. *All Our Years.* New York, 1948.

Memoirs by a long-time member of the English faculty.

Mathews, Shailer

P114 Mathews, Shailer. *New Faith for Old: An Autobiography.* New York, 1936.

Mathews was a leading figure in the divinity school.

P115 Wuster, Stephen H. "'The Modernism' of Shailer Mathews: A Study in American Religious Progressivism, 1894-1924." U.C. unpub. Ph.D. thesis, 1972.

Merriam, Charles E.

See also: T74.

P116 Karl, Barry Dean. *Charles E. Merriam and the Study of Politics.* Chicago, 1974.

P117 Tinzmann, Otto J. "The Education of Charles E. Merriam." DeP.U. unpub. M.A. thesis, 1969.

A study of Merriam's "education" as a Chicago city alderman, 1909-1917.

Michelson, Albert A.

P118 Livingston, Dorothy Michelson. *The Master of Light: A Biography of Albert A. Michelson.* New York, 1973.

Michelson was a physicist at U.C. in the first third of the 20th century.

Moulton, Richard G.

P119 Moulton, W. Fiddian. *Richard Green Moulton . . . A Memoir.* New York, 1926.

An Englishman who taught literary theory and interpretation at U.C.

Pierce, Bessie L.

P120 Duis, Perry R. "Bessie Louise Pierce: Symbol and Scholar." *CH,* n.s., V, 3 (Fall 1976), 130-140.

Pierce was the foremost historian of Chicago. A careful examination of her work and a brief biographical sketch.

Rockefeller, John D.

P121 Nevins, Allan. *John D. Rockefeller: The Heroic Age of American Enterprise.* 2 vol. New York, 1940.

P122 __________. *Study in Power: John D. Rockefeller, Industrialist and Philanthropist.* 2 vol. New York, 1953.

Both books deal with Rockefeller's role in the founding of U.C.

P123 Rockefeller, John D. *Random Reminiscences of Men and Events.* New York, 1909.

P124 Deleted

Small, Albion W.

P125 Goodspeed, Thomas W. "Albion Woodbury Small." *Am. J. of Soc.*, XXXII, 1 (July 1926), 1-14.

Small was head of U.C.'s sociology department in the early years and founder of the *American Journal of Sociology.*

Stagg, Amos A.

P126 Stagg, Amos A. *Touchdown! As Told by Coach Amos Alonzo Stagg to Wesley Winans Stout.* New York, 1927.

Stagg was the great U.C. coach.

Talbot, Marion

P127 Talbot, Marion. *More Than Lore: Reminiscences of Marion Talbot, Dean of Women, The University of Chicago, 1892-1925.* Chicago, 1936.

Talbot was the first dean of women in any American university.

Veblen, Thorstein

P128 Dorfman, Joseph. *Thorstein Veblen and His America.* Rev. ed. New York, 1961.

Wallace, Elizabeth

P129 Wallace, Elizabeth. *The Unending Journey.* Minneapolis, 1952.

An important woman in the academic life of the University.

Northwestern University

P130 Arey, Leslie B. *Northwestern University Medical School, 1859-1959*. Evanston, 1959.

The standard work.

P131 Dalgety, George S. *Evanston and Northwestern University*. Evanston, 1934.

P132 Howe, Jonathan T. "The Northwestern University Fraternity System: A History, 1951-1963." N.U. unpub. B.A. Honors thesis, 1963.

P133 Jacobson, Jacob Zavel. *Scott of Northwestern: The Life Story of a Pioneer in Psychology and Education*. Chicago, 1951.

A central figure at Northwestern as a psychologist and as president.

P134 James, James Alton. "Graduate Study and the Development of the Graduate School, 1856-1931." N.U. archives.

P135 Loucks, Vernon R. *James Alton James, a Short Biography*. [Evanston?], 1963.

A major figure in the life of Northwestern.

P136 Paulison, Walter. *The Tale of the Wildcats*. Evanston, 1951.

P137 Rahl, James A. and Kurt Schwerin. *Northwestern University School of Law: A Short History*. Chicago, 1960.

P138 Sedlak, Michael W. "The Emergence and Development of Collegiate Business Education in the United States 1881-1974: Northwestern University as a Case Study." N.U. unpub. Ph.D. thesis, 1977.

P139 Sheppard, Robert D. *A Historical Sketch of Northwestern University*. Evanston, 1903.

P140 Sheppard, Robert D. and Harvey B. Hurd, ed. *History of Northwestern University and Evanston*. Chicago, 1906.

P141 Swanson, Richard A. "Edmund J. James, 1855-1925: A Conservative Progressive in American Higher Education." U.I.U. unpub. Ph.D. thesis, 1966.

P142 Wells, Harry L. *Northwestern University's Evanston: An Irrevocable Trust*. Evanston, 1948.

P143 Wilde, Arthur H., ed. *Northwestern University, 1855-1905*. 4 vol. New York, 1905.

P144 Williamson, Harold F. and Payson S. Wild. *Northwestern University: A History, 1850-1975*. Evanston, 1976.

A long, detailed institutional history of the University.

Other Colleges and Universities

See also: E40; N139

P145 Berchtold, Theodore A. *To Teach, To Heal, To Serve: The Story of the Chicago College of Osteopathic Medicine: The First 75 Years (1900-1975)*. Chicago, 1975.

P146 Deleted

P147 Deleted

P148 Dunn, Frederick R. "The Central YMCA Schools of Chicago: A Study in Urban History." U.C. unpub. Ph.D. thesis, 1940.

P149 Erickson, Clifford G. *Chicago's TV College: Final Report of a Three Year Experiment of the Chicago City Junior College in Offering College Courses for Credit Via Open Circuit Television*. Chicago, 1960.

P149a Hendricks, Walter. "Historical Sketch of Armour Institute of Technology." *Am. Engineer and Alumnus*, II, 4 (1937), 34-40.

See P156.

P150 Hetherington, Norriss S. "Financing Education and Science in Nineteenth-Century America: The Case of Cleveland Abbe, The Chicago Astronomical Society and the University of Chicago." *JISHS*, 4 (Sept. 1975), 319-323.

A short piece describing how the first University of Chicago attempted to gain the services of a trained astronomer without paying him a salary.

P151 Kaufman, Agnes Joslyn. "Lewis Institute." Chicago, n.d.

See P156.

P152 Kearney, Edmund W. *Chicago State College, 1869-1969: A Centennial Retrospective*. [Chicago, 1969].

A short text with illustrations in a lavish oversize binding.

P153 Lelon, Thomas Charles. "The Emergence of Roosevelt College of Chicago: A Search for an Ideal." U.C. unpub. Ph.D. thesis, 1973.

A well-documented survey with good bibliography.

P154 Merrill, Marie Georgetta. *The History of St. Luke's Hospital School of Nursing, Chicago*. Chicago, [1946?].

P155 Peebles, James Clinton. "A History of the Armour Institute of Technology." Typescript. Chicago, [1955?].

Peebles was a student and faculty member for most of the period 1898-1948. The narrative was duplicated after his death. See P156.

P156 Rogers, Fred A. "Lewis Institute." Chicago, 1939.

Lewis and Armour Institutes merged to become Illinois Institute of Technology.

P157 Schryver, Grace Fay. *A History of the Illinois Training School for Nurses, 1880-1929*. Chicago, 1930.

P158 Weaver, George H. "Beginnings of Medical Education in and Near Chicago: The Institutions and the Men." *Bull. of the Soc. of Med. H. Chicago,* III, 4 (Sept. 1925), 340-470.

A long account reprinting much primary evidence.

P159 Weinstein, M. M., M. B. Mrtek, R. L. Lambert and M. G. Mrtek. "From These Ashes: Parts I and II." *Pharmacy in H.,* XV, 2/3 (Spring/Summer 1973), 54-66, 107-116.

Traces the rebirth of the Chicago College of Pharmacy after the Civil War.

Q
ARTS AND CULTURE

The literature on Chicago's arts is vast, including thousands of pieces of literary criticism alone. In general, pure criticism of work in any media was not included. Emphasis is placed on those works that give a good introduction to a subject or artist and which present good bibliographies.

General

See also: A31; E15, 125; H80

Q1 Duncan, Hugh Dalziel. *Culture and Democracy: The Struggle for Form in Society and Architecture in Chicago and the Middle West during the Life and Times of Louis H. Sullivan.* Totowa, 1965.

A strong argument for Chicago's importance in the ". . . struggle to achieve a new democratic society . . ." and in creating new ". . . *forms* of American expression . . ." It is a far-ranging study of Chicago's intellectual history, treating many areas outside of architecture, e.g.: theater, retailing, industry, labor, social reform, various schools of "Chicago" thought, etc.

Q2 Engelbrecht, Lloyd. "The Association of Arts and Industries: The Background and Origins of the Bauhaus Movement in Chicago." U.C. unpub. Ph.D. thesis, 1973.

A detailed study of many aspects of the art world in Chicago from the Chicago Arts and Crafts Society (1897) to the 1940s. Includes a good bibliography and 122 illustrations.

Q3 Hanks, David. "The Midwest." *The Arts and Crafts Movement in America 1876-1916.* Edited by Robert Judson Clark. Princeton, 1972.

Q4 Madden, Betty I. *Art, Crafts, and Architecture in Early Illinois.* Urbana, 1974.

There is a fair amount of Chicago material on many kinds of arts and crafts. Moreover, it is worked into a larger context.

Q4a Murphy, Mary Elizabeth. "Cultural Interests Indicated by Lectures Before the Chicago Lyceum, 1837-1897." U.C. unpub. M.A. thesis, 1929.

Q5 Palles, Leon L. "Urban Gateways." *Arts in Society*, XII, 1 (1975), 44-49.

Q6 Seymour, Ralph Fletcher. *Some Went This Way: A Forty Year Pilgrimage Among Artists, Bookmen and Printers.* Chicago, 1945. An important document for the Chicago Renaissance.

Q7 Smith, Alson Jesse. *Chicago's Left Bank*. Chicago, 1953.

A survey of Chicago's intellectual life in which he makes the curious comparison of Chicago and Florence, and New York and Rome.

Q8 Szuberla, Guy. "Urban Vistas and the Pastoral Garden: Studies in the Literature and Architecture of Chicago, 1893-1909." U.M. unpub. Ph.D. thesis, 1972.

He argues that Chicago's growth was viewed by the leading architects and writers as infinite. This brought about a rejection of the pastoral ideal and the development of a new aesthetic to account for the city's attraction.

Q9 Williams, Kenny J. *In the City of Men: Another Story of Chicago*. Nashville, 1974.

Essentially a study of post-Fire Chicago intellectual life focused by the careers of Fuller in letters and by Sullivan in architecture. "It is the partial story of the writers and architects who - conditioned by the business culture of Chicago - attempted to create an art for those destined to remain in the city." Long bibliography and a list of Chicago novels.

Literary

(General)

See also: A30; H211; K27, 31, 34, 42; T146.

Q10 Amadea Wirtz, Sister M., C.S.A. "Chicago as a Literary Center - 1890-1940." DeP.U. unpub. M.A. thesis, 1943.

Q11 Angle, Paul M. "Literature in Chicago, Beginnings and Renaissance." *CH*, VIII, 2 (Winter 1966-1967), 33-45.

Argues that Kramer overstates the case for a Chicago Renaissance because there was a strong literary tradition in Chicago long before the so-called Renaissance.

Q12 Dondore, Dorothy Anne. *The Prairie and the Making of Middle America: Four Centuries of Description*. Cedar Rapids, 1926.

There is some material on Chicago writers.

Q13 Duffey, Bernard. *The Chicago Renaissance in American Letters*. East Lansing, 1954.

A scholarly study of the movement in the late 19th and early 20th centuries. A standard work; bibliography.

Q14 Duncan, Hugh Dalziel. *The Rise of Chicago as a Literary Center from 1855 to 1920: A Sociological Essay in American Culture*. Totowa, 1964.

He argues that "In Chicago patronage of literature passed from the hands of the traditional elites to the new elites of business and politics . . ."

Q15 Fleming, Herbert E. " . . . Literary Interests of Chicago." *Am. J. of Soc.* XI, 3 (Nov. 1905), 377-408.

A long study (continued in subsequent issues of the journal) of Chicago as a producer of literary material that influenced a large hinterland.

Q16 Fleming, Robert Edward. "The Chicago Naturalistic Novel: 1930-1966." U.I.U. unpub. Ph.D. thesis, 1967.

Fleming argues that Chicago's writers have tended more towards naturalism - documentation and emphasis on detail - than towards realism. He deals with four major themes of the naturalists: adjustment of the immigrant; efforts of blacks to rise; corrupting influence of the city; labor-management struggle.

Q17 Gookin, Frederick William. *The Chicago Literary Club: A History of Its First Fifty Years*. Chicago, 1926.

A narrative with some lists and documents.

Q18 Grey, Lenox B. "Chicago and the Great American Novel." U.C. unpub. Ph.D. thesis, 1935.

The fundamental work on Chicago in fiction. The long analysis is moderate and carefully grounded in scholarship. It provides a discussion of a variety of different themes, e.g., "the Business Baron and the new feudalism," the Haymarket Riot. The bibliography and other appendixes are a dissertation in themselves. Finding aids for Chicago are listed - as is "a representative list of Chicago novels portraying various periods," and an index that supplies references to novels and Chicago references, authors, subject and events.

Q19 Grosch, Anthony R. "Social Issues in Early Chicago Novels." *CH*, n.s., IV, 2 (Summer 1975), 68-77.

A look at some of the themes in the literature of the Chicago Renaissance.

Q20 Howells, William Dean. "Certain of the Chicago School of Fiction." *North Am. R.*, CLXXVI, (May 1903), 734-746.

A famous early piece recognizing the development of the Midwestern School.

Q20a Henne, Francis E. "The Chicago Novel." U.I.U. unpub. M.A. thesis, 1934.

A general survey.

Q21 Kramer, Dale. *Chicago Renaissance*. New York, 1966.

Covers the writers in the period 1900-1930; it makes less pretense to scholarship than Bernard Duffey's book (Q13).

Q22 Mencken, H. L. *The Literary Capital of the United States*. Chicago, 1920.

A version of his essay of April 17, 1920 in the *Nation* which was important in gaining recognition for the Chicago School.

Q23 Smith, Carl S. "Fearsome Fiction and the Windy City: Or, Chicago in the Dime Novel." *CH*, n.s., VII, 1 (Spring 1978), 2-11.

A description of how the genre dealt with Chicago.

Q24 Stronks, James Bernard. "The Early Midwestern Realists and William Dean Howells." U.C. unpub. Ph.D. thesis, 1956.

". . . reconstructs in detail the facts of Howells' relationships - as novelist, theorist, editor, reviewer and literary friend - with Edward Eggleston, E. W. Howe, Joseph Kirkland, and Hamlin Garland from 1870 through 1895." Bibliography.

Q25 Tucker, John I. "Tarzan was Born in Chicago." *CH*, n.s., I, 1 (Spring 1970), 18-31.

About the Chicago connections of the creator Edgar Rice Burroughs, the first illustrator James Allen Saint John, and Johnny Weismuller.

Q26 Weiss, Robert M. "The Shock of Experience: A Group of Chicago's Writers Face the Twentieth Century. U.W. unpub. Ph.D. thesis, 1966.

In large part a biographical study of Henry Fuller, Hamlin Garland, George Ade, and Robert Herrick. His principal conclusion is that the changes of the early 20th century had a profound affect and altered the lives and styles of his subjects. Bibliography.

Q27 Yatron, Michael. *America's Literary Revolt*. New York, 1959.

An interesting piece on Sandburg, Masters and Lindsay.

(Periodicals)

General

Q28 Mott, Frank Luther. *A History of American Magazines.* 5 vol. Cambridge, 1938-1968.

The beginning point for the study of any American magazine, it is no less so for Chicago. The index is sound and useful, but in particular see the passages listed below:

"Chicago as a Magazine Center," IV, 98-100
"Chapbook," IV, 450-452
"Dial," III, 539-543
"Little Review," V, 116-178
"Poetry," V, 225-245

Individual Studies

(The Chap Book, 1894-1898)

The most influential Chicago magazine. It was a major force in the book arts and graphics as well as literature.

Q29 Calkins, Earnest Elmo. "The Chap Book." *Colophon,* III, pt. 10 (1932), [not paginated].

Q30 Kramer, Sidney David. *Stone & Kimball, 1893-1897, and Herbert S. Stone & Co. 1893-1905: With a Bibliography of Their Publications.* Chicago, 1940.

A narrative with a full dress descriptive bibliography.

Q31 Regnery, Henry. "Stone, Kimball and *The Chap-Book*." *CH,* n.s., IV, 2 (Summer 1975), 87-95.

A good, clear narrative.

(The Dial, 1880-1929)

The Dial was a distinguished and established magazine of criticism in Chicago until it removed to New York in 1916.

Q32 Joost, Nicholas. "Culture vs. Power: Randolph Bourne, John Dewey, and 'The Dial'." *Midwest Q.,* IX, 3 (Ap. 1968), 245-259.

Shows how *The Dial*'s editorial policy moved from neutrality to pacifism under Randolph Bourne's influence.

Q33 Joost, Nicholas. "'The Dial' in Transition, the End of the Browne Family's Control, 1913-1916." *JISHS*, LIX, 3 (Autumn 1966), 272-288.

The changing of owners after the death of Francis Fisher Browne and the subsequent change in editorial policy.

Q34 Mosher, Fredric John. "Chicago's 'Saving Remnant': Francis Fisher Browne, William Morton Payne, and the *Dial* (1880-1892)." U.I. unpub. Ph.D. thesis, 1950.

(Friday Literary Review, 1890-1932)

Q35 Tanselle, G. Thomas. "The 'Friday Literary Review' and the Chicago Renaissance." *Journalism Q.*, XXXVIII, 3 (Summer 1961), 332-336.

(Little Review, 1914-1929)

The *Little Review* was a force beyond Chicago in literary life. It sponsored a number of causes - among them feminism - which were not strictly literary.

Q36 Hoffman, Frederick J., Charles Allen and Carolyn F. Ulrich. *The Little Magazine: A History and a Bibliography*. Princeton, 1946.

(Poetry, 1912-)

Founded by Harriet Monroe, it quickly became the most important periodical for poetry in the United States. See Literary Biography, Q86-88.

(Biography)

The biographies marked with an asterisk below are part of a series published by Twayne. They are, as a group, well-researched and written by a journeyman scholar in the area. The bibliographies of primary and secondary materials are uniformly long and useful. See also: B46, 58.

Ade, George

See also: Q59.

Q37 *Coyle, Lee. *George Ade*. New York, 1964.

Q38 Kelly, Fred C. *George Ade: Warmhearted Satirist*. Indianapolis, 1947.

An undocumented narrative.

Algren, Nelson

Q39 Algren, Nelson. *Conversations with Nelson Algren.* Edited by H. E. F. Donohue. New York, 1964.

Autobiographical conversations with a major post-WWII Chicago writer.

Q40 *Cox, Martha Healsy and Wayne Chatteron. *Nelson Algren.* Boston, 1975.

Anderson, Margaret

Q41 Anderson, Margaret C. *The Fiery Fountains.* New York, 1951.

A continuation of the author's autobiography, *My Thirty Years War.*

Q42 __________. *My Thirty Years War.* New York, 1930.

Autobiography of the publisher of *The Little Review.*

Anderson, Sherwood

Q43 Anderson, Sherwood. *Sherwood Anderson's Memoirs: A Critical Edition.* Edited by Ray Lewis White. Chapel Hill, 1969.

The best edition, with a useful selected bibliography.

Q44 *Burbank, Rex. *Sherwood Anderson.* New York, 1964.

Q45 Howe, Irving. *Sherwood Anderson.* Stanford, 1966 (c1951).

A reprint of the 1951 edition of this biography of Anderson. Not wholly friendly.

Q46 Schevill, James E. *Sherwood Anderson, His Life and Work.* [Denver, 1951].

Baum, L. Frank

Q47 Baum, L. Frank. *The Annotated Wizard of Oz.* Introduction, notes and bibliography by Michael Patrick Hearn. New York, 1973.

Q48 Greene, David L. and Dick Martin. *The Oz Scrapbook.* New York, 1977.

Much material on Baum's personal and public life. A good overview.

Bellow, Saul

Q49 Bellow, Saul. "Starting Out in Chicago." *Am. Scholar*, XLIV, 1 (Winter 1974-1975), 71-77.

Q50 *Dutton, Robert R. *Saul Bellow*. New York, 1971.

Browne, Maurice

Q51 Browne, Maurice. *Too Late to Lament*. Bloomington, 1956.

An autobiography by the co-founder of the Chicago Little Theater.

Butcher, Fanny

Q52 Butcher, Fanny. *Many Lives - One Love*. New York, 1972.

Fanny Butcher was active in Chicago's literary life as book editor of the *Tribune*.

Dell, Floyd

Q53 Dell, Floyd. *Homecoming, an Autobiography*. New York, 1933.

About 50 pages are devoted to his life in Chicago.

Q54 *Hart, John E. *Floyd Dell*. New York, 1971.

Q55 Tanselle, George Thomas. "Faun at the Barricades: The Life and Works of Floyd Dell." N.U. unpub. Ph.D. thesis, 1959.

A good work with an extraordinary bibliography.

Dreiser, Theodore

Q56 Dreiser, Helen. *My Life with Dreiser*. Cleveland, 1951.

A fundamental memoir for the study of Dreiser by his wife.

Q57 Elias, Robert H., ed. *Theodore Dreiser, Apostle of Nature*. New York, 1949.

A good scholarly biography.

Q58 *Gerber, Philip L. *Theodore Dreiser*. New York, 1964.

A good, short narrative with an annotated critical bibliography.

Dunne, F. Peter

Q59 DeMuth, James David. "Small Town Chicago: The Comic Perspective of Finley Peter Dunne, George Ade, and Ring Lardner (1890-1920)." U.M. unpub. Ph.D. thesis, 1975.

Q60 Ellis, Elmer. *Mr. Dooley's America: A Life of Finley Peter Dunne*. New York, 1941.

A popular work.

Q61 Fanning, Charles. *Mr. Dooley and the Chicago Irish: An Anthology*. New York, 1976.

Aimed at a more scholarly audience than most collections.

Q62 Schaaf, Barbara C. *Mr. Dooley's Chicago*. Garden City, 1977.

A biographical introduction and selections with careful notes. More useful for the casual reader than Fanning.

Farrell, James T.

Q63 *Branch, Edgar Marquess. *James T. Farrell*. New York, 1971.

Field, Eugene

Q64 Conrow, Robert. *Field Days: The Life, Times and Reputation of Eugene Field*. New York, 1974.

Q65 Thompson, Slason. *Eugene Field: A Study in Heredity and Contradictions*. 2 vol. New York, 1901.

Fuller, Henry B.

Q66 Bowron, Bernard R., Jr. *Henry B. Fuller of Chicago: The Ordeal of a Genteel Realist in Ungenteel America*. Westport, 1974.

The standard work on an important Chicago novelist, editorialist and member of *Poetry's* staff. Bibliography.

Garland, Hamlin

A very full personal record was left by Garland in his autobiographical works and diaries listed below. One must use care, however, for there are different accounts of the same event.

Q67 *Afternoon Neighbors*. New York, 1921.
Q68 *Back Trailers from the Middle Border*. New York, 1928.
Q69 *Companions on the Trail*. New York, 1931.

Q70 *Diaries*. Edited by Donald Pizer. San Marino, 1968.
Q71 *My Friendly Contemporaries*. New York, 1932.
Q72 *Roadside Meetings*. New York, 1930.
Q73 *A Son of the Middle Border*. New York, 1921.

Q74 Holloway, Jean. *Hamlin Garland: A Biography*. Austin, 1960.

A long, well-documented life with an excellent bibliography.

Hackett, Francis

Q75 Hackett, Francis. *American Rainbow: Early Reminiscences*. New York, 1970.

Hecht, Ben

Q76 Hecht, Ben. *A Child of the Century*. New York, 1954.

A fascinating autobiography of a major figure in journalism and letters.

Q77 __________. *Gaily, Gaily*. Garden City, 1963.

Hecht's memoirs of his early days in Chicago. Hecht was a newpaperman, novelist, founder of the *Literary Times*, etc.

Herrick, Robert

Q78 *Budd, Louis J. *Robert Herrick*. New York, 1971.

Q79 Nevius, Blake. *Robert Herrick: The Development of a Novelist*. Berkeley, 1962.

Herrick, a U.C. faculty member, wrote important novels about middle-class Chicago. The standard life.

Howells, William D.

Q80 Brooks, Van Wyck. *Howells: His Life and World*. New York, 1959.

Howells' criticism was important in the recognition of the Chicago School.

Kirkland, Joseph

Q81 *Henson, Clyde E. *Joseph Kirkland*. New York, 1962.

Lardner, Ring

See also: Q59.

Q82 Yardley, Jonathan. *Ring: A Biography of Ring Lardner.* New York, 1977.

Now the standard work on his life.

Lindsay, Vachel

Q83 Massa, Ann. *Vachel Lindsay, Fieldworker for the American Dream.* Bloomington, 1970.

Bibliography.

Q84 Masters, Edgar Lee. *Vachel Lindsay.* New York, 1935.

A life by a fellow poet, one who had known Lindsay and who was sympathetic to his work. He used Lindsay's correspondence in writing the book.

Masters, Edgar Lee

Q85 Masters, Edgar Lee. *Across Spoon River.* New York, 1936.

Masters' autobiography.

Monroe, Harriet

Q86 *Cahill, Daniel J. *Harriet Monroe.* New York, 1973.

Q87 Monroe, Harriet. *A Poet's Life: Seventy Years in a Changing World.* New York, 1938.

A basic document by the editor of *Poetry* magazine.

Q88 Williams, Ellen. *Harriet Monroe and the Poetry Renaissance: The First Ten Years of Poetry 1912-22.* Urbana, 1977.

A well-documented, scholarly narrative. Bibliography. For a sketch see her article in *CH*, n.s., IV, 4 (Winter 1975-1976), 204-213.

Moody, Harriet

Q89 Dunbar, Olivia Howard. *A House in Chicago.* Chicago, 1947.

A study of William Vaughn Moody's widow, Harriet Converse Tilden Moody, and her remarkable set of literary friends.

Moody, William V.

Q90 *Halpern, Martin. *William Vaughn Moody*. New York, 1964.

Q91 Henry, David D. *William Vaughn Moody: A Study*. Boston, 1934.

Motley, Willard

Q91a Giles, James R. and Jerome Klinkowitz. "The Emergence of Williard Motley in Black Literature." *Negro Am. Lit. Forum*, VI, 2 (Summer 1972), 31-38.

Norris, Frank

Q92 *French, Warren. *Frank Norris*. New York, 1962.

Q93 Walker, Franklin Dickerson. *Frank Norris, a Biography*. New York, 1963 (c1960).

An undocumented narrative.

Read, Opie P.

Q94 Read, Opie Percival. *I Remember*. New York, 1930.

Memoirs of a Chicago humorist.

Sandburg, Carl

Q95 Chu, James C. Y. "Carl Sandburg: His Association with Henry Justin Smith." *Journalism Q.*, L, 1 (Spring 1973), 43-47.

Q96 *Crower, Richard. *Carl Sandburg*. New York, 1964.

Q97 Golden, Harry. *Carl Sandburg*. Cleveland, 1961.

A popular life.

Q98 Haas, Joseph and Gene Lovitz. *Carl Sandburg: A Pictorial Biography*. New York, 1967.

Q99 Sandburg, Carl. *Always the Young Strangers*. New York, 1953.

Autobiography of his early life.

Sell, Henry B.

Q100 Gardner, Virginia. "A Literary Editor Reminisces: Henry Blackman Sell." *CH*, n.s., III, 2 (Fall 1974), 101-110.

Sell created the *Daily News* book review section in 1916.

Terkel, Louis "Studs"

Q101 Powers, John James. "Studs Terkel, a Free Spirit of Mass Media: A Case History and Analysis of the Mass Media Career of Studs Terkel." N.U. unpub. Ph.D. thesis, 1975.

A narrative.

Q102 Terkel, Louis "Studs." *Talking to Myself*. New York, 1978.

Autobiography.

Tietjens, Eunice

Q103 Tietjens, Eunice. *The World at My Shoulder*. New York, 1938.

Autobiography of a woman involved in Chicago's literary life in the first four decades of this century.

Wright, Richard

Q104 Bakish, David. *Richard Wright*. New York, 1973.

Q105 Wright, Richard. *Black Boy: A Record of Childhood and Youth*. New York, 1945.

Richard Wright's life in the South before he moved to Chicago.

Q106 __________. *American Hunger*. New York, 1977.

The second half of his autobiography.

Wyatt, Edith

Q107 Kirk, Clara M. and Rudolf. "Edith Wyatt: The Jane Austen of Chicago." *CH*, n.s., I, 3 (Spring 1971), 172-178.

Howells, the leading critic of his day, admired her but he could not "make" her career.

Theater

(General)

Q108 Johnson, Genevieve Goodman. "A History of the Chicago Theater, October 21, 1871-1872." U.C. unpub. M.A. thesis, 1932.

Discusses the theaters, the companies' management and productions, the popular types of productions; appendixes contain summaries of programs, daily programs, stars and theater buildings.

Q109 McCaslin, Nellie. *Theatre for Children in the United States: A History*. Norman, 1971.

Some material on Chicago.

Q110 Mackay, Constance D'Arcy. *The Little Theatre in the United States*. New York, 1917.

Has several chapters on Chicago.

Q111 McVicker, James H. *The Theater: Its Early Days in Chicago*. Chicago, 1884.

McVicker was the leading figure in early Chicago theater.

Q112 Sherman, Robert Lowery. *Chicago Stage, Its Records and Achievements*. Chicago, 1947.

"Gives a complete record of all entertainment and substantially, the cast of every play presented in Chicago, in its first production in the city, from the beginning of theatricals in 1834 down to the last before the fire of 1871."

Q113 Sturtevant, Catherine. "A Study of the Dramatic Productions of Two Decades in Chicago: 1847-1857 and 1897-1907." U.C. unpub. Ph.D. thesis, 1931.

A general discussion of the theater and the plays presented, with a chapter of comparison of the two decades. The bibliography is 80 pages long and includes references to the texts of plays presented in Chicago. A chronological appendix of 70+ pages is also useful.

Q114 Wilt, Napier. "The History of the Two Rice Theatres in Chicago from 1847 to 1857." U.C. unpub. Ph.D. thesis, 1923.

"This study was made, primarily, to collect, organize and present in a form usable by students of the American theatre such material as exists for the two Rice theatres in Chicago from 1847 to 1857, and with no intention to prove or disprove any theory." Bibliography.

Q115 Winterbottom, Goddard. "Theater in Chicago: Growing, Ambitious and Floundering." *FOCUS/Midwest,* VI, 41 (1968), 14-15.

(Studies of Special Topics)

Q116 Flanagan, Hallie. *Arena.* New York, 1940.

On the Federal Theater Project in Chicago during the 1930s.

Q117 Isaacs, Edith J. R. *The Negro in the American Theater.* New York, 1947.

Many Chicago references.

Q118 Kerber, Harold J. "The Administration of the Federal Theater." U.C. unpub. M.A. thesis, 1939.

Q119 Schiffler, Harold. "The Chicago Church-Theater Controversy of 1881-1882." *JISHS,* LIII, 4 (Winter 1960), 361-375.

Describes the religious opposition to theatrical productions in the late 19th century.

(Biography - Individuals and Theaters)

Browne, Maurice

Q120 Dukore, Bernard Frank. "Maurice Browne and the Chicago Little Theatre." U.I.U. unpub. Ph.D. thesis, 1957.

Browne was co-founder with his wife of the Chicago Little Theater.

Goodman Theater

Q121 Newell, James Samuel. "A Critical Analysis of the Development and Growth of the Kenneth Sawyer Goodman Memorial Theatre and School of Drama, Chicago, Illinois, 1925-1971." Wayne S.U. unpub. Ph.D. thesis, 1973.

McVicker's Theater

Q122 Bergstrom, Lois Mildred. "The History of McVicker's Theater from 1857-61." U.C. unpub. M.A. thesis, 1930.

A narrative. There is a long list of "Daily History of Plays and Actors at McVicker's During 1857-1861."

Q123 Ludwig, Jay Ferris. "McVicker's Theatre, 1857-1896." U.I.U. unpub. Ph.D. thesis, 1958.

Morgan, Anna

Q124 Morgan, Anna. *My Chicago*. Chicago, 1918.

A memoir by a woman deeply involved in the arts - particularly the theater - in the period of the Chicago Renaissance.

Second City

Q125 Sweet, Jeffrey. *Something Wonderful Right Away*. New York, 1978.

Interviews with stars of the Second City and Compass Players.

Artists and Craftsmen

(General)

See also: N155

Q126 *The Chicago Art Review*. Edited by Leslie J. Krantz. Chicago, c1977.

A guide to galleries and museums, it gives a few historical notes and describes the high points of the collections.

Q127 Illinois. Arts Council. *Painters and Sculptors in Illinois, 1820-1945*. [Chicago, 1971].

Catalog for an exhibit.

Q128 Whitridge, Eugenia. "Art in Chicago: The Structure of the Art World in a Metropolitan Community." U.C. unpub. Ph.D. thesis, 1946.

The most important single work on art in Chicago. Part one is a sociological-historical survey from 1833 to 1940. This is followed by an interesting section on the ecology of the art world in Chicago which considers topics such as the location of artists, Chicago as a center of Midwestern arts, etc. Part three deals with the social organization of the art world in Chicago and the final part discusses "artist types and the professional career."

(Studies of Special Topics)

Q129 Darling, Sharon S. "Arts and Crafts Shops in the Fine Arts Building." *CH,* n.s., VI, 2 (Summer 1977), 79-86.

A brief description of some of the craftsmen who occupied the Fine Arts Building.

Q130 __________. *Chicago Metalsmiths: An Illustrated History.* Chicago, 1977.

An award-winning study of 19th and 20th century Chicago craftsmen and the objects they created in silver, gold and copper.

Q131 Faulkner, Joseph W. "Painters at the Hall of Expositions: 1890." *CH,* n.s., II, 1 (Spring 1972), 14-16.

Explains how Sara C. F. Hallowell brought Impressionism to Chicago in the 1890s.

Q132 *Guide to Chicago Murals: Yesterday and Today.* Chicago, 1978.

Q133 Hammer, Ethel Joyce. "Attitudes Toward Art in the Nineteen Twenties in Chicago." U.C. unpub. Ph.D. thesis, 1975.

". . . the primary goal . . . is an investigation of the functions served by art in Chicago" in the 1910s and '20s.

Q134 Hanson, Olive E. "Educational and Social Values in the W.P.A. Art Project." DeP.U. unpub. M.A. thesis, 1941.

Q135 Hey, Kenneth Robert. "Five Artists and the Chicago Modernist Movement, 1909-1928." Emory U. unpub. Ph.D. thesis, 1973.

Attempts to show how cultural taste was affected by civic cultural institutions. The five artists studied are Ralph Clarkson, Jerome Blum, Manierre Dawson, Stanislaus Szukalski, and Rudolph Weisenborn.

Q136 Hoyt, Roger Eric. "The Explosion of a Dormant Art Form: Chicago's Murals." *CH,* n.s., III, 1 (Spring-Summer 1974), 28-35.

Beginning with William Walker's *Wall of Respect* in 1967, Chicago's black and Hispanic people have revived the art form of the mural. Hoyt argues that Chicago's murals are the most important in the United States.

Q137 Law, Hazel Jane. "Chicago Architectural Sculpture." U.C. unpub. Ph.D. thesis, 1935.

Treats the period of the Columbian Exposition and after. There is a set of brief biographical notes on Chicago sculptors in an appendix.

Q138 Petraitis, Paul. "The Portrait Art on Calling Cards." *CH,* n.s., II, 1 (Spring 1972), 31-33.

Reprints eighteen Chicago cartes-de-viste.

Q139 Ricker, Jewett E., ed. *Sculpture at a Century of Progress, Chicago, 1933, 1934.* Chicago, 1934.

A pamphlet.

Q140 Rogovin, Mark and Marie Burton. *Mural Manual.* [Chicago, 1973].

Q141 Schulze, Franz. *Fantastic Images: Chicago Art Since 1945.* Chicago, 1974 (c1972).

A brief essay followed by pictures and text.

Q142 Seineke, Katherine Wagner. "Mucha's Chicago Poster." *CH,* n.s., II, 1 (Spring 1972), 26-30.

Mucha was an important Art Nouveau artist. This article describes the making of his famous portrait of Zdenka Cerny.

Q143 Smith, Clark Sommer. "Nine Years of Federally Sponsored Art in Chicago, 1933-42." U.C. unpub. M.A. thesis, 1965.

A documented survey of the project and an analysis of some particular kinds of work. Useful bibliography of newspaper and magazine articles.

Q144 [Special Chicago Issue]. *Apollo: The Magazine of the Arts,* LXXXIV, 55 (Sept. 1966).

Articles on Great Chicago Collectors, Buckingham's print collection, etc.

Q145 Tingley, Donald F. "The 'Robin's Egg Renaissance': Chicago and the Arts, 1910-1920." *JISHS,* LXIII, 1 (Spring 1970), 34-35.

An essay on the interaction between artists and Chicago.

Q146 *WPA and the Black Artist, Chicago and New York.* Chicago, 1978.

An exhibit of which this is the catalog.

(Biography)

Bradley, Will

Q147 Hornung, Clarence, ed. *Will Bradley: His Graphic Art.* New York, 1974.

Bradley designed some well-known work for Chicago publishers.

Denslow, W. W.

Q148 Greene, Douglas G. and Michael P. Hearn. *W. W. Denslow.* Mt. Pleasant, MI, 1977.

Denslow drew the illustrations for *The Wizard of Oz* and other Chicago works.

Healy, George P.

Q149 De Mare, Marie. *G. P. A. Healy, American Artist: An Intimate Chronicle of the Nineteenth Century.* New York, 1954.

The standard life.

Q150 Healy, George Peter. *Reminiscences of a Portrait Painter.* Chicago, 1894.

Healy was probably the first resident artist in Chicago with a wide circle of customers and friends.

Leyendecker, J. C.

Q151 Schau, Michael. *J. C. Leyendecker.* New York, 1974.

Leyendecker worked as an illustrator in Chicago for a brief period.

Mosher, Charles D.

Q152 Viskochil, Larry A. "Chicago's Bicentennial Photographer: Charles D. Mosher." *CH,* n.s., V, 2 (Summer 1976), 95-104.

Mosher moved to Chicago in 1863 where be became a leading photographer, winning a gold medal at the 1893 World's Fair; he also became a civic leader.

Taft, Lorado

Q153 Taft, Ada. *Lorado Taft, Sculptor and Citizen.* Greensboro, 1946.

A short life of the best-known Chicago sculptor by his wife.

Q154 Williams, Lewis. "Lorado Taft: American Sculptor and Art Missionary." U.C. unpub. Ph.D. thesis, 1958.

Music

See also: I37

(Studies of Special Topics)

Q155 Angle, Paul M. "Chicago, a Musical Accompaniment." *CH,* VIII, 12 (Summer 1969), 353-374.

". . .[A] small sampling of music concerned with events, places, and people in Chicago."

Q156 Cassidy, Claudia. "The Years of Splendor: Chicago's Music and Theater." *CH,* n.s., II, 1 (Spring 1972), 4-13.

Shows that Chicago has a long tradition of excellence in its musical productions. Mostly a description of the flourishing of the symphony and opera in the 1920s.

Q157 Edlund, Lawrence L. *The Apollo Musical Club of Chicago: A Historical Sketch.* Chicago, 1946.

The Apollo Club has been a leading singing society for many years.

Q158 Manna, Sal. "The Complete Guide to Chicago Concert Halls." *Ill. Entertainer,* II, 51 (June 1978), 16-18.

Q159 Schoepko, Alfred. "The History of the Chicago Singverein 1910-1960." N.U. unpub. M.A. thesis, 1961.

A narrative history of the Society is preceded by a short account of choral music in the Midwest.

Q160 Staater, H. Ray. "The First Quarter Century of Music in Chicago (1835-1860)." DeP.U. unpub. M.A. thesis, 1940.

Q161 Thorson, Theodore W. "A History of Music Publishing in Chicago 1850-1960." N.U. unpub. Ph.D. thesis, 1961.

(Blues and Jazz)

Q162 Bushnell, George D., Jr. "When Jazz Came to Chicago." *CH,* n.s., I, 3 (Spring 1971), 132-141.

Identifies the elements in jazz unique to Chicago, traces its heyday and the cause of its decline in the city.

Q163 Hansen, Chadwick. "Social Influences on Jazz Style: Chicago 1920-1930." *Am. Q.,* XII, 4 (Winter 1960), 493-507.

Argues that the white dominant culture of the North was open to black men and this effected a change in jazz style.

Q164 Hennessey, Thomas J. "The Black Chicago Establishment 1919-1930." *J. of Jazz Studies*, II, 2 (June 1975), 15-45.

Based on his 1973 Northwestern University Ph.D. thesis to which the reader is referred for greater detail.

Q165 Lax, John. "Chicago's Black Jazz Musicians in the Twenties: Portrait of an Era." *J. of Jazz Studies*, I, 2 (June 1974), 107-127.

An anlysis of developments in Chicago. He argues that "[t]echnical and stylistic innovations in jazz were spawned by a need for self-expression that simply could not be wholly accommodated within the musical tradition of another age and another culture . . . to regard it merely as a black reaction to the fact of white oppression is to reduce and distort its meaning. In reality jazz represented a far more profound expression that came not only from the core of black society but also from the core of American society." The notes provide bibliographical information.

Q166 Litweiler, John T. "New Music in Chicago: The Free Jazz Movement." *FOCUS/Midwest*, VI, 41 (1968), 26-29.

Q167 Metcalfe, Ralph, Jr. "The Blues, Chicago Style." *CH*, n.s., III, 1 (Spring-Summer 1974), 4-13.

Argues that jazz was not a distinctively black music, but that the blues were. The blues were created by Southern musicians who came to Chicago and modified their style from country to an urban style.

(Opera)

Q168 Davis, Ronald. *Opera in Chicago*. New York, 1966.

A narrative with appendixes, it is intended to be a scholarly study. See a hostile review in *Saturday Review*, September 17, 1966, p. 59.

Q169 *Lyric Opera of Chicago: Twenty Years*. Chicago, 1974.

Pictures and text.

Q170 Moore, Edward C. *Forty Years of Opera in Chicago*. New York, 1930.

A popular history with some appendixes of performances.

Q171 Wood, Maude Aurilla. "The Early History of Grand Opera in Chicago." U.C. unpub. M.A. thesis, 1926.

(Symphony)

Q172 Belt, Byron. "The Chicago Symphony Orchestra and Its Repertoire." N.U. unpub. M.M. thesis, 1952.

Q173 Furlong, William Barry. *Season with Solti: A Year in the Life of the Chicago Symphony Orchestra*. New York, 1974.

A popular account of his year with the orchestra.

Q174 Johnson, Ellis A. "The Chicago Symphony." U.C. unpub. M.A. thesis, 1951.

The standard history.

Q175 Lightfoot, Robert M. *The Chicago Symphony Orchestra*. Chicago, 1974.

Really a book of photographs.

Q176 Otis, Philo Adams. *The Chicago Symphony Orchestra: Its Organization, Growth and Development, 1891-1924*. Freeport, 1972 (c1924).

(Biography)

Collins, Lee

Q177 Collins, Lee. *Oh, Didn't He Ramble: The Life Story of Lee Collins*. Edited by Frank J. Gillis and John W. Miner. Urbana, 1974.

A short biography of an important figure in Chicago's jazz history.

Garden, Mary

Q178 Fletcher, Richard D. "'Our Own' Mary Garden." *CH*, n.s., II, 1 (Spring 1972), 34-46.

A short narrative of the Chicago native who became a famous opera singer. Her engagements in Chicago always prompted large audiences.

Q179 Garden, Mary and Louis Biancolli. *Mary Garden's Story*. New York, 1951.

Petrillo, James

Q180 Leiter, Robert D. *The Musicians and Petrillo*. New York, 1953.

Petrillo was the head of the Chicago Federation of Musicians.

Root, George F.

Q181 Root, George Frederick. *The Story of a Musical Life: An Autobiography*. Cincinnati, c1891.

Root published and wrote popular music in Chicago between 1858 and 1871.

Stock, Frederick

Q182 Berglund, Donald Herbert. "A Study of the Life and Work of Frederick Stock During the Time He Served as Musical Director of the Chicago Symphony Orchestra, with Particular Reference to His Influence on Music Education." U.C. unpub. Ph.D. thesis, 1955.

Thomas, Theodore

Q183 Russell, Charles. *The American Orchestra and Theodore Thomas*. Garden City, 1927.

The standard life of the man who brought good symphonic music to Chicago.

Q184 Thomas, Theodore. *A Musical Autobiography*. 2 vol. Chicago, 1905.

An autobiography, an appreciation by the editor, and in volume 2, the programs of his concerts.

Upton, George P.

Q185 Upton, George P. *Musical Memories: My Recollections of Celebrities of the Half Century 1850-1900*. Chicago, 1908.

A standard work.

Motion Pictures

See also: E142

(General)

Q186 Jahant, Charles A. "Chicago: Center of the Silent Film Industry." *CH*, n.s., III, 1 (Spring-Summer 1974), 45-53.

An account of Chicago's flourishing movie-making industry during the first two decades of the 20th century.

Q187 Scheetz, George. "The Chicago Film Industry: The Beginnings to 1918." U.I.U. unpub. ms.

The most detailed work on this subject.

(Studies of Special Topics)

Q188 Haaley, Lois. "A Study of the Motion Pictures in Chicago as a Medium of Communication." U.C. unpub. M.A. thesis, 1924.

A good description of the size, distribution, etc., of the movie theater business in Chicago.

Q189 McCarthy, Kathleen D. "Nickel Vice and Virtue: Movie Censorship in Chicago, 1907-1915." *J. of Popular Film*, V, 1 (? 1976), 37-55.

Argues that the same drive that appeared in the temperance movement worked a basic and long-lasting change in movies. Unlike saloons, the movie theater's product could be molded to conform to a set of values. "By 1915 movies were well on their way to becoming 'respectable' . . ."

(Biography - Firms)

Selig Polyscope Co.

Q190 LaHue, Kalton. *Motion Picture Pioneer: The Selig Polyscope Company*. South Brunswick, 1973.

Chicago was an important center in the early days of the motion picture industry. This is a collection of articles, reviews, photographs, etc., held together by a short text about one of the major firms in Chicago.

Museums and Libraries

(General)

Q191 *Chicago's Museums are in Trouble.* Chicago, 1969.

Q192 Horowitz, Helen Lefkowitz. *Culture and the City: Cultural Philanthropy in Chicago from the 1880s to 1917.* Lexington, 1976.

A study of some of the major cultural institutions of the city, centering on the Art Institute. She argues that " . . . they were largely organized, sustained, and controlled by a group of businessmen who served, with considerable overlapping on their boards of trustees . . . Their trustees had turned to cultural philanthropy not so much to satisfy personal aesthetics or scholarly yearnings as to accomplish social goals. Disturbed by social forces they could not control and filled with idealistic notions of culture, these businessmen saw in the museum, the library, the symphony orchestra, and the university a way to purify their city and to generate a civic renaissance."

Q193 Smithsonian Institution. *Annual Report . . . June 30, 1903 . . . National Museum.* Washington, 1905.

Includes a section on Chicago museums.

(Biography - Individuals and Institutions)

Adler Planetarium

Q194 Fox, Philip. *Adler Planetarium and Astronomical Museum of Chicago.* Chicago, 1933.

The Art Institute of Chicago

Q195 Cierpik, Anne Felicia. "History of the Art Institute of Chicago from its Incorporation on May 24, 1879 to the Death of Charles L. Hutchinson." DeP.U. unpub. M.A. thesis, 1957.

Narrative chapters arranged by subject: administration, school, museum, exhibitions, and the library.

Q196 Maxon, John. *The Art Institute of Chicago.* New York, 1971.

A very short narrative of the Institute and major gifts to it is followed by photographs and text of the major holdings of the museum.

Q197 Pankovich, Helen. "The Libraries of the Art Institute of Chicago." U.C. unpub. M.A. thesis, 1964.

She lays stress on the institutional aspects rather than the collections.

Q198 Rich, Daniel Catton. "The Art Institute of Chicago and Chicago." *Art in Am.,* XXXII, 4 (Oct. 1944), 246-253.

A friendly in-house article.

Q199 Wardwell, Allen. "The Thorne Miniature Rooms at the Art Institute of Chicago." *Historic Preservation,* XIX, 1 (1967), 14-17.

A history of this unusual collection.

Q200 Zolberg, Vera Lenchner. "The Art Institute of Chicago: The Sociology of a Cultural Organization." U.C. unpub. Ph.D. thesis, 1974.

A study of the institution as it is but with a considerable historical component.

Chicago Academy of Sciences

Q201 Higley, William Kerr. *Historical Sketch of the Academy.* Chicago, 1902.

A short narrative of the Academy of Sciences that was also published in Blanchard (A19).

Chicago Historical Society

Q202 Angle, Paul M. *The Chicago Historical Soceity, 1856-1956: An Unconventional Chronicle.* New York, 1956.

A series of excerpts from various commentaries on the Society.

Q203 Brubaker, Robert L. "The Development of an Urban History Research Center: The Chicago Historical Society's Library." *CH,* n.s., VII, 1 (Spring 1978), 22-36.

A narrative of the setbacks and growth of the library.

Chicago Public Library

Q204 Chicago. Public Library. *The Treasures of All Knowledge.* Chicago, 1972.

Q205 Chicago. Public Library. *Treasures of the Chicago Public Library: A Contribution Toward a Descriptive Catalog.* Chicago, 1977.

A descriptive list of the high spots of the Chicago Public Library's Special Collections.

Q206 Joeckel, Carleton Bruns and Leon Carnovsky. *A Metropolitan Library in Action: A Survey of the Chicago Public Library.* Chicago, 1940.

Q207 Martin, Lowell Arthur. *Library Response to Urban Change: A Study of the Chicago Public Library.* Chicago, 1969.

An evaluation with recommendations for the future.

Q208 Schlipf, Frederick Allen. "The Geographical Distribution of Urban Public Library Use and Its Relationship to the Location of Branch Libraries." U.C. unpub. Ph.D. thesis, 1973.

Useful for its descriptions of the branch system and the use of the library system.

Q209 Spencer, Gwladys. *The Chicago Public Library: Origins and Backgrounds.* Reprint. Chicago, 1972.

The standard work.

Field Museum

Q210 Collier, Donald. "Chicago Comes of Age: The World's Columbian Exposition and the Birth of the Field Museum." *Bul. of the Field Museum of Natural H.*, XL, 5 (May 1969), 2-7.

This and the following articles (Q211, 212) are official accounts written for anniversaries.

Q211 Field, Stanley. "Fifty Years of Progress: Some of the History of the Field Museum (1893-1943) - and a Forecast of its Future." *Field Museum News*, XIV, 9-10 (Sept.-Oct. 1943), 3-10.

Q212 Williams, Patricia M. "The Burnham Plan and the Field Museum." *Bul. of the Field Museum of Natural H.*, XXXIX, 5 (May 1968), 8-12.

John Crerar Library

Q213 Bay, Jens Christian. *The John Crerar Library, 1895-1944.* Chicago, 1945.

A topical narrative.

Museum of Contemporary Art

Q214 **Schulze, Franz. "The View from the MCA." *Art in Am.*, LX, 3 (May/June 1960), 96-99.**

An overview of the origins of the Museum of Contemporary Art.

Museum of Science and Industry

Q215 Kogan, Herman. *A Continuing Marvel: The Story of the Museum of Science and Industry*. Garden City, 1973.

A popular narrative.

Newberry Library

Q216 "The Second Father of the Newberry." *Newberry Library Bul.*, I, 7 (June 1947), 3-18.

On the Eliphalet Wickes Blatchford papers.

Q217 Finkelman, Paul. "Class and Culture in Late Nineteenth-Century Chicago: The Founding of the Newberry Library." *Am. Studies*, XVI, 1 (Spring 1975), 5-22.

W218 Towner, Lawrence W. *The Newberry Library . . . A Brief History*. Chicago, 1977.

A short pamphlet with a bibliography.

Q219 __________. *An Uncommon Collection of Uncommon Collections: The Newberry Library*. Chicago, 1970.

Poole, Frederick William

Q220 Williamson, William Landram. *William Frederick Poole and the Modern Library Movement*. New York, 1963.

Poole was one of the best known 19th century librarians. In Chicago he served as head of the Chicago Public Library and as the first librarian of the Newberry Library. Outside of Chicago he is known as the originator of *Poole's Index to Periodical Literature*.

R
COMMUNICATION

Book Arts and Trade

(General)

See also: H78; I44, 81; K31

R1 Byrd, Cecil K. *A Bibliography of Illinois Imprints 1814-58*. Chicago, 1966.

An improvement over McMurtrie (R4) for the period that it covers.

R2 Haffner, C. C., Jr. "Chicago - Printing Capital of the United States." *Chicago Schools J.*, XXXVI, 5 (Jan./Feb. 1955), 109-114.

R3 Historical Records Survey. *Checklist of Chicago Ante-Fire Imprints 1851-1871*. Chicago, 1938.

A long list but not definitive.

R4 McMurtrie, Douglas C. *The First Printers of Chicago, with a Bibliography of the Issues of the Chicago Press, 1836-1850*. Chicago, 1927.

A very short narrative precedes the bibliography.

R5 Regan, James L. *The Story of Chicago in Connection with the Printing Business*. Chicago, 1912.

A substantial part of the work is given over to a general history but more than half of the volume is devoted to an account of printing in Chicago, the daily newspapers, and miscellaneous periodical publications, which gives the publisher, dates of publication and name changes.

R6 Sereiko, George Eugene. "Chicago and Its Book Trade, 1871-1893." C.W.R.U. unpub. Ph.D. thesis, 1973.

Part one of this account examines the general book trade in the U.S.; part two treats activities related to the trade. The conclusion summarizes Chicago's rise to the second most important book city in the U.S. A series of appendixes records active firms in the period.

(Studies of Special Topics)

R7 Bay, Jens C. "Scarce and Beautiful Imprints of Chicago." *The Papers of the Bibliographical Society of America*, XV (1921), 88-102.

R8 Deleted

R9 Compton, Frank E. "Subscription Books." *Bowker Lectures on Book Publishing*. New York, 1939.

Chicago was the center of this type of publishing in the Midwest.

R10 Davis, Carl DeWitt. "A Study of the School for Apprentices of the Lakeside Press, Chicago." U.C. unpub. M.A. thesis, 1921.

A short, simple description of the School without much critical analysis.

R11 Norris, Joe L. "Pioneer Marketing Associations of the American Book Trade, 1873-1901." U.C. unpub. Ph.D. thesis, 1938.

A national study which has some Chicago references.

R12 Wallihan, James Rodgers. "Workplace Politics and Leadership in a Chicago Printing Trades Union." Ind.U. unpub. Ph.D. thesis, 1974.

A study in labor relations. The paper handlers' union is his test case.

(Biography - Individuals and Firms)

Andreas, Alfred T.

R13 Ristow, Walter W. "Alfred T. Andreas and His Minnesota Atlas." *Minnesota H.*, XL, 1 (Fall 1966), 120-129.

A good, short life of Andreas who was an important publisher and cartographer, as well as historian, in Chicago in the late 19th century. The publication of the Minnesota atlas was the apex of his career.

Brent, Stuart

R14 Brent, Stuart. *The Seven Stairs*. Boston, 1962.

Brent is a successful Chicago book dealer.

Donnelley, R. R.

R15 Chicago Typothetae. *A Memorial of R. R. Donnelley*. Chicago, 1899.

Donnelley, R. R. & Co.

R16 Donnelley, Gaylord. "Donnelley History." *The Donnelley Printer*, Spring 1965/Fall 1967.

Foresman, Hugh Austin
(Scott, Foresman, & Co.)

R17 Foresman, Hugh Austin. *These Things I Remember*. Chicago, 1949.

Recollections of a major Chicago publisher.

Griggs, S. C. & Co.

R18 Morris, Jack C. "The Publishing Activities of S. C. Griggs and Company, 1848-1896; Jansen, McClurg and Company, 1872-1886; and A. C. McClurg and Company, 1886-1900; with Lists of Publications." U.I.U. unpub. M.S.L.S. thesis, 1941.

Ransom, Will
(Village Press)

R19 Schwartz, Philip John. "Will Ransom: The Early Years." *J. of Library H.*, III, 2 (Ap. 1968), 138-155.

Deals with the Village Press in Chicago.

Scott, Foresman & Co.

R20 Scott, Foresman and Company, Publishers. *A Half-Century of Scott, Foresman Progress*. Chicago, c1934.

Starrett, Vincent

R21 Ruber, Peter. *The Last Bookman: A Journey into the Life and Times of Vincent Starrett . . .* New York, 1968.

A short biography of a famous Chicago literary journalist and bookman.

R22 Starrett, Vincent. *Born in a Bookshop: Chapters from the Chicago Renascence*. Norman, 1965.

University of Chicago Press

R23 Chicago. University. *The University of Chicago Press Catalogue of Books and Journals, 1891-1965*. Chicago, 1967.

There is a short introductory essay.

Village Press

See: R19, Will Ransom

Newspapers

(General)

See also: I51, 59, 123; N7; T27, 95

R24 Abbot, Willis J. "Chicago Newspapers and Their Makers." *R. of Reviews*, XI, 6 (June 1895), 646-665.

An article of great importance for the history of Chicago journalism.

R25 Deleted

R26 Illinois Press Association. *Illinois Newspaper Directory. History of Illinois Association*. Springfield, 1934- .

R27 McPhaul, John J. *Deadlines and Monkeyshines: The Fabled World of Chicago Journalism*. Westport, CT, 1973 (c1962).

A popular history of the Chicago press, frequently cited.

R28 Scott, Franklin William. *Newspapers and Periodicals of Illinois, 1814-1879*. Springfield, IL, 1910.

The most complete guide to Illinois papers. A very short introduction is followed by the bibliography, which is arranged by county. There is a brief description of the circumstances for most of the papers.

R29 Simmons, W. R. and Associates Research, Inc. *Chicago Imprint: A Study of Daily and Sunday Newspapers, Newspaper Magazines and Selected Nationals*. Chicago, 1967.

Also see the later issues.

(Studies of Special Topics)

R30 Ball, James Harland. "A Study of Typical Crusades Undertaken by Chicago Newspapers." N.U. unpub. M.A. thesis, 1940.

The principal value of this thesis comes from providing newspaper material on 40 topics.

R31 Barger, Harold M. "Political Content of Black Newspapers." N.U. unpub. Ph.D. thesis, 1970.

Barger compares and analyzes a sample of national black newspapers with those of Chicago.

R32 Blair, Cecil Clyde. "The Chicago Democratic Press and the Civil War." U.C. unpub. Ph.D. thesis, 1947.

Blair's thesis is that the Democratic press in Chicago during the War had an alternative policy to Lincoln's, which was grounded in the Crittenden Compromise. The Democrats, however, were loyal to the Union, which they feared Lincoln's policy would destroy by its extremism. He studies the *Times* under Storey, and to a lesser extent, the *Post*.

R33 Davis, Fred and George J. Nollet. "The Community Newspaper in Metropolitan Chicago." U.C. unpub. M.A. thesis, 1951.

They give a generalized description of Chicago area community newspapers. Good list of papers.

R34 Dornfeld, A. A. "The City News Bureau." *CH*, n.s., V, 2 (Summer 1976), 76-84.

A short account of the "associated press" of the city of Chicago which had its origins in the late 19th century.

R35 Engleman, Beryl Frederick. "The Rise and Development of Community Newspapers in the Chicago Metropolitan Area." N.U. unpub. M.A. thesis, 1932.

Similar in many respects to Davis and Nollet's thesis (R33) but with a difference in detail.

R36 Erickson, John Edward. "Newspapers and Social Values: Chicago Journalism, 1890-1910." U.I.U. unpub. Ph.D. thesis, 1973.

Follows several themes in Chicago journalism and finds that newspapers reported and were affected by changing social values.

R37 Flanery, James Allen. "Chicago Newspapers' Coverage of the City's Major Civil Disorders of 1968." Ind.U. unpub. Ph.D. thesis, 1971.

Flanery attempted to answer these questions: (1) What really happened? (2) What did the Chicago press report? (3) Why did they report what they did?

He interviewed over 200 newsmen. In general, he found that Chicago papers played up demonstrator violence and played down police violence.

R38 Freeman, William H. *The Press Club of Chicago: A History with Sketches of Other Prominent Press Clubs of the United States.* Chicago, 1894.

A very formal, fact-filled account of the club with photographs of the members.

R39 Janowitz, Morris. *The Community Press in an Urban Setting: The Social Elements of Urbanism.* Chicago, 1967.

A study of ethnic, community and other special newspapers using metro-Chicago evidence.

R40 Johns, Elizabeth Dewey. "Chicago's Newspapers and the News: A Study of Public Communication in a Metropolis." U.C. unpub. Ph.D. thesis, 1942.

There is a brief history of the major papers in 1942; a chapter on the newspaper and the public, e.g., where they circulated; the kinds of news in the various papers; sources of news; and a final chapter on news in the metropolis.

R41 Jung, Norman Oliver. "Chicago's Foreign Language Press in World War I." U.C. unpub. M.A. thesis, 1959.

Deals with the efforts of the Bohemian, German and Polish press in Chicago to influence opinion in America.

R42 Lawson, Lawrence Breslin. "Treatment of the Negro by White Newspapers of Chicago." U.C. unpub. M.A. thesis, 1949.

A study of the five major Chicago papers which concludes that blacks received better treatment in the 1940s than before.

R43 Matré, Richard A. "The Chicago Press and Imperialism, 1899-1902." N.U. unpub. Ph.D. thesis, 1961.

Traces the rise and fall of imperialist sentiment in Chicago papers. There is a useful appendix which provides a thumbnail sketch of the major papers.

R44 Sheppard, Edward L. "The Radical and Labor Periodical Press in Chicago: Its Origin and Development to 1890." Urbana, 1949.

There is a checklist of Chicago labor and trade union periodicals, 1850-1890, and a list of their publishers. Neither list is complete.

R45 Skrupskelis, Enata. "The Lithuanian Immigrant Press in the U.S. after World War II." U.C. unpub. M.A. thesis, 1961.

(Biography - Individuals and Firms)

See also: A39; P1

Abbott, Robert S.

R46 Ottley, Roi Vincent. *The Lonely Warrior: The Life and Times of Robert S. Abbott.* Chicago, 1955.

A biography of Robert S. Abbott the founder of the Chicago *Defender*, an important black newspaper.

Abott, Willis J.

R47 Abott, Willis J. *Watching the World Go By.* Boston, 1933.

Abott was a Chicago reporter in the 19th century.

American

R48 Murray, Jesse George. *The Madhouse on Madison Street.* Chicago, 1965.

A popular history of the Hearst paper, the *Chicago American*, from its beginning to the time that it ceased to be a Hearst paper.

Baker, Ray Stannard

R49 Baker, Ray Stannard. *American Chronicle, the Autobiography of Ray Stannard Baker.* New York, 1945.

Baker was a leading progressive journalist. Bannister's book treats his entire life, Semonche's (R51) his early period which included his work in Chicago. Both have bibliographies - Bannister's is annotated, Semonche's longer, with a list of Baker's own work.

R50 Bannister, Robert C. *Ray Stannard Baker: The Mind and Thought of a Progressive*. New Haven, 1966.

See annotation for R59

R51 Semonche, John E. *Ray Stannard Baker: A Quest for Democracy in Modern America, 1870-1918*. Chapel Hill, 1969.

See annotation for R49.

Bell, Edward Price

R52 Zobrist, Benedict Karl. "Edward Price Bell and the Development of the Foreign Press Service of the *Chicago Daily News*. N.U. unpub. Ph.D. thesis, 1953.

A study of the establishment of the foreign news service rather than a biography of Bell. Based on three important manuscript collections at the Newberry Library.

Borough, Reuben W.

R53 Borough, Reuben W. "The Chicago I Remember, 1907." *JISHS*, LIX, 2 (Summer 1966), 117-130.

Borough is best known as a reporter for the Chicago *Daily Socialist*.

Daily News

R54 Abramoske, Donald J. "The Chicago Daily News: A Business History, 1875-1901." U.C. unpub. Ph.D. thesis, 1963.

A study in the emergence of 20th century organization in newspapers.

R55 __________. "The Founding of the *Chicago Daily News*." *JISHS*, LIX, 4 (Winter 1966), 341-353.

A brief account of Stone's effort to start the *Daily News* and the role of Victor Lawson in helping him do so.

R56 Chicago Daily News. *1876 . . . Today: Historical Highlights*. Chicago, 1959.

A brief chronology, lists of the *Daily News'* prizes, etc.

R57 *Done in a Day*. Edited by Dick Griffin and Rob Warden. Chicago, c1977.

An anthology of *Daily News* columns.

R58 Schmidt, Royal Jae. "The Chicago Daily News and Illinois Politics, 1876-1920." U.C. unpub. Ph.D. thesis, 1957.

An attempt to show how the *Daily News* viewed leading issues 1876-1920 and to discover the role of self-interest in those positions. He concludes that the *Daily News* editorials were a reflection of proprietor Victor Lawson's personality and his business interests. Despite support for some liberal causes, Lawson was, at bottom, a conservative member of the upper class business community. The paper grew in political influence. Lawson was not inflexible and his views frequently changed with the times.

R59 __________. "The *Chicago Daily News* and Traction Politics 1876-1920." *JISHS*, LXIV, 3 (Autumn 1971), 312-326.

Shows how over a 45 year period the question of street railroads influenced the *Daily News* editorial stance.

Defender

R60 Davis, Ralph. "The Negro Newspaper in Chicago." U.C. unpub. M.A. thesis, 1939.

A description of the historical development and content of black Chicago papers from the 1870s to the 1930s.

R61 Jones, Wendell Primus. "The Negro Press and the Higher Education of Negroes, 1933-1952: A Study of News and Opinion on Higher Education in the Three Leading Negro Newspapers." U.C. unpub. Ph.D. thesis, 1954.

An interesting study of black attitudes as seen in black newspapers. Three newspapers were studied, one of which was the Chicago *Defender*.

R62 Lochard, Metz T. P. "The Negro Press in Illinois." *JISHS*, LVI, 3 (Autumn 1963), 570-591.

Really an account of the Chicago *Defender* and how it emerged as the state's dominant black paper.

R63 Seemann, Howard L. "Keeping the Gates at the Chicago *Defender*." *Journalism Q.*, XLVIII, 2 (Summer 1971), 275-278.

Seemann reached the conclusion that the content of the city's leading black newspaper was determined by racial awareness and a desire to participate in the civil rights movement.

R64 Tallackson, Stephen R. "The Chicago Defender and Its Reaction to the Communist Movement in the Depression Era." U.C. unpub. M.A. thesis, 1967.

Argues that the *Defender's* chief goal was civil rights for blacks in the existing system. Only when the CP could aid in that goal would the *Defender* endorse them.

Doherty, Bill

R65 Doherty, Bill. *Crime Reporter: Autobiography*. New York, 1964.

Doherty was a crime reporter in Chicago for almost thirty years in the middle third of the 20th century.

Doherty, Edward J.

R66 Doherty, Edward Joseph. *Gall and Honey: The Story of a Newspaperman*. New York, 1941.

He was a reporter for the *Examiner*, *Tribune* and *Record Herald*.

Field, Marshall III

R67 Becker, Stephen. *Marshall Field III*. New York, 1964.

A popular life of the founder of the Chicago *Sun* and later publisher of the *Daily News*.

Fetridge, William H.

R68 Fetridge, William Harrison. *With Warm Regards: A Reminiscence*. Chicago, c1976.

A Chicago businessman and publisher active in Republican politics.

Hermann, Charles

R69 Hermann, Charles H. *Recollections of Life and Doings in Chicago from the Haymarket Riot to the End of World War I*. Chicago, 1945.

Hermann knew many key figures of the era and relates many interesting stories.

Jewish Daily Forward

R70 Hareven, Tamara K. "Un-American American and the *Jewish Daily Forward*." *Yivo Annual of Jewish Social Science*, XIV (1969), 234-250.

A study of the early editorial policy of the paper towards several important policy questions and its attitude towards the government. A New York paper, the *Forward* was read in Chicago.

Keeley, James

R71 Linn, James Weber. *James Keeley, Newspaperman.* Indianapolis, c1937.

Keeley had an important career at the *Tribune* and the short-lived *Herald*. A popular account.

Knox, Frank

R72 Beasley, Norman. *Frank Knox, American: A Short Biography.* Garden City, 1936.

Knox was many things in his life, but his strongest Chicago connection was as owner of the *Daily News*. A popular life.

Lawson, Victor

R73 Dennis, Charles Henry. *Victor Lawson, His Time and His Work.* Chicago, 1935.

A long undocumented life of the man who made the *Daily News* a great paper. Dennis knew him.

R74 Tree, Robert Lloyd. "Victor Fremont Lawson and His Newspapers, 1890-1900: A Study of the Chicago Daily News and the Chicago Record." N.U. unpub. Ph.D. thesis, 1959.

A friendly account, concluding that Lawson made his papers successful while maintaining a very high level of quality. Success came because: (1) the papers early established a reputation for trust and worthiness; (2) there were "many features, stories, and special columns that appear . . ."; (3) the papers maintained a "moderately liberal editorial policy . . . on social and government matters . . ."

Lloyd, Henry Demarest

R75 Destler, Chester McArthur. *Henry Demarest Lloyd and the Empire of Reform.* Philadelphia, 1963.

Lloyd was an editor and writer for the *Tribune* and a major figure in Chicago in the late 19th century.

Lindstrand, Francis Albin

R76 Lindquist, Emory. "'Onkel Ola' and His Letters in 'Svenska Amerikanaren': One Aspect of the Career of Francis Albin Lindstrand." *Swedish Pioneer H. Q.*, XIV, 4 (Oct. 1968), 245-258.
A brief account of F. A. Lindstrand who was a writer for and then owner of the leading Chicago Swedish paper.

MacArthur, Charles

R77 Hecht, Ben. *Charlie: The Improbable Life and Times of Charles MacArthur*. New York, 1957.

The first quarter of the book deals with Chicago.

McCormick, Robert

R78 O'Reilly, Alice M. "Colonel Robert Rutherford McCormick, His *Tribune* and Mayor William Hale Thompson." U.C. unpub. M.A. thesis, 1963.

A chapter on McCormick and one on Thompson is followed by an account of their struggle. She argues that they disliked each other so intensely, although both were Republicans, because of the issues of race, labor, ethnics, and foreign policy.

R79 Waldrop, Frank C. *McCormick of Chicago: An Unconventional Portrait of a Controversial Figure*. Englewood Cliffs, 1966.

A popular biography.

McCutcheon, John T.

R80 McCutcheon, John T. *Drawn from Memory*. Indianapolis, 1950.

Autobiography of a well known Chicago newspaper cartoonist.

Medill, Joseph

R81 Bennett, James O'Donnell. *Joseph Medill: A Brief Biography and Appreciation*. Chicago, 1947.

A friendly account.

R82 Moriarty, F. T. "The Life and Public Service of Joseph Medill." N.U. unpub. M.A. thesis, 1933.

Useful mainly for a few pieces of information not found in Bennett (R81).

R83 Strevey, Tracy Elmer. "Joseph Medill and the Chicago Tribune during the Civil War Period. U.C. unpub. Ph.D. thesis, 1930.

A survey of the views and role of Joseph Medill and the *Tribune* before and during the Civil War. Medill's role in forming the Republican party is laid out as is his increasing radicalism. For more detail on the *Tribune's* policies, see Norman O. Carlson, "A Study of Editorial Comment in the *Chicago Tribune* 1861-1862," U.C. unpub. M.A. thesis, 1950.

Moore, William T.

R84 Moore, William T. *Dateline Chicago: A Veteran Newspaperman Recalls Its Heyday*. New York, 1973.

Memoirs of a reporter for the *Herald Examiner* and the *Tribune*.

Prairie Farmer

See: R119, WLS

Rascoe, Burton

R85 Rascoe, Burton. *Before I Forget*. Garden City, 1937.

Memoirs of an important Chicago literary journalist.

Ray, Charles H.

R86 Monaghan, James. *The Man Who Elected Lincoln*. Indianapois, 1956.

On *Tribune* editor Charles H. Ray, who gave early and important aid to Lincoln.

Smith, Henry Justin

R87 Chu, Chi-Ying. "Henry Justin Smith (1875-1936), Managing Editor of the *Chicago Daily News*." S.I.U. unpub. Ph.D. thesis, 1970.

A narrative and analysis.

Stahl, John M.

R88 Stahl, John Meloy. *Growing with the West: The Story of a Busy, Quiet Life*. London, 1930.

Stahl was editor of the *Illinois Farmer and Farmers Call*, president of the Farmers' National Congress, etc.

Stone, Melville E.

R89 *"M.E.S.", His Book: A Tribute and a Souvenir of the Twenty-Five Years 1893-1918 of the Service of Melville E. Stone as General Manager of the Associated Press*. New York, 1918.

A collection of material relating to Stone and the Associated Press.

R90 Stone, Melville E. *Fifty Years a Journalist*. Garden City, 1921.

The memoir of the founder of the *Daily News* and first General Manager of the Associated Press.

Storey, Wilbur F.

R91 Walsh, Justin E. *To Print the News and Raise Hell: A Biography of Wilbur F. Storey*. Chapel Hill, 1968.

Storey was the major force behind the *Times*. For a short article on Storey's Chicago career see *Journalism Quarterly*, XL, 4 (Autumn 1963), 497-510.

Thompson, Slason

R92 Thompson, Slason. *Way Back When*. Chicago, 1931.

The autobiography of a *Daily News* writer in the 1880s and 1890s.

Times

R93 Crowell, Alfred A. "The History of the *Chicago Daily Times* [1929-1940]." N.U. unpub. M.A. thesis, 1940.

Tribune

R94 Basich, George. "The Opinion of the *Chicago Tribune* Concerning Internationalism in 1939 and 1946." U.C. unpub. M.A. thesis, 1947.

Describes the attitudes in 1939 and 1946 and compares them. The *Tribune* was still an isolationist paper in 1946.

R95 *Chicago Tribune*. *A Century of Tribune Editorials, 1847-1947*. Chicago, 1947.

An interesting collection on a wide variety of topics.

R96 __________. *Pictured Encyclopedia of the World's Greatest Newspaper . . .* Chicago, 1928.

"A handbook of the newspaper as exemplified by the *Chicago Tribune*." An interesting insight into the operations of a newspaper in the 1920s.

R97 __________. *The WGN*. Chicago, 1922.

A house publication for its 75th year. The history of the

R98 Dante, Harris L. "The *Chicago Tribune's* 'Lost' Years, 1865-1874." *JISHS,* LXVIII, 2 (Summer 1965), 139-164.

Describes the period of the editorial direction of Horace White (1865-1874) when the *Tribune* moved towards more liberal Republican doctrines.

R99 Edwards, Jerome E. *The Foreign Policy of Col. McCormick's Tribune, 1929-1941.* Reno, 1971.

Edward's analysis carries him farther than the title indicates. He argues that the *Tribune's* "fundamental concepts" between 1929 and 1941 "remained the same. The newspaper continued to emphasize its belief in the superiority of the United States over any other nation, and the superiority of midwestern culture over that of the Eastern seaboard. Chicago still survived as the apex of civilization. The United States continued to be played for an international sucker by the brilliance of European diplomacy." Bibliography.

R100 Jenkins, Warren Gard. "The Foreign Policy of the Chicago Tribune, 1914-1917: A Program of National Self Interest." U.W. unpub. Ph.D. thesis, 1943.

R101 Keefe, Thomas M. "The Catholic Issue in the Chicago Tribune before the Civil War." *Mid-America*, LVII, 4 (Oct. 1975), 227-245.

He argues that in the decade before the Civil War ". . . the *Tribune* consistently held to the position that Catholics, leaders and communicants were perverse and alien elements in American society and forces of evil in the world at large."

R102 Kinsley, Philip. *The Chicago Tribune: Its First Hundred Years.* 3 vol. New York, 1943.

The official history of the *Tribune* but it extends only to 1900. It is not a useful work. No notes. No bibliography.

R103 Lorenz, Alfred L. "Lincoln, Medill and the Republican Nomination of 1860." *Lincoln Herald,* LXVIII, 4 (Winter 1966), 199-205.

An account of the events leading to Medill's endorsement of Lincoln.

R104 Rothman, Robert A. and Donald W. Olmsted. "Chicago 'Tribune' Cartoons During and After the McCormick Era." *Journalism Q.,* XLIII, 1 (Spring 1966), 67-72.

Argues that the *Tribune* front page editorial cartoons were much the same before and after McCormick. Several themes are identified - one is that national concerns are the subject of most cartoons.

R105 Tebbel, John. *An American Dynasty: The Story of the McCormicks, Medills, and Pattersons*. Garden City, 1947.

An account of the families who have owned the *Tribune*. The book is in general hostile to the owners and their paper.

Weekly News

R106 Abramoske, Donald J. "Victor Lawson and the Chicago 'Weekly News': A Defeat." *Journalism Q.*, XLIII, 1 (Spring 1966), 43-48.

A description of Victor F. Lawson's failure to market a weekly edition of the *Daily News*.

Wilkie, Frank B.

R107 Wilkie, Franc B. *Personal Reminiscences of Thirty-Five Years of Chicago Journalism*. Chicago, 1891.

A memoir of the earlier period of Chicago's press.

Wright, John S.

R108 Lewis, Lloyd. *John S. Wright, Prophet of the Prairies*. Chicago, 1941.

Wright was an early settler and founder of the *Prairie Farmer*. Lewis was publisher of the *Farmer* when this life was written.

Radio and Television

R109 Barnouw, Erik. *A History of Broadcasting in the United States*. 3 vol. New York, 1966-1970.

The standard history of American radio and television. Extensive bibliographies in each volume. Vol. 1, *A Tower in Babel*, to 1933; vol. 2, *The Golden Web*, 1933-1953; vol. 3, *The Image Empire*, from 1953.

(Radio)

General

See also: K51; N29; P26a

R110 **Deleted**

R111 Dunning, John. *Tune in Yesterday: The Ultimate Encyclopedia of Old-Time Radio 1925-1976*. Englewood Cliffs, 1976.

Short articles on Chicago shows and people, but it is not always wholly accurate.

R112 Riley, Donald W. "A History of American Radio Drama from 1919 to 1944." O.S.U. unpub. Ph.D. thesis, 1944.

National in scope, but with important material on Chicago.

\ R113 Weinrott, Lester A. "Chicago Radio: The Glory Days." *CH*, n.s., III, 1 (Spring-Summer 1974), 14-22.

A description of Chicago radio in the second quarter of this century. Among the shows mentioned are "Vic and Sade," "Amos and Andy," "Lum and Abner," "The Three Doctors," and Don MacNeil's "Breakfast Club."

Biography - Individuals, Firms and Programs

("Amos and Andy")

R114 *All About Amos 'N' Andy and Their Creators Correll and Gosden*. New York, 1929.

"Amos and Andy" was the most popular Chicago radio show. This book is a popular piece of fan literature.

("Vic and Sade")

R115 Rhymer, Paul. *The Small House Half-Way Up in the Next Block: Paul Rhymer's Vic and Sade*. Edited with an introduction by Mary Frances Rhymer. New York, 1972.

"Vic and Sade" was one of the best-loved Chicago radio programs. The introduction is a useful essay by his wife.

(WBKB)

R116 WBKB. *WBKB, Chicago's Pioneer Television Station*. Peoria, 1949.

(WGN)

R117 WGN. *The Wonderful World of WGN*. Chicago, 1966.

R118 Fink, John. *WGN: A Pictorial History*. Chicago, c1961.

An ordinary photographic history of the radio station.

(WLS)

R119 Evans, James F. *Prairie Farmer and WLS: The Burridge B. Butler Years.* Urbana, 1969.

A biography of Burridge Butler and his two great media empires, WLS radio and the *Prairie Farmer.* Bibliography.

(WMAQ)

R120 Caton, Chester. "WMAQ - Her Independent Years." N.U. unpub. Ph.D. thesis, 1950.

A detailed narrative from the origins of the station to 1931.

R121 Linton, Bruce A. "A History of Chicago Radio Station Programming, 1921-1931, with Emphasis on Stations WMAQ and WGN." N.U. unpub. Ph.D. thesis, 1953.

The study was limited to the years 1921-1931 before either station became affiliated with a network. He describes how owners affected the pattern of programs, which in turn led to a "philosophy of each station."

R122 WMAQ-TV. *WMAQ-TV: 1948-1968.* Chicago, 1968.

(Television)

General

R123 Greenfield, Jeff. *Television: The First Fifty Years.* New York, c1977.

Some attention is paid to the early period when Chicago was a television center.

R124 Nielsen, Theodore Lynn. "Television: Chicago Style." *J. of Broadcasting,* IX, 4 (Fall 1965), 305-312.

R125 Sternberg, Joel Barry. "A Descriptive History and Critical Analysis of the Chicago School of Television - Chicago Network Programming in the Chicago Style from 1948 and 1954." N.U. unpub. Ph.D. thesis, 1973.

The fundamental work on early television in Chicago, a long (four volumes), detailed account. Also, much on Chicago radio. The essay on the implications of such strong network control for a democratic society is thought-provoking.

R126 Sternberg, Joel Barry. "Television Town." *CH*, n.s., IV, 2 (Summer 1975), 108-117.

An interesting, short article by the master of the subject.

Studies of Special Topics

R127 Mulder, Ronald Dean. "The Effects of Televised Political Advertising: The 1975 Chicago Mayoral Election." U.C. unpub. Ph.D. thesis, 1975.

Mulder argues that " . . . televised political advertisements appear to have made a significant impact upon voters' political attitudes during the 1975 Chicago mayoral election."

R128 Nielsen, Theodore Lynn. "A History of Chicago Television News Presentation (1948-1968)." U.W. unpub. Ph.D. thesis, 1971.

Describes the period when Chicago was a "partner" in the presentation of national programming and the period of decline.

R129 Schwarzwalder, John Carl. "An Historical Study of the Technical, Legal, and Financial Development of Television." U.H. unpub. Ph.D. thesis, 1953.

Chicago was still a major producing city at the time of this study.

R130 Stewart, Robert Hammel. "The Development of Network Television Program Types to January, 1953." O.S.U. unpub. Ph.D. thesis, 1954.

Biography - Individuals and Programs

(Brookter, Marie)

R131 Brookter, Marie. *Here I Am - Take My Hand*. New York, 1974.

Brookter is a television producer, active in Civil Rights work, who campaigned for Mayor Daley.

(Ding-Dong School)

R132 Kirkorian, Donald George. "An Historical-Descriptive Study of the National Broadcasting Company's Preschool Television Program Ding Dong School." N.U. unpub. Ph.D. thesis, 1972.

A brief biographical sketch of "Miss Frances" with chapters on the conception of the show, its "set up," music, etc.

("Garroway at Large")

R133 Rothaar, Edward Raymond. "An Evaluation and Historical Survey of the Television Program Series 'Garroway at Large'." O.S.U. unpub. M.A. thesis, 1959.

There is a nearly equally long section about this program in Sternberg (R125).

S33 Hotchkiss, Wesley Akin. "Geography of Chicago Churches." U.C. unpub. M.A. thesis, 1948.

→ Uses Hyde Park as a case study in religious sociology.

S34 Noreen, Robert G. "Ghetto Worship: A Study of the Names of Chicago Storefront Churches." *Names*, XIII, 1 (March 1965), 19-38.

S35 Reep, Samuel Nicholas. *The Organization of the Ecclesiastical Institutions of a Metropolitan Community*. Minneapolis, 1910.

S36 Rowe, Stephen C. "Denominational Practices and the Religion of Democracy: The Church Federation of Greater Chicago and Metropolitan Issues - 1945-1968." U.C. unpub. Ph.D. thesis, 1974.

The Federation began the period with high hopes. Rowe examines the ways that were employed to realize these hopes.

S37 Sutherland, Robert Lee. "An Analysis of Negro Churches in Chicago." U.C. unpub. Ph.D. thesis, 1930.

A description resting on some unpublished studies at the University of Chicago as well as other material. Useful maps.

S38 Swisher, Okey R. "A Church in a Moving Population." U.C. unpub. M.A. thesis, 1949.

The study concentrates on West Ridge. There is a description of the community, its individual churches, and a case study of St. James United Church.

S39 Umbeck, Sharvy Greiner. "The Social Adaptations of a Selected Group of the German-Background Protestant Churches in Chicago." U.C. unpub. Ph.D. thesis, 1940.

The first three chapters are narratives of the churches in Chicago 1835-1938. These are followed by chapters on adaptations to the language and in the parochial school. Maps and graphs.

S40 **Vitrano, Steven P.** *An Hour of Good News: The Chicago Sunday Evening Club, a Unique Preaching Ministry*. Chicago, 1974.

A narrative of an organization that was a leading force in modern Protestant evangelism. A list of speakers is included.

S41 Wiltsee, Herbert Leon. "Religious Developments in Chicago, 1893-1915." U.C. unpub. M.A. thesis, 1953.

S42 Zimmerman, Joseph Francis. "The Downtown City Church: Religious Response to Urbanization in Chicago.: HaU. unpub. Ph.D. thesis, 1974.

(Individual Protestant Denominations and Leaders)

Baptist

S43 Bousman, Gary A. "Inclusive Membership in the Churches of the Chicago Baptist Association." U.C. unpub. M.A. thesis, 1937.

The issue that he deals with is the question of who should be admitted to membership, but the most useful part is the sketches of Baptist churches in Chicago and the metropolitan area.

S44 Dillow, Myron D. "A History of Baptists in Illinois, 1786-1845." Southwestern Baptist Theological Seminary unpub. Ph.D. thesis, 1965.

S45 **Ericson, C. Oscar George. *Harvest on the Prairies: Centennial History of the Baptist Conference of Illinois 1856-1956.* Chicago, 1956.**

There are several Chicago references, with lists, biographical sketches, etc.

S46 Hine, Leland D. "Aspects of Change in the Churches of the Chicago Baptist Association, 1931-1935." U.Penn. unpub. Ph.D. thesis, 1958.

S47 Stackhouse, Perry J. *Chicago and the Baptists.* Chicago, 1933.

The standard narrative.

Congregational

S48 Thompson, Warren Elstob. *Building a Christian Chicago: A History of the Chicago Congregational Union, 1882-1932.* Chicago, 1932.

Episcopal

S49 Hall, Francis J. *A History of the Diocese of Chicago, Including a History of the Undivided Diocese of Illinois from Its Organization in A.D. 1835.* Dixon, Ill., n.d.

Short.

S50 Hopkins, John Henry. *The Great Forty Years in the Diocese of Chicago, A.D. 1893 to 1934.* Chicago, 1936.

S51 Shoemaker, Robert W. "The Diocese of Chicago and the Movement to Change the Name of the Church." *H. Mag. of the Protestant Episcopal Church,* XXXII, 4 (Dec. 1963), 349-359.

Evangelical

S52 Schwab, John G., *et.al. History of the Illinois Conference of the Evangelical Church, 1837-1937.* Harrisburg, 1937.

S53 Umbeck, Sharvy Greiner. "An Analysis of the Evangelical Synod Churches in Chicago: A Study in Social Adaptation." U.C. unpub. M.A. thesis, 1938.

Narrates the history and background and then describes their distribution in Chicago, finances, organization, etc.

Latter Day Saints

S54 Taylor, Larene. "The Cook County Latter-Day Saint Disapora." U.C. unpub. M.A. thesis, 1948.

Defines the Latter Day Saints, locates them in the metropolitan area and describes their church and family life.

Lutheranism

S55 Hess, Leland Elmer. "Lutheranism in Chicago (1893-1918)." U.C. unpub. M.A. thesis, 1940.

A narrative with chapters on education and the social gospel. Bibliography.

S56 Kloetzli, Walter. *Lutheran Central Area Study of Chicago.* 2 vol. Chicago, 1960.

Contains a good history of Lutheranism in Chicago as well as an important sociological survey of the city.

S57 Schwartzkopf, Louis J. *The Lutheran Trail: A History of the Synodical Conference Lutheran Churches in Northern Illinois.* St. Louis, 1950.

S58 Wagner, Martin Luther. *The Chicago Synod and Its Antecedents.* Waverly, Iowa, [1909?].

Methodism

S59 Chicago. First Methodist Church. *Centennial Program. First Methodist Episcopal Church of Chicago. Commemorating One Hundred Years of Methodist History in Chicago, 1831-1931.* [Chicago, 1931].

S60 Pennewell, Almer M. *The Methodist Movement in Northern Illinois.* Sycamore, Ill., 1942.

S61 Thompson, John. *The Soul of Chicago.* Chicago, 1920.

Mission Covenant

S62 Backlund, Oscar Theodore. "Survival Factors of the Mission Covenant Churches in Chicago." U.C. unpub. M.A. thesis, 1935.

A study of the sect with statistical tables.

Moody Bible Institute

S63 Getz, Gene A. *MBI: The Story of Moody Bible Institute.* Chicago, 1969.

A topical, documented history, with a chronological table, reprints of official documents, a list of the trustees, and an appendix on the buildings and grounds. Bibliography.

S64 Martin, Dorothy. *Moody Bible Institute: God's Power in Action.* Chicago, 1977.

A friendly history of MBI and its presidents from Moody to the present.

Moody, Dwight L.

S65 Curtis, Richard K. *They Called Him Mister Moody.* Garden City, 1962.

A well-documented general life.

S66 Day, Richard Ellsworth. *Bush Aglow: The Life Story of Dwight Lyman Moody, Commoner of Northfield.* Philadelphia, 1936.

A popular life.

S67 Findlay, James F. *Dwight L. Moody.* Chicago, 1969.

Well documented; based on his Northwestern University Ph.D. thesis of 1961.

S68 Moody, Paul. *My Father: An Intimate Portrait of Dwight Moody*. Boston, 1938.

An account of Dwight L. Moody by the younger son.

S69 Moody, William R. *The Life of Dwight L. Moody by His Son*. New York, 1900.

S70 __________. *D. L. Moody*. New York, 1930.

An important document on evangelical religion in Chicago. A revised edition of the 1900 work.

S71 Pollock, John C. *Moody: A Biographical Portrait of the Pacesetter in Modern Mass Evangelism*. New York, 1963.

Well-documented general life.

(Presbyterianism)

S72 Writers' Program. Illinois. *A History of the First Presbyterian Church of Chicago, 1833-1941*. Chicago, 1941.

S73 Stevenson, Andrew. *Chicago: Pre-Eminently a Presbyterian City*. Chicago, 1907.

An interesting book which describes the Presbyterians in various occupations, e.g., banking, with sketches of leading Presbyterian institutions.

Other Religions

(Buddhist)

S74 [Ichikawa, Michiko]. "Midwest Buddhist Temple, Chicago, Illinois." *Buddhist Churches of America*. 2 vol. Chicago, 1974.

(Koreshan Unity)

See also: N153

S75 Fine, Howard D. "The Koreshan Unity: The Chicago Years of a Utopian Community." *JISHS*, LXVIII, 3 (June 1975), 213-227.

The Unity was a communistic millennial community founded by Cyrus Read Teed, which was centered in Chicago from 1886-1903.

T

POLITICS

See also: G, Government; I24; R, Communication (newspapers).

Studies of More Than One Period

T1 Allswang, John M. *Bosses, Machines, and Urban Voters: An American Symbiosis*. Port Washington, NY, 1977.

There are two Chicago essays - one on Mayors Thompson and Cermak, and one on Mayor Daley.

T2 __________. *A House for All Peoples: Ethnic Politics in Chicago, 1890-1936*. Lexington, 1971.

The impact of the ethnic vote became much greater in this period. This is particularly true of the period after WWI when masses of immigrants became citizens and registered for the first time. By the election of 1932 a clear pattern of ethnic support for the Democratic party had developed. "The ethnics entered the Democracy because their support was sufficiently reciprocated to make it reasonable for them to do so . . ." Bibliography.

T3 Bradley, Donald S. *The Historical Trends of the Political Elites in Metropolitan Central City: The Chicago Mayors*. Chicago, 1963.

Studies the selection of mayors in the city to determine the distribution of political power among groups within the community.

T4 Clifford, Thomas P. *The Political Machine: An American Institution*. New York, 1975.

A chapter on Chicago and a comparison of New York and Chicago.

T5 Ellis, Lewis E. "A History of the Chicago Delegation in Congress, 1843-1925." U.C. unpub. Ph.D. thesis, 1927.

Sought to answer the questions of whether the delegation was united, whether it was partisan, the usefulness of the legislation to Chicago, and how the group managed itself. See also his article of the same title in *Transactions of the Illinois State Historical Society*, XXXVII, (1930), 52-149.

T6 Green, Paul Michael. "The Chicago Democratic Party, 1840-1920: From Factionalism to Political Organization." U.C. unpub. Ph.D. thesis, 1975.

Politics before the early 1890s are briefly described, followed by a detailed narrative of the period 1893-1920. The principal source was a close reading of newspapers. Green argues that Chicago politics were as disorganized as the young city before the election of Carter Harrison I, the first professional politician, as mayor. He questions Allswang's emphasis on ethnicity and the myth of an unbeatable monolithic Irish bloc. The political importance of reformers is also disputed because the machine incorporated their ideas.

T7 Kantowicz, Edward R. *Polish-American Politics in Chicago.* Chicago, 1975.

An account of the beginning of a "Polish vote" in the 1880s and its growth, change and impact to 1940. Kantowicz gives a statistical review of this bloc vote with descriptions of the neighborhoods in which it centered. Maps and graphs.

T8 Levine, Edward M. *The Irish and Irish Politicians: A Study of Cultural and Social Alienation.* Notre Dame, 1966.

Argues that their background in Ireland made the Irish particularly able to master politics. Much of the material bears directly on Chicago.

T9 MacRae, Duncan, Jr. and J. A. Meldrum. "Critical Elections in Illinois, 1888-1958." *Am. Pol. Science R.,* LIV, 3 (Sept. 1960), 669-683.

T10 Mazur, Edward H. "Minyans for a Prairie City: The Politics of Chicago Jewry, 1850-1940." U.C. unpub. Ph.D. thesis, 1974.

He argues that " . . . before the huge Democratic vote, there was a large Republican vote and the movement from one political allegience to another was more gradual than abrupt. Both the Republican Jewish vote and the Democratic Jewish vote reflected the responses to the conditions of the time, country of origin, time of arrival, economic position, religious philosophies and degree of acculturation." Mazur documents his argument in a long narrative history of Chicago Jewry into the era of FDR.

T11 Peterson, Paul Elliott. "City Politics and Community Action: The Implementation of the Community Action Program in Three American Cities." U.C. unpub. Ph.D. thesis, 1967.

An early attempt to evaluate the Economic Opportunity Act of 1964 in Chicago, Philadelphia and New York.

T12 Philip, William B. "Chicago and the Down State: A Study of Their Conflicts, 1870-1934." U.C. unpub. Ph.D. thesis, 1940.

Still the standard work.

T13 Pinderhughes, Dianne Marie. "Interpretations of Racial and Ethnic Participation in American Politics: The Cases of the Black, Italian and Polish Communities in Chicago 1910-1940." 2 vol. U.C. unpub. Ph.D. thesis, 1977.

A long, detailed examination of the idea that blacks can be treated as "ethnics" in historical research and policy formulation. She found " . . . that blacks simply do not fit into the categories that have been applied to immigrant groups with mixed success." Bibliography.

T14 ["Polish Americans and the Democratic Party"]. *Polish Am. Studies*, XXIX, 1/2 (Spring/Autumn 1972).

The entire issue is given over to this topic. Two articles by Edward Kantowicz and Victor Greene treat Chicago.

T15 Rex, Frederick. *The Mayors of the City of Chicago from March 4, 1837 to April 13, 1933*. Chicago, 1947.

The best general reference resource for the mayors.

T16 Thurner, Arthur W. "Polish American in Chicago Politics, 1890-1930." *Polish Am. Studies*, XXVIII, 1 (Spring 1971), 20-42.

Explains why Poles were so slow in becoming involved in Chicago politics.

T17 White, John Patrick. "Lithuanians and the Democratic Party: A Case Study of Nationality Politics in Chicago and Cook County." U.C. unpub. Ph.D. thesis, 1953.

A short analysis of the Lithuanian community of Chicago is followed by chapters on various aspects of its political acitivity: Lithuanian political groups, ticket making, patronage, Lithuanians and the parties, etc.

Before WWI

See also: B21, 24; D35, 39; H164; I66; K46, 47, 49, 50; M27, 56, S4; N111, 167, 177, 189; P4, 22; R103

T18 Ahern, Michael Loftus. *The Great Revolution: A History of the Rise and Progress of the People's Party in the City of Chicago and County of Cook, with Sketches of the Elect in Office*. Chicago, 1874.

A sketch of the Populist Party in Chicago.

T19 Ahern, Michael Loftus. *Political History of Chicago [1837-1887]*. Chicago, 1886.

Useful for the collected biographical sketches of many 19th century political and governmental figures.

T20 Bennett, Fremont O. *Politics and Politicians of Chicago, Cook County and Illinois*. Chicago, 1886.

A detailed narrative with lists of officials, excerpts from documents, etc.

T21 Bergquist, James Manning. "The Political Attitudes of the German Immigrant in Illinois, 1848-1860." N.U. unpub. Ph.D. thesis, 1966.

Bergquist describes the transition from the Democratic Party to the new Republican Party that the Germans made in the 1850s. This shift was particularly noteworthy in Chicago. He regards this as part of a national movement of free-soil Jacksonians into the Republican Party.

T22 Buenker, John D. "Chicago's Ethnics and the Politics of Accommodation." *CH*, n.s., III, 2 (Fall 1974), 92-100.

A short account of how a need for services and fear of WASP cultural domination brought about ethnic participation in politics. The movement of ethnic groups to the Democratic Party is also covered. No notes. For a documented article on the same topic see: *Journal of the Illinois State Historical Society*, LXVII, 2 (Ap. 1974), 175-199.

T23 __________. "The New-Stock Politicians of 1912." *JISHS*, LXII, 1 (Feb. 1969), 35-52.

Less Chicago material than in his other articles, but important.

T24 __________. "Urban Immigrant Lawmakers and Progressive Reform in Illinois." *Essays in Illinois History*. Edited by Donald F. Tingley. Carbondale, IL, 1968.

See annotation for T25.

T25 __________. *Urban Liberalism and Progressive Reform*. New York, 1973.

Buenker, a student of Huthnacher, argues that ". . . machine politicians did indeed make valuable contributions to reform efforts before the First World War." This is a national study, but with much Chicago material.

T26 Cardwell, Gary Lee. "The Rise of the Stalwarts and the Transformation of Illinois Republican Politics, 1860-1880." U.Va. unpub. Ph.D. thesis, 1976.

T43 Nelli, Humbert S. "John Powers and the Italians: Politics in a Chicago Ward, 1896-1921." *J. of Am. H.*, LVII, 1 (June 1970), 67-84.

Shows how Powers established a political base in his ward and what benefits it brought him.

T44 Roberts, Sidney I. "Businessmen in Revolt: Chicago, 1874-1900." N.U. unpub. Ph.D. thesis, 1960.

Really a history of reform in that period which he argues came in waves as citizens went from apathy to a frenzied zeal when faced with a major outrage. Only in the last chapter is there analysis. Bibliography.

T45 __________. "The Municipal Voters' League and Chicago's Boodlers." *JISHS*, LIII, 2 (Summer 1960), 117-148.

Describes the reaction against flagrant graft in the 1890s. Other articles by Roberts in *Union League Men and Events, 1957-1958* are listed in typescript in the Chicago Historical Society Library.

T46 Scott, Anne Firor. "Saint Jane and the Ward Boss." *Am. Heritage*, XII, 1 (Dec. 1960), 12-17, *passim*.

A popular account of Jane Addams and Johnny "de Pow" Powers.

T46a Sommers, Lawrence Edmund. "Lawyers and Progressive Reform: A Study of Attitudes and Activities in Illinois 1890-1920." N.U. unpub. Ph.D. thesis, 1967.

Argues that ". . . local progressivism was a conscious attempt to balance industrial [injustice] . . . with social justice."

T47 Steffens, Lincoln. *The Shame of the Cities*. New York, 1905.

A famous muckraking work, dealing with Chicago in a chapter called "Chicago: Half Free and Fighting On."

T48 Tarr, Joel A. "The Urban Politician as Entrepreneur." *Mid-America*, XLIX, 1 (Jan. 1967), 55-67.

Bosses, Tarr argues, were involved in businesses to gain personal profits. He reviews the careers of some of Chicago's political leaders to support his theory.

T49 __________. "William Kent to Lincoln Steffens: Origins of Progressive Reform in Chicago." *Mid-America*, XLVII, 1 (Jan. 1965), 48-57.

A brief account of the origins of the Municipal Voters League, some important members, and its successful technique (concentration on one thing, the election of honest aldermen). He reprints a long letter from Kent which describes roughly the same thing.

T50 **Tingley, Ralph Russell. "From Carter Harrison II to Fred** Busse: A Study of Chicago Political Parties and Personages from 1896 to 1907." U.C. unpub. Ph.D. thesis, 1950.

A general survey of politics in the period. Tingley identifies the issues, describes them, and weighs their influence on elections. He concludes their personalities were more important than issues.

T51 Tompkins, D. David. "John Peter Altgeld as a Candidate for Mayor of Chicago in 1899." *JISHS*, LVI, 4 (Winter 1963), 654-676.

An account of Altgeld's race against Harrison in 1899.

T52 Wheeler, Joanne Elizabeth. "The Origins of Populism in the Political Structure of a Midwestern State: Partisan Preference in Illinois, 1876-1892." SUNY Buffalo unpub. Ph.D. thesis, 1976.

1917-1945

See also: F140; H156-158; M27, 56; N53, 167, 177; P22

T53 Allswang, John M. "The Chicago Negro Voter and the Democratic Consensus: A Case Study, 1918-1936." *JISHS*, LX, 2 (June 1967), 145-175.

Allswang argues that the black vote remained Republican well into the New Deal.

T54 Andersen, Kristi Jean. "How Realignments Happen: Mobilization and the Creation of a Democratic Majority, 1928-1936." U.C. unpub. Ph.D. thesis, 1976.

T55 Bean, Philip Garth. "Illinois Politics During the New Deal." U.I.U. unpub. Ph.D. thesis, 1976.

Useful for the struggle between Governor Horner and the Kelly-Nash machine.

T56 Blaisdell, Fred W. *The Republican Party in Chicago*. Chicago, 1939.

T56a Bugan, Kenneth Gregory. "Women in Public Affairs of Illinois 1916-1920." U.I.U. unpub. M.A. thesis, 1952.

T57 **Deleted**

T58 Dobyns, Fletcher. *The Underworld of American Politics.* New York, c1932.

Links the machine, Cermak and corruption.

T59 Dorsett, Lyle W. *Franklin D. Roosevelt and the City Bosses.* Port Washington, NY, 1977.

See his essay "Roosevelt is My Religion" on Mayor Edward J. Kelly.

T60 Zeigler, Ruth. "The Chicago Civil Liberties Committee, 1929-1938." U.C. unpub. M.A. thesis, 1938.

An account of the founding and first years of the Chicago branch of the ACLU.

T61 Forthal, Sonya. *Cogwheels of Democracy: A Study of the Precinct Captain.* Westport, 1972 (c1946).

She studies over 600 captains in the late 1920s. Twenty-five of them are described in some detail but the bulk of them appear in several chapters of generalization about the methods and results of the lowest part of the machine.

T62 Gordon, Rita Werner. "The Change in the Political Alignment of Chicago's Negroes During the New Deal." *J. of Am. H.*, LVI, 3 (Dec. 1969), 584-603.

She argues that the New Deal was the principal cause of the switch of blacks to the Democratic party.

T63 Gosnell, Harold F. "The Chicago Black Belt as a Political Background." *Am. J. of Soc.*, XLIX, (Nov. 1933),

A description of the composition of the black vote, black party ties, etc.

T64 __________. *Getting Out the Vote.* Chicago, 1927.

The analysis of who voted and why retains interest, but the bulk of this reforming study is dated.

T65 __________. *Machine Politics: Chicago Model.* Chicago, 1968 (c1937).
Out of the Chicago school of "scientific" analysis, with the expected jargon. It is still a useful study of the nuts and bolts of the "machine" in the 1920s and 1930s.

T66 __________. *Negro Politicians: The Rise of Negro Politics in Chicago.* Chicago, 1935.
Surveys the role of blacks in Chicago politics before Mayor Thompson. Much greater detail thereafter. Essays on the "machine", Ed. H. Wright, Oscar DePriest and patronage. Bibliography.

T67 Gosnell, Harold F. "Political Meetings in the Chicago 'Black Belt'." *Am. Pol. Science R.*, XXXVIII, 2 (Ap. 1934), 254-258.

A short, fascinating description of mass Republican meetings in Chicago's black belt.

T68 Gosnell, Harold F. and N. N. Gill. "An Analysis of the 1932 Presidential Vote in Chicago." *Am. Pol. Science R.*, XXIX, 6 (Dec. 1935), 967-984.

Gosnell and Gill found that the election of 1932 confirmed a move towards the Democratic party that had begun in 1928.

T69 Hachey, Thomas, ed. "A Confidential Account of Mayor Kelly's Visit to London, November, 1945." *JISHS,* LXX, 4 (Nov. 1977), 276-282.

A confidential British account of Kelly's trip to London to secure the United Nation's headquarters for Chicago.

T70 Henderson, Elmer William. "A Study of the Basic Factors Involved in the Change in the Party Alignment of Negroes in Chicago, 1932-1938." U.C. unpub. M.A. thesis, 1939.

An early study of this question, now useful for the primary evidence that he quotes.

T71 Hoffman, Daniel Ronald. "Whose Kind of Town? An Examination of the Pluralist Thesis and the Power Elite in Chicago." U.Ca.-Santa Barbara unpub. Ph.D. thesis, 1973.

A complex examination of a "power elite" that ruled Chicago's politicians.

T71a Jones, Gene Delon. "The Origin of the Alliance Between the New Deal and the Chicago Machine." *JISHS,* LXVII, 3 (June 1974), 253-274.

"Government relief to the unemployed was important in Chicago politics, and it is the politics of relief that explains the alliance of the Chicago machine with Roosevelt." See his Ph.D. thesis, "The Local Political Significance of New Deal Relief Legislation in Chicago," Northwestern University, 1970, for a complete analysis of this subject. He believes that the works program of the Federal government helped shore up the financial situation of the city of Chicago and thus, bolstered the machine in its only area of weakness.

T72 Logsdon, Joseph A. "The Rev. Archibald J. Carey and the Negro in Chicago Politics." U.C. unpub. M.A. thesis, 1961.

A short paper but interesting for its description of the beginning of black politics in Chicago.

T73 McCourt, Kathleen. *Working-Class Women and Grass-Roots Politics*. Bloomington, 1977.

". . . reports on the involvement of these women in such [Chicago] community organizations and how their participation has affected them."

T74 Merriam, Charles E. *Chicago: A More Intimate View of Urban Politics*. New York, 1970 (c1929).

Merriam was a University of Chicago faculty member, but this book grew more from his practical experience in city politics. It, like the work of Gosnell (T63-68) and Rakove (T126), tries to give a picture of the reality of politics. His point of view is reformist, however.

T75 Morris, Harry W. "The Chicago Negro and the Major Political Parties, 1940-1948." U.C. unpub. M.A. thesis, 1950.

More useful for its summary of black voting in the 1940s than for its interpretation.

T76 Neher, Leonardo. "The Political Parties in Chicago's 42nd Ward." U.C. unpub. M.A. thesis, 1952.

A description of a Northside organization.

T77 Rhodes, Benjamin D. "Anglophobia in Chicago: Mayor William Hale Thompson's 1927 Campaign Against King George V." *Ill. Q.*, XXXIX, 4 (Summer 1977), 5-14.

T78 Sadler, Charles. "'Political Dynamite': The Chicago Polonia and President Roosevelt in 1944." *JISHS*, LXXI, 2 (May 1978), 119-132.

Shows how FDR established and maintained a working relationship with Polish-Americans in the face of changing conditions in Europe.

T79 Stuart, William H. *The Twenty Incredible Years*. Chicago, 1935.

Useful for details of the Thompson administration.

T80 Thurner, Arthur W. "The Impact of Ethnic Groups on the Democratic Party in Chicago, 1920-1928." U.C. unpub. Ph.D. thesis, 1966.

Studies Chicago politics 1920-1928 with special emphasis on the influence of various ethnic groups and the causes of their movement to the Democratic Party.

T81 Williams, Elmer Lynn. *The Fix-It Boys: The Inside Story of the New Deal and the Kelly-Nash Machine*. Chicago, 1940.

Vigorous attack on "corruption;" a partisan document.

T82 Wooddy, Carroll Hill. *The Chicago Primary of 1926: A Study in Election Methods*. Chicago, 1926.

A detailed narration of the campaign, the participants and the issues.

T83 __________. "The Direct Primary in Chicago." U.C. unpub. Ph.D. thesis, 1926.

Describes the background of Chicago's primary system, followed by an analysis of current issues.

1945-

See also: L14; M23; P20, 32, 34, 43, 44; O25, 67; R127; U, Civil Disorders (Democratic Convention)

T84 Deleted

T85 Banfield, Edward C. *Political Influence*. Glencoe, Ill., 1961.

Banfield studied all major public questions in 1957-1958 that generated controversy in Chicago. These include the expansion of the Cook County Hospital, the proposal to merge the welfare departments of the county and the city, the financial problem of the CTA, the Fort Dearborn Project, the construction of Circle campus, and the proposals to build a lake front exhibition hall. Chapters of generalization about the structure, process, mythology of influence, and its effect on the public good end the book. The case studies are useful.

T86 Banfield, Edward C. and James Q. Wilson. *City Politics*. Cambridge, 1963

A study of the role of politics, in its broadest sense, in the governing of cities. Much of the evidence is drawn from Chicago.

T87 Bryer, Gladys N. "Politics in a Public Housing Project." U.C. unpub. M.A. thesis, 1967.

T88 Cherry, Horace Dicken. "Effective Precinct Organization." U.C. unpub. M.A. thesis, 1952.

"This is a sample survey of effective precinct captains throughout Chicago. It is an attempt to discover the determination of effective precinct work and organization."

T89 Colfax, J. David. "The Big City Voter: A Study of Political Participation in Chicago." U.C. unpub. Ph.D. thesis, 1964.

A good, radical interpretation.

T90 Deleted

T91 *The Daley Record*. Chicago, 1970.

T92 Deleted

T93 Geisler, Roy G. "Chicago Democratic Voting, 1947-1957." U.C. unpub. Ph.D. thesis, 1958.

The period was one of decline for the Democratic Party. This was the result of the weakening of the Democratic Party and its machine, which was due to: (1) unwise machine strategy, particularly in registration; (2) "the failure of the machine to slate candidates who could retain the loyalty of old Democratic partisans or attract new ones;" (3) a shift in ethnic and racial group loyalties; (4) a decline in absolute and relative size of the machine vote; (5) a declining market for machine patronage. These conclusions are discussed at considerable length in the text of the paper.

T94 Guysenir, Maurice G. "Jewish Vote in Chicago." *Jewish Social Studies*, XX, 4 (Oct. 1958), 195-214.

T95 Hooper, Michael. "Party and Newspaper Endorsement as Predictors of Voter Choice." *Journalism Q.*, XLVI, 2 (1969), 302-305.

An attempt to measure the impact of newspaper and party endorsements on the 1964 at-large elections.

T96 Kasperson, Roger E. "Toward a Geography of Urban Politics: Chicago, a Case Study." *Econ. Geography*, XLI, 2 (Ap. 1965), 95-107.

T97 Knauss, Peter R. *Chicago: A One-Party State*. Champaign, 1974.

Knauss argues that Chicago is a "one party state" and that this is due to an alliance of many of the elements of the establishment, including the church, mass media, the major bureaucracies, the regular Democratic Party, and sometimes the Republican Party.

T98 Leahy, William J. *Non-Issues in the Present Mayoral Campaign and Several Campaigns to Come.* Chicago, 1967.

A strong anti-Daley, anti-machine piece.

T99 McGriggs, Lee Augustus. "Black Legislative Politics in Illinois: A Theoretical and Structural Analysis." U.I.U. unpub. Ph.D. thesis, 1975.

A study of the Chicago machine and black politicians. The study concluded that black legislators followed the lead of the machine in voting, but that they failed to secure as many benefits for their group as did white machine members.

T100 McKeough, Kevin Laurence. "Suburban Voting Behavior in the 1960 Presidential Election: The Case of Cook County, Illinois." U.Kan. unpub. Ph.D. thesis, 1967.

In general, he argues that Kennedy's vote in the suburbs came from people of the lower classes, ethnics, and those with prior residence in Chicago. Many questionable theses are set out from this finding.

T101 Michaelson, Ronald Dwight. "The Politics of Gubernatorial Endorsements in Cook County, Illinois: An Empirical Analysis." S.I.U. unpub. Ph.D. thesis, 1970.

The scope of his study is limited to the endorsement of the Republican Party in the 1968 gubernatorial race.

T102 Piety, Harold R. "Independents Elect Democrat Paul Simon." *FOCUS/Midwest,* VII, 46 (Nov. 1969), 22-25.

A narrative of Simon's successful bid for the post of Lt. Governor.

T103 Rust, James A. "The Ward Committeeman in Chicago." U.C. unpub. M.A. thesis, 1953.

Describes who was likely to become a Committeeman, why, and how they did so, their method of operation and the consequences of this.

T104 Sandquist, Elroy C., Jr. *Chicago - Typical Republican Problem.* Chicago, 1967.

T105 Snowiss, Leo M. "Chicago and Congress: A Study of Metropolitan Representation." 2 vol. U.C. unpub. Ph.D. thesis, 1965.

T106 Snowiss, Leo M. "Congressional Recruitment and Representation." *Am. Pol. Science R.*, LX, 3 (Sept. 1966), 627-639.

T107 Swartz, Sherwin A. "Massive Precinct Work by Coalition of Independents Beats Daley Organization." *FOCUS/Midwest*, VII, 46 (Nov. 1969), 14-17.

Swartz argues that the election of William S. Singer, which is analyzed, showed that the Daley machine could be beaten.

T108 Vocino, Thomas Joseph. "Assessing the Impact of the 1965 Reapportionment on the Politics and Policies of the Illinois General Assembly." S.I.U. unpub. Ph.D. thesis, 1973.

T109 Walton, John and Luis M. Salces. *The Political Organization of Chicago's Latino Communities*. Evanston, 1977.

T110 Wilson, James Q. *The Amateur Democrat*. Chicago, 1962.

A study of independent Democrats, whom he calls amateurs, and their role and potential in the Democratic party. The book is now useful for the case studies of Chicago politics that he uses as evidence.

T111 __________. *Negro Politics: The Search for Leadership*. Glencoe, 1960.

A well-known study which describes Chicago's black politics before the civil rights movement made fundamental changes in it.

Biography

(Altgeld, John P.)

T112 Christman, Henry M., ed. *The Mind and Spirit of John Peter Altgeld: Selected Writings and Addresses*. Urbana, 1960.

T113 Barnard, Harry. *Eagle Forgotten: The Life of John Peter Altgeld*. Indianapolis, 1938.

A long, straightforward narrative. Bibliography.

(Bross, William)

T114 Yount, Charles Allen. *William Bross, 1813-1890*. Lake Forest, Ill., 1940.

A short biography, mindful that Bross was a benefactor of Lake Forest College.

(Carey, Archibald J.)

T115 Kilstrom, John P. "The Politics of Principle: A Political Portrait of Archibald J. Carey." N.I.U. unpub. M.A. thesis, 1969.

See also Joseph Longsdon, "The Rev. Archibald Carey and the Negro in Chicago Politics," U.C. unpub. M.A. thesis (T72).

(Cermak, Anton)

T116 Gottfried, Alex. *Boss Cermak of Chicago: A Study of Political Leadership*. Seattle, 1962.

A detailed narrative of the career of Chicago's only foreign-born mayor. Gottfried's views on Cermak's psycho-history can be separated from his other conclusions about the central role of ethnic groups in Chicago politics, the importance of the "wet" issue to Cermak, and Cermak's high level of political and administrative ability. See also Paul Michael Green on the significance of ethnicity (T6). Bibliography.

(Cole, George)

T117 King, Hoyt. *Citizen Cole of Chicago*. Chicago, 1931.

Biography of a civic reformer during the 1890s and early 1900s.

(Coughlin, John)

T118 Wendt, Lloyd and Herman Kogan. *Lords of the Levee: The Story of Bathhouse John and Hinky Dink*. Paper edition published under title *Bosses in Lusty Chicago*. Indianapolis, 1943.

A good, popular history of "Bathhouse John" Coughlin and "Hinky Dink" Michael Kenna who acted as bosses in the vice-filled first ward from the late 19th century until well into the 20th.

(Daley, Richard J.)

There is no scholarly life of Daley. Eugene Kennedy's book (T122) is the best, followed closely by O'Connor's *Clout* (T124). Rakove's book is good for a broader view of the organization.

T119 Bowen, William. "Chicago: They Didn't Have to Burn it Down After All." *Fortune*, LXXI, 1 (Jan. 1965), *passim*.
A friendly review of the improvements in Chicago during Daley's first two terms.

T120 Daley, Richard J. *Quotations from Mayor Daley.* Compiled by Peter Yessne. New York, 1969.

A collection of very brief quotations.

T121 Gleason, William Francis. *Daley of Chicago: The Man, the Mayor, and the Limits of Conventional Politics.* New York, 1970.

T122 Kennedy, Eugene. *Himself: The Life and Times of Mayor Richard J. Daley.* New York, 1978.

T123 Mathewson, Joe. *Up Against Daley.* La Salle, Ill., 1974.

Mathewson argued (in the early '70s) that the Daley machine was vulnerable to attack by independents. He describes several instances of this in support of his argument. No notes, no bibliography.

T124 O'Connor, Len. *Clout - Mayor Daley and His City.* Chicago, 1975.

T125 __________. *Requiem: The Decline and Demise of Mayor Daley and His Era.* Chicago, 1977.

A detailed account of Daley's last years, but not as good as *Clout* (T124).

T126 Rakove, Milton L. *Don't Make No Waves . . . Don't Back No Losers: An Insider's Analysis of the Daley Machine.* Bloomington, 1975.

Rakove, a trained scholar and participant in Chicago politics, attempts to describe the machine as it is or was under Mayor Daley. He argues that urban problems are political and that the machine attempts to deal with these problems in a pragmatic way. The book has no formal documentation and rests on Rakove's own authority as a student and practitioner of Chicago politics.

T127 Royko, Mike. *Boss: Richard J. Daley of Chicago.* New York, 1971.

A hostile, amusing, one-sided work.

T128 Spurlock, James L., ed. *Richard J. Daley, In Memory.* Chicago, 1977.

A picture book tribute to the Mayor.

T129 Whitehead, Ralph, Jr. "The Organization Man Mayor Richard Daley." *Am. Scholar*, XCVI (Summer 1977), 351-357.

(Dawes, Charles)

T130 Pixton, John E. "The Early Career of Charles G. Dawes." U.C. unpub. Ph.D. thesis, 1952.

Concentrates on the period around the turn of the 19th century. One chapter is on Chicago.

(Dever, William)

T131 Bukowski, Douglas. "William Dever and Prohibition: The Mayoral Election of 1923 and 1927." *CH*, n.s., VII, 2 (Summer 1978), 109-118.

A useful summary of Dever's rise and fall.

(Douglas, Paul)

T132 Anderson, Jerry M. "Paul H. Douglas: Insurgent Senate Spokesman for Humane Causes, 1949-1963." Mich. State U. unpub. Ph.D. thesis, 1964.

The first quarter is a narrative of Douglas' career, the remainder an analysis of his form and opinions as a speaker in the U.S. Senate. The bibliography has a long list of Douglas' own writings.

T133 Douglas, Paul H. *In the Fullness of Time: The Memoirs of Paul H. Douglas*. New York, 1972.

Most of the first part of the book deals with Douglas in Chicago and the rest has much material relevant to Chicago's history.

T134 Schapsmeier, Edward L. and Frederick H. Schapsmeier. "Paul H. Douglas: From Pacifist to Soldier-Statesman." *JISHS*, LXVII, 3 (June 1974), 307-323.

A short biography.

(Dunne, Edward)

T135 Becker, Richard. "Edward Dunne, Reform Mayor of Chicago 1905-1907." U.C. unpub. Ph.D. thesis, 1971.

Argues that Dunne was not a typical reformer because he was less concerned with fiscal and administrative concerns than he was with social problems. He was not totally successful, but he was able ". . . to redefine the agenda of urban reform . . ." Dunne thus made a lasting impact on "reform" by expanding its base to include the laboring class.

T136 Buenker, John D. "Edward F. Dunne: The Urban New Stock Democrat as Progressive." *Mid-America*, L, 1 (Jan. 1968), 3-21.

T137 Sullivan, William L., comp. *Dunne: Judge, Mayor, Governor*. Chicago, 1916.

(Farwell, Arthur B.)

T138 Clayton, John. "The Scourge of Sinners: Arthur Burrage Farwell." *CH*, n.s., III, 2 (Fall 1974), 68-77.

Farwell was the head of the Hyde Park Protective Association and a foe of political and moral corruption in the late 19th and early 20th centuries.

(Fisher, Walter)

T139 Deleted

T140 Fisher, Walter T. "Walter L. Fisher." *U. of Chicago Law School Record*, X, 1 (1964-1965), 3-11.

T141 Gould, Alan B. "Walter L. Fisher: Profile of an Urban Reformer, 1880-1910." *Mid-America*, LVII, 3 (July 1975), 157-172.

(Harrison, Carter I)

T142 Abott, Willis J. *Carter Henry Harrison: A Memoir*. New York, 1895.

An undocumented narrative of the first Harrison.

T143 Johnson, Claudius O. *Carter Henry Harrison I: Political Leader*. Chicago, 1928.

Still the standard life, but see also Green (T6) and Allswang (T2). Bibliography.

(Harrison, Carter II)

T144 Harrison, Carter H. *Stormy Years: The Autobiography of Carter H. Harrison, Five Times Mayor of Chicago*. Indianapolis, c1935.

See T145.

T145 Harrison, Carter H. *Growing Up with Chicago.* Chicago, 1944.

The second Carter H. Harrison. The first volume (T144) is the more useful for political history.

T146 Nugent, Walter T. K. "Carter H. Harrison and Dreiser's 'Walden Lucas'." *Newberry Library Bul.*, VI, 7 (Sept. 1966), 222-230.

Compares Dreiser's Mayor Cowperwood with Harrison.

(Ickes, Harold L.)

T147 Ickes, Harold L. *The Autobiography of a Curmudgeon.* New York, 1943.

Ickes was an active Republican lawyer who came out for FDR in 1932 and entered the national administration.

(Kennelly, Martin)

T148 Duis, Perry R. and Glen E. Holt. "The Real Legacy of 'Poor Martin' Kennelly." *Chicago*, XXVII, 7 (July 1978), 162-165.

A brief description of the real achievements of Martin Kennelly.

(Kenna, Michael)

See: T118, John Coughlin

(Kent, William)

T149 Kent, Elizabeth. *William Kent, Independent: A Biography.* Typescript. 1950.

The first half of the book describes his career in Chicago as an important reform figure.

T149a Woodbury, Robert Louis. "William Kent: Progressive Gadfly, 1864-1928." Yale U. unpub. Ph.D. thesis, 1967.

(Lorimer, William)

T150 Tarr, Joel A. "The Expulsion of Chicago's 'Blond Boss' from the United States Senate." *CH*, n.s., II, 2 (Fall 1972), 78-85.

Adapted from the book (T151).

T151 Tarr, Joel A. *A Study in Boss Politics: William Lorimer of Chicago*. Urbana, 1971.

Tarr argues that Lorimer, an immigrant, built a machine in Chicago to fill the vacuum created by the chaos of rapid industrialization, population growth, etc., in the late 19th century. Since his supporters were immigrants, etc., and he was a professional politician, he was opposed by the progressives who were native-born, pious in religion, and who sought reform government by giving it into their hands. Once they gained power, the progressive reformers wanted to install corporate models of efficient government administration by experts. Lorimer's case in the Senate played out this tension on a national scale. Bibliography.

(Lowden, Frank O.)

T152 Hutchinson, William T. *Lowden of Illinois: The Life of Governor Frank O. Lowden*. 2 vol. Chicago, 1957.

(Mann, James R.)

T153 Mitchell, Rena. "The Congressional Career of James R. Mann." U.C. unpub. M.A. thesis, 1938.

Mann represented Hyde Park for several terms in Congress. Some Chicago material, but it is mostly national.

(Mitchell, Arthur)

T154 Duis, Perry R. "Arthur W. Mitchell, New Deal Negro in Congress." U.C. unpub. M.A. thesis, 1966.

A short life of Chicago's first black democratic Congressman.

(O'Leary, Jim)

T155 Griffin, Richard T. "Big Jim O'Leary: 'Gambler Boss iv th' Yards'." *CH*, n.s., V, 4 (Winter 1976-1977), 213-222.

An undocumented short biography.

(Thompson, William "Big Bill")

T156 Bright, John. *Hizzoner, Big Bill Thompson: An Idyll of Chicago*. New York, 1930.

A popular, satirical biography.

T157 Hoffmann, George C. "Big Bill Thompson, His Mayoral Campaigns and Voting Strength." U.C. unpub. M.A. thesis, 1956.

Downplays the importance of Thompson's personality and argues the greater cohesion of the GOP was the crucial factor.

T158 Schottenhamel, George. "How Big Bill Thompson Won Control of Chicago." *JISHS*, XLV, 1 (Spring 1952), 30-49.

A short narrative description of his electoral life.

T159 Wendt, Lloyd and Herman Kogan. *Big Bill of Chicago*. Indianapolis, 1953.

A good, popular account.

(Wentworth, John)

T160 Fehrenbacher, Don E. *Chicago Giant: A Biography of "Long John" Wentworth*. Madison, 1957.

The standard life.

U
CIVIL DISORDERS

In the list below labor related incidents have been excluded. For those accounts see Chapter I, Labor.

Lager Beer Riot - 1855

U1 Renner, Richard Wilson. "In a Perfect Ferment." *CH,* n.s., V, 3 (Fall 1976), 161-170.

A short, clear summary.

Race Riot - 1919

U2 Chicago. Commission on Race Relations. *The Negro in Chicago: A Study of Race Relations and a Race Riot in 1919.* New York, 1968 (c1922).

The official report, it presents the most detailed account of the riot. A comparison of the facts in the report and the newspaper accounts shows the unreliability of the latter.

U3 Sandburg, Carl. *The Chicago Race Riots, July, 1919.* New York, 1969 (c1919).

Sandburg was a young reporter when he wrote these essays.

U4 Tuttle, William M., Jr. "Contested Neighborhoods and Racial Violence: Prelude to the Chicago Riot of 1919." *J. of Negro H.,* LV, 4 (Oct. 1970), 266-288.

Tuttle touches again on the growing tension that predated the riot in 1919, expanding his analysis beyond the labor market (see I79-80).

U5 __________. *Race Riot: Chicago in the Red Summer of 1919.* New York, 1970.

A documented monograph, in which Tuttle is at considerable pain to show the origin of the riot in the years before. The best summary.

U6 __________. "Views of a Negro During 'The Red Summer' of 1919 - A Document." *J. of Negro H.,* LI, 3 (July 1966), 209-218.

Reprints a letter of a Chicago black man sent after the riots.

U7 Waskow, Arthur. *From Race Riot to Sit-In*. Garden City, 1966.

Includes two chapters on the riots, based on his 1963 University of Wisconsin Ph.D. thesis.

U8 Williams, Lee E. *Anatomy of Four Race Riots*. Hattiesburg, Miss., 1972.

A brief essay on the Chicago riot.

Trumbull Park Homes - 1950s

U9 Chicago. Commission on Human Relations. *The Trumbull Park Homes Disturbances: A Chronological Report August 4, 1953 to June 30, 1955*. Chicago, 1955.

A straightforward narrative. This report was preceded by two "documentary" reports in 1954.

Chicago Black Riots - 1960s

These have not yet received scholarly attention. There is a mass of material available, however, through the periodical indexes listed in the introduction. See also: G40.

Democratic Convention Riots and Trials - 1968

U10 Chicago. Department of Law. *The Strategy of Confrontation: Chicago and the Democratic National Convention, 1968*. Chicago, 1968.

The official defense of the city's conduct by the Daley organization.

U11 Chicago. Riot Study Committee. *Report . . . to the Hon. Richard J. Daley*. Chicago, 1968.

U12 *The Conspiracy*. Edited by Peter and Deborah Babcox and Bob Abel. New York, 1969.

A series of pieces by the defendants in the conspiracy trial.

U13 *Contempt: Transcript of the Contempt Citations, Sentences, and Responses of the Chicago Conspiracy 10*. Chicago, 1970.

U14 Dellinger, David T. *The Conspiracy Trial.* Indianapolis, 1970.

Very long excerpts from the trial.

U15 __________. *The Tales of Hoffman.* New York, 1970.

Excerpts from the transcript with drawings by an NBC artist.

U16 Epstein, Jason. *The Great Conspiracy Trial: An Essay on Law, Liberty, and the Constitution.* New York, 1970.

A popular account. He attempts to set the trial in a broader context of American history, life and law.

U17 Feiffer, Jules. *Pictures at a Prosecution: Drawings & Text from the Chicago Conspiracy Trial.* New York, 1971.

U18 Hayden, Thomas. *Trial.* New York, 1970.

An account of convention week and the trial by a participant.

U19 Lane, Mark. *Chicago Eyewitness.* New York, c1968.

U20 *Law & Disorder: The Chicago Convention and Its Aftermath.* Edited by Donald Myrus. Chicago, 1968.

Pictures and essays by well-known observers.

U21 Lukas, J. Anthony. *The Barnyard Epithet and Other Obscenities Notes on the Chicago Conspiracy Trial.* New York, 1970.

By a reporter for the *New York Times.*

U21a Mailer, Norman. *Miami and the Siege of Chicago: An Informal History of the Republican and Democratic Conventions of 1968.* New York, 1968.

U22 Reeves, Mary Martha. "The Chicago-Eight Conspiracy Trial: A Rhetorical Analysis of the Societal Context and Interpersonal Dynamic." U.Wash. unpub. Ph.D. thesis, 1975.

Somewhat less arcane than similar studies.

U23 Robinson, John P. "Public Reaction to Political Protest: Chicago 1968." *Public Opinion Q.,* XXXIV, 1 (Spring 1970), 1-9

A survey of national response to the 1968 convention disorders

U24 Sadock, Verna. *Verdict: The Exclusive Picture Story of the Trial of the Chicago 8.* Text by Joseph Opaku. New York, 1970 She was an artist for NBC.

U25 Schneir, Walter, comp. *Telling It Like It Was: The Chicago Riots.* New York, 1969.

U26 Schultz, John. *Motion Will be Denied: A New Report on the Chicago Conspiracy Trial.* New York, 1972.

A popular account of the trial.

U27 __________. *No One Was Killed: Documentation and Meditation Convention Week, Chicago, August 1968.* Chicago, 1969.

Schultz was a reporter for *Evergreen Review* during the convention.

U28 Stein, David Lewis. *Living the Revolution: The Yippies in Chicago.* Indianapolis, 1969.

A newspaperman describes the Yippies in Chicago.

U29 U. S. Congress. House. Committee on Un-American Activities. *Subversive Involvement in Disruption of 1968 Democratic Party National Convention. Hearings.* 2 vol. Washington, 1968.

Testimony of Tom Hayden and Rennie Davis, among others.

U30 Walker, Daniel. *Rights in Conflict: The Violent Confrontation of Demonstrators and Police in the Parks and Streets of Chicago During the Week of the Democratic National Convention of 1968.* Chicago, 1968.

The famous report of Daniel Walker, *et.al.*, which termed the convention a police riot.

Black Panther Raid and Trials

U31 Arlen, Michael J. *An American Verdict.* Garden City, 1973.

An account of the trials resulting from the raid on Panther headquarters.

U32 Commission of Inquiry into the Black Panthers and the Police. *Search and Destroy: A Report.* New York, 1973.

A thorough work, hostile towards the police.

U33 United States. District Court. Illinois (Northern District, Eastern Division). *Report of the January 1970 Grand Jury.* Washington, 1970.

The corrected edition of the Grand Jury's investigation of the raid on the Panthers.

V
DISASTERS

General

V1 Kartman, Ben, ed. *Disaster*. New York, 1948.

Among the short disaster accounts are three Chicago stories: the Great Fire, the Iroquois Theater Disaster and the Eastland sinking.

Eastland

V2 Billow, Jack J. "The Tragedy of the Eastland." *Inland Seas*, XVI, 3 (Fall 1960), 190-195.

A first-hand account by a crewman on one of the Eastland's sister boats.

V3 Boyer, Dwight. *True Tales of the Great Lakes*. New York, 1971.

Another summary essay.

V4 Cook County, (Ill.). Coroner. *Transcript of Testimony . . .* Chicago, [1915].

A good primary source.

V5 Dowling, Edward J. "Tragedy at Clark Street Bridge." *Steamboat Bill*, XCIV, 2 (Summer 1965), 43-49.

A careful study of the disaster and its causes; one of the best summaries.

V6 Elliott, J. L. "The Eastland - A Half-Century Ago." *Inland Seas*, XXI, 2 (Summer 1965), 115-121.

Elliott was taken by his father to watch the rescue effort as a small boy. He argues that the ship sank when too many passengers went to the side.

V7 Hoehling, A. A. *Disaster: Major American Catastrophes*. New York, 1973.

Includes a short account of the Eastland sinking, but is not wholly accurate.

V8 *Investigation of Accident to the Steamer "Eastland" Containing a Copy of Testimony and Report of Board of Inquiry made to the Secretary of Commerce . . . Also . . . Preliminary Report of the Committee of Supervisors and Inspectors . . . of the Steamboat Inspection Service . . .* Washington, 1916.

V9 Red Cross. Chicago Chapter. Eastland Relief Committee. *Eastland Disaster Relief: American Red Cross 1915-1918.* Chicago, 1918.

Outlines the aid to the families of the victims and lists all of the dead with brief biographical sketches.

V10 Ross, Irwin. "The Eastland Disaster." *Am. H. Illus.*, VI, 7 (Nov. 1971), 17-22.

A short, illustrated article.

V11 Thompson, Merwin S. "Just What Was the Cause of the Steamer *Eastland* Disaster?" *Inland Seas*, XV, 3 (Fall 1959), 200-206.

Argues that the cause ". . . was a misunderstanding between the bridge officers and the engine room department regarding the distribution of water ballast."

Iroquois Theater Fire

V12 Everett, Marshall (pseud.). *The Great Chicago Theater Disaster*. Chicago, 1904.

Some narrative, excerpts from documents, a list of the dead. Northrop's (V16) is much the same sort of book.

V13 Guenzel, Louis. *Retrospects: The Iroquois Fire*. Chicago, 1945.

Guenzel had access to the building for many days after the fire and made a report with drawings and photographs.

V14 McGibeny, Ruth Thompson. "The Iroquois Theater Fire." *CH*, n.s., III, 3 (Winter 1974-1975), 177-180.

A first-hand account by a survivor.

V15 Neil, Henry. *Chicago's Awful Theater Horror by the Survivors and Rescuers*. Chicago, 1904.

V16 Northrop, Henry Davenport. *World's Greatest Calamities*. [Chicago?, 1904].

See annotation for Everett (V12).

V17 Stanger, Wesley A. *Rescued from Fiery Death*. Chicago, 1904.

A long account of the fire.

Fire of 1871

There are a multitude of primary, secondary and fictional accounts of the Great Chicago Fire. Primary and contemporary accounts differ greatly on the facts of the Fire. Paul Angle's selection of primary accounts (V18) is a good one and in an accessible format. Elias Colbert's (V20) is another useful account, in a paperback binding. Goodspeed's work (V22) is good for the fires in Wisconsin and Michigan that occurred on the same day. Among secondary accounts attention should be called to the issue of *Chicago History* devoted wholly to the Fire (V27), to Musham's careful account (V33), and to the photographs in Herman Kogan's work (V31). Duis and Holt have written the best short history (V29). Richard Shepro's (V37) and T. J. Naylor's (V35) papers treat an interesting facet of the Fire. None of the fictional works are distinguished.

(Primary and Contemporary Accounts)

V18 Angle, Paul M. *The Great Chicago Fire, October 8-10, 1871, Described by Eight Men and Women Who Experienced Its Horrors and Testified to the Courage of Its Inhabitants.* New and enlarged ed. Chicago, 1971.

V19 Chicago Relief and Aid Society. *Report of the Chicago Relief and Aid Society of Disbursement of Contributions for the Sufferers by the Chicago Fire.* Cambridge, 1874.

V20 Colbert, Elias and Everett Chamberlin. *Chicago and the Great Conflagration.* New York, 1971 (c1871).

V21 Foster, Thomas Dove. *A Letter from the Fire: Being an Account of the Great Chicago Fire, Written in 1871.* Cedar Rapids, 1949.

V22 Goodspeed, Edgar Johnson. *History of the Great Fires in Chicago and the West . . . with a History of the Rise and Progress of Chicago . . . To Which is Appended a Record of the Great Fires in the Past.* Chicago, 1871.

V23 McIlvaine, Mable, comp. *Reminiscences of Chicago During the Great Fire.* Chicago, 1915.

V24 Ranalletta, Kathy. "'The Great Wave of Fire' at Chicago - The Reminiscences of Martin Stamm." *JISHS*, LXX, 2 (May 1977), 149-160.

A popular account in a convenient format.

V25 Sheahan, James Washington and George Putnam Upton. *The Great Conflagration. Chicago: Its Past, Present and Future, Embracing a Detailed Narrative of the Great Conflagration in the North, South and West Divisions.* Philadelphia, 1871.

(Secondary Accounts)

V26 Angle, Paul M. "What Survived the Fire?" *CH,* VI, 5 (Fall 1961), 137-138.

V27 *Chicago History.* n.s., I, 4 (Fall 1971), 196-244.

V28 Cromie, Robert Allen. *The Great Chicago Fire.* New York, 1958.

A popular history.

V29 Duis, Perry R. and Glen E. Holt. "Kate O'Leary's Sad Burden." *Chicago,* XXVII, 10 (Oct. 1978), 220-222.

V30 Heise, Kenan. "Who Paid for the Chicago Fire?" *Chicago,* XXIV, 10 (Oct. 1975), 92-95.

V31 Kogan, Herman and Robert Cromie. *The Great Fire: Chicago 1871.* New York, 1971.

V32 Larson, Lowell Dean. "Constitutionalism in Crisis: The Case of the Great Chicago Fire." U.C. unpub. Ph.D. thesis, 1962.

V33 Musham, H. A. "The Great Chicago Fire: October 8-10, 1871." *Papers, ISHS,* IV (1941), 69-189.

V34 Naden, Corinne J. *The Chicago Fire, 1871: The Blaze That Nearly Destroyed a City.* New York, 1969.

V35 Naylor, Timothy J. "Responding to the Fire: The Work of the Chicago Relief and Aid Society." *Science & Society,* XXXIX, 4 (Winter 1975-1976), 450-464.

V36 Phelan, Mary Kay. *The Story of the Great Chicago Fire, 1871.* New York, 1971.

V37 Shepro, Richard Warren. "The Reconstruction of Chicago After the Great Fire of 1871." Ha.U. unpub. B.A. thesis, 1974.

W
WORLD'S FAIRS

World's Columbian Exposition, 1893

More material was published for and about the 1893 World's Fair than for any other fair or event in Chicago's history. Material was selected for this section on the basis of how much it would contribute to an overview of the Fair, how it would relate to topics of current interest, and aid in the identification of books, pamphlets, objects and other materials from the Fair. The best guides to printed material on the Fair are the bibliographies of the dissertations listed and the catalogs of the Chicago Historical Society Library, the Chicago Public Library, the John Crerar Library and the Library of Congress.

(General)

W1 Bancroft, Hubert Howe. *The Book of the Fair*. 2 vol. Chicago, 1895.

A long text with many photographs. One of the standard works on the Fair.

W2 Burg, David F. *Chicago's White City of 1893*. Lexington, c1976.

A sound, documented narrative that has now become the standard account.

W3 Cameron, William E. *World's Fair, Being a Pictorial History of the Columbian Exposition . . .* Boston, c1893.

A long, well-documented history.

W4 *The Chicago Record's History of the World's Fair*. Chicago, 1893.

A newspaper's history of the Fair.

W5 Curti, Merle. "America at the World's Fairs, 1851-1893." *Am. H. R.*, LV, 4 (July 1950), 833-856.

He argues that ". . . increasing American participation in world fairs reflected the expansion of American patriotism and enterprise in the last half of the nineteenth century." He adds that these fairs were an important factor in changing world attitudes toward America and that recognition of American technical progress came earlier than has been thought.

W6 Doenecke, Justus D. "Myths, Machines and Markets: The Columbian Exposition of 1893." *J. of Popular Culture,* VI, 3 (Spring 1972), 535-549.

An interesting article about the use of the Fair in popularizing industrial development and in "selling" it in a pastoral guise.

W7 Johnson, Rossiter, ed. *A History of the World's Columbian Exposition Held in Chicago in 1893.* 4 vol. New York, 1897-1898.

One of the standard, long, detailed accounts. The place to start in tracking down a specific piece of information.

W8 Knutson, Robert L. "The White City: The World's Columbian Exposition of 1893." Col.U. unpub. Ph.D. thesis, 1956.

W9 Parmet, Robert D. and Francis L. Lederer, II. "Competition for the World's Columbian Exposition: The New York Campaign and the Chicago Campaign." *JISHS,* LXV, 4 (Winter 1972), 364-394.

A narrative of how Chicago beat out New York for the Fair. It was during this rivalry that Chicago acquired the nickname "Windy City."

(Special Topics)

W10 Andrews, William D. "Women and the Fairs of 1876 and 1893." *Hayes H. J.,* I, 3 (Spring 1977), 173-184.

W11 Angle, Paul M. "The Columbus Caravels." *CH,* VIII, 9 (Fall 1968), 257-269.

A short account of their construction and use.

W12 Barnes, Sisley. "George Ferris' Wheel: The Great Attraction of the Midway Plaisance." *CH,* n.s., VI, 3 (Fall 1977), 177-182.

The story of the Ferris Wheel at the 1893 Fair.

W13 Barrows, John Henry, ed. *The World's Parliament of Religions: An Illustrated and Popular Story of the World's First Parliament of Religions, Held in Chicago in Connection with the Columbian Exposition of 1893.* 2 vol. Chicago, 1893.

W14 Broun, Elizabeth. "American Paintings and Sculpture in the Fine Arts Building of the World's Columbian Exposition Chicago, 1892." U.Kan. unpub. Ph.D. thesis, 1976.

W15 Cleary, James F. "Catholic Participation in the World's Parliament of Religions, Chicago, 1893." *Catholic H. R.*, LV, 4 (Jan. 1970), 585-609.

He argues that the church came to the World's Parliament to show its acceptance of pluralism in American religious life.

W16 *The Congress of Women Held in the Woman's Building, World's Columbian Exposition, Chicago, U.S.A., 1893 . . . With Portraits, Biographies and Addresses*. 2 vol. Edited by Mary Kavanaugh Oldham Eagle. Chicago, 1894.

The official account.

W17 Dornfeld, A. A. "The *Viking* in Lincoln Park." *CH*, n.s., III, 2 (Fall 1974), 111-116.

The ship sailed across the North Atlantic for the 1893 Fair. It was a hit and has remained in Chicago ever since.

W18 Houghton, Walter R., ed. *Neely's History of the Parliament of Religions and Religious Congresses at the World's Columbian Exposition*. Chicago, 1893.

W19 Hume, Paul and Ruth. "The Great Chicago Piano War." *Am. Heritage*, XXI, 6 (Oct. 1970), 16-21.

Awards at the Fair meant a great deal. This article deals with competition in one area.

W20 Massa, Ann. "Black Women in the 'White City'." *J. of Am. Studies*, VIII, 3 (Dec. 1974), 319-337.

She recounts the efforts of black women to be represented at the Fair, ending in the publication of *The Reason Why the Colored American is Not in the Columbian Exposition* (W23).

W21 Riedy, James L. "Sculpture at the Columbian Exposition." *CH*, n.s., IV, 2 (Summer 1975), 99-107.

A description of the sculpture created for the 1893 Fair.

W22 Rudwick, Elliott M. and August Meier. "Black Man in the 'White City': Negroes and the Columbian Exposition, 1893." *Phylon*, XXVI, 4 (Winter 1965), 354-361.

A useful survey of the discrimination experienced by blacks at the Fair.

W23 Wells, Ida B. *The Reason Why the Colored American is Not in the World's Columbian Exposition*. Chicago, 1893.
Published as part of a campaign to achieve a proper place for black people at the Fair.

W24 Weimann, Jeanne Madeline. "A Temple to Women's Genius: The Woman's Building of 1893." *CH*, n.s., VI, 1 (Spring 1977), 23-33.

The Woman's Building at the Columbian Exposition was a visible sign of the women's movement of that period. It was designed by a woman, administered by a woman's committee, and housed exhibits showing women's achievements.

W25 Wilson, Robert E. "The Infanta at the Fair." *JISHS,* LIX, 3 (Autumn 1966), 252-271.

Wilson makes an interesting connection between the Infanta's rude behavior and the growth of anti-Spanish feeling in Chicago.

W26 *World's Congress of Representative Women: A Historical Resume for Popular Circulation of the World's Congress of Representative Women, Convened in Chicago on May 15, and Adjourned on May 22, 1893, under the Auspices of the Woman's Branch of the World's Congress Auxiliary* . . . Edited by May Wright Sewall. Chicago, 1894.

The Congress was an important step in the feminist movement. This report reprints some of the proceedings and documents.

(Columbian Exposition Architecture)

See also: E, Architecture

W27 Deleted

W28 Hoffman, Donald. "Clear Span Rivalry: The World's Fairs of 1889-1893." *JSAH,* XXIX, 1 (Mar. 1970), 48-50.

An illustration of the international competition that went on at the Fairs of the 19th century.

W28a Karolowicz, Titus M. "The Architecture of the World's Columbian Exposition." N.U. unpub. Ph.D. thesis, 1965.

This is a study of how the buildings came to look as they did, *not* a study of the architectural influence of the Fair. An appendix reproduces some primary material, including plans and photographs.

W29 __________. "D. H. Burnham's Role in the Selection of Architects for the World's Columbian Exposition." *JSAH,* XXIX, 3 (Oct. 1970), 247-254.

W30 Olmsted, Frederick Law. "The Landscape Architecture of the World's Columbian Exposition." *Inland Arch.*, XXII, 2 (Sept. 1893), 18-21.

An important descriptive article by the principal designer.

W31 Shankland, E. C. "The Construction of the Buildings, Bridges, etc., at the World's Columbian Exposition." *Inland Arch.*, XXII, 1 (Aug. 1893), 8-9.

An account of engineering at the Fair by the chief engineer.

W32 Tselos, Dimitri. "The Chicago Fair and the Myth of the 'Lost Cause'." *JSAH*, XXVI, 4 (Dec. 1967), 259-268.

An interesting re-evaluation of the choice of a classical style for the Fair.

(Catalogs, Awards)

W33 Chicago. World's Columbian Exposition, 1893. *Classification of the World's Columbian Exposition, Chicago, U.S.A., 1893.* Chicago, 1891.

W34 __________. *List of Awards*. 2 vol. Typescript. n.p., n.d.

The volumes cover domestic (vol. 1) and foreign (vol. 2) awards. Held at the Chicago Historical Society.

W35 __________. *Official Guide to the World's Columbian Exposition in the City of Chicago, State of Illinois, May 1 to October 26, 1893, by Authority of the U. S. of America . . .* Souvenir ed. Compiled by John J. Flinn. Chicago, 1893.

W36 __________. *Report of the President to the Board of Directors of the World's Columbian Exposition*. Chicago, 1898.

W37 __________. *The People's Ready Reference Guide to Chicago and the World's Columbian Exposition: What to See and How to See It; Every Question Answered*. Chicago, 1893.

W38 __________. *World's Columbian Exposition, 1893: Official Catalogue*. 17 parts. Chicago, 1893.

W39 *Rand, McNally & Co.'s A Week at the Fair, Illustrating the Exhibits and Wonders of the World's Columbian Exposition, with Special Descriptive Articles by Mrs. Potter Palmer, the Countess of Aberdeen, Mrs. Schuyler Van Rensselaer . . .* Chicago, 1893.

(Views)

W40 Buel, James W. *The Magic City*. New York, 1974 (c1894).

Included because it appears as a reprint.

W41 Chicago. World's Columbian Exposition, 1893. *Official Views of the World's Columbian Exposition Issued by the Department of Photography, C. D. Arnold, H. D. Higinbotham, Official Photographers*. Chicago, 1893.

W42 Chicago. World's Columbian Exposition, 1893. Department of Photography. *State Buildings: Portfolio of Views*. Chicago, 1893.

W43 *The Dream City: A Portfolio of Photographic Views of the World's Columbian Exposition*. St. Louis, 1893.

W44 Walton, William. *Art and Architecture*. Philadelphia, 1893.

A large, lavish work.

W45 Shepp, James W. and D. B. Shepp. *Shepp's World's Fair Photographed . . .* Chicago, c1893.

Very long captions make this book of special value.

Century of Progress, 1933-1944

A Century of Progress was on a scale similar to the Columbian Exposition but it has generated far fewer publications. See also: E149; Q126

W46 Cahan, Cathy and Richard. "The Lost City of the Depression." *CH*, n.s., V, 4 (Winter 1976-1977), 233-242.

A short account of the 1933-1934 Chicago World's Fair.

W47 Chicago. Century of Progress International Exposition, 1933-1934. *Official Book of the Fair, Giving Pre-Exposition Information, 1932-1933, of a Century of Progress International Exposition, Chicago, 1933*. Chicago, 1932.

The first guide book was followed by at least five other editions, revisions, etc. They are all useful, particularly in tracing changes in the Fair. Many of the exhibits also had guide books and some of these went into different editions.

W48 __________. *Official Pictures of a Century of Progress Exposition: Photographs by Kaufmann & Fabry Co., Official Photographers*. Chicago, c1933.

W49 Chicago. Century of Progress International Exposition. 1933-34. *Report of the President of a Century of Progress to the Board of Trustees.* Chicago, 1936.

This and Lohr's book (W50) are the two standard surveys of the 1933-1934 Fair.

W50 Lohr, Lenox Riley. *Fair Management, the Story of A Century of Progress Exposition: A Guide for Future Fairs.* Chicago, 1952.

The best narrative.

W51 Meier, August and Elliott M. Rudwick. "Negro Protest at the Chicago World's Fair, 1933-1934." *JISHS*, LIX, 2 (Summer 1966), 161-171.

An account of discrimination against blacks and the resulting protest.

W52 *Progress.* Chicago, 1931-1934.

From May to November, 1933 it appeared as the *Official World's Fair Weekly.*

X
ENVIRONS

Chicago's environs were not a part of the research for this bibliography. The list below was compiled from the holdings of the Chicago Historical Society and is not comprehensive. See also: F, Transportation (surface); T100

General

X1 Business Executives' Research Council of Greater Chicago. *Chicago's Metropolitan Growth: Patterns, Problems, Prospects.* [Evanston, 1955?].

X2 Chapin, Louella. *Round About Chicago.* Chicago, [c1907].

X3 Chicago and North-Western Railway Company. *The Beautiful Country Near Chicago.* Chicago, 1900.

X4 __________. *Beautiful Suburban Towns.* Chicago, c1909.

X5 *Chicago Daily News. Chicago and Its Suburbs . . . The Future.* Chicago, 1977.

X6 Freeman, Hal M. *Desegregation of Chicago Suburbs.* [Chicago?], 1965.

Offprint from the *J. of Intergroup Relations*, IV, 4.

X7 Illinois Central Railroad. *Country Clubs on the Suburban Line of the Illinois Central Railroad.* Chicago, 1906.

X8 Deleted

X9 League of Women Voters of Cook County. *Survey of Community Action Programs, Suburban Cook County.* [Chicago], 1967.

X10 Northeastern Illinois Metropolitan Area Planning Commission. *A Social Geography of Metropolitan Chicago. Trends and Characteristics of Municipalities in the Chicago Metropolitan Area.* Chicago, [1960].

X11 __________. *Suburban Factbook, 1950-1960. A Socio-Economic Data Inventory for 100 Municipalities in Northeastern Illinois.* Chicago, [1960].

X12 Northeastern Illinois Planning Commission. *Urban Esthetics and Civic Design in Northeastern Illinois.* [Chicago, 1966].

X13 [Runnion, James B.] *Out of Town: Being a Descriptive, Historical and Statistical Account of the Suburban Towns and Residences of Chicago.* Chicago, 1869.

X14 Taylor, Graham Romeyn. *Satellite Cities: A Study of Industrial Suburbs.* New York, 1915.

X15 White, Marian. *Book of the Western Suburbs: Homes, Gardens, Landscapes, Highways and Byways, Past and Present.* Chicago, 1912.

Cook County

X16 Andreas, Alfred T. *History of Cook County, Illinois. From the Earliest Period to the Present Time . . .* Chicago, 1884.

X17 Barge, William D. *The Genesis of Cook County.* Typescript. Chicago, 1919.

X18 Bateman, Newton. *Historical Encyclopedia of Illinois.* 2 vol. Chicago, 1901-1905.

X19 Goodspeed, Weston Arthur, ed. *History of Cook County, Illinois.* Chicago, [1911?].

X20 Johnson, Charles B. *Growth of Cook County: A History of the Large Lake-Shore County That Includes Chicago.* Chicago, 1960.

X21 *Portrait and Biographical Record of DuPage and Cook Counties, Illinois . . .* Chicago, 1894.

X22 Waterman, Arba Nelson. *Historical Review of Chicago and Cook County and Selected Biography.* 3 vol. Chicago, 1908.

Studies of Two or More Suburbs

X23 Adair, Anna B. and Adele Sandberg. *Indian Trails to Tollways: The Story of the Homewood-Flossmoor Area.* Homewood, 1968.

X24 Beaudette, E. Palma. *Des Plaines, Park Ridge, Mt. Prospect.* [Chicago?, 1916?].

X25 __________. *Niles Township: Niles Center, Morton Grove, Niles Village, Tessville.* [Chicago?, 1916?].

X26 Calumet Federation for the Promotion of Calumet Waterways. *Calumet Waterway Victory Celebration, September 8, 1935. Sponsored by Calumet Federation for the Promotion of Calumet Waterways.* Chicago, 1935.

X27 Ettema, Ross. *From the Land of Windmills and Wooden Shoes: Early Dutch Settlers of South Holland, Thornton, Lansing and Dolton, Illinois Buried in the Old Holland Section of the Homewood Memorial Gardens, Homewood, Illinois.* [South Holland, IL?], 1976.

X28 Illinois Historic Structures Survey. *Inventory of Architecture Before W. W. II in Calumet City, Chicago Heights, Country Club Hills, Flossmoor, Harvey, Homewood, Lansing, Matteson, Olympia Fields, Thornton [in] Cook County.* [Chicago], 1973.

X29 League of Women Voters of Hinsdale, Illinois. *This is Your Community, Hinsdale, Clarendon Hills.* [Hinsdale], 1961.

X30 Libertyville-Mundelein Historical Society. *Historical Libertyville-Mundelein from 1835.* [Libertyville, 1970?].

X31 Life Printing and Publishing Company, Cicero. *35 Years of Progress: Cicero, Berwyn, Stickney and Forest View Life.* [Cicero, 1961].

X31a Yackley, Joseph. *Reminiscences of Naperville and Lisle.* n.p., 1916.

X32 Young, Frank E. J. *Historical Sketches of Towns on the Chicago, Burlington and Quincy Railroad in Cook and DuPage Counties.* Typescript. Chicago, 1919.

Individual Suburbs

(Batavia)

X33 Gustafson, John S. *Historic Batavia, Illinois.* Batavia, 1962.

X34 Shumway, Eunice K. *Batavia, Illinois Past and Present.* Chicago, 1965.

(Bellwood)

X35 *Bellwood Golden Jubilee, 1900-1950. Commemorating 50 Years of Development and Progress of the Village of Bellwood, Illinois, August 13, thru 20. Official Souvenir Book.* [Bellwood, 1950].

(Braidwood)

X36 Donna, Modesto Joseph. *The Braidwood Story.* [Braidwood, 1957].

(Bridgeview)

X37 Peksa, Rich. *History of Bridgeview, Illinois.* [Bridgeview], 1972.

(Broadview)

X38 *The Story of Broadview, 1914-1964.* [Broadview, 1964].

(Brookfield)

X39 Illinois Historic Structures Survey. *Inventory of Historic Structures in Brookfield, Cook County. Interim Report.* [Chicago], 1972.

(Chicago Heights)

X40 Beaudette, E. Palma, comp. *Chicago Heights, Illinois, 1914 . . .* [Chicago?], 1914.

X41 Caldwell, Edward. *The Founding and the Founders of the Village of Thorn Grove in 1833 That Became the Town of Bloom in 1850 and the City of Chicago Heights in 1892.* 2 vol. New York, 1947.

X42 Chicago Heights, Illinois. *Programme the Historical Pageant of Bloom Township Chicago Heights, Illinois, 1833-1933 Pageant Days.* Chicago Heights, 1933.

(Deerfield)

X43 Reichelt, Marie. *History of Deerfield, Illinois.* [Glenview, Ill.], 1928.

X44 Rosen, Harry M. and David H. *But Not Next Door.* New York, 1962.

(Des Plaines)

X45 Des Plaines Chamber of Commerce. *Des Plaines, Illinois. 125th Anniversary, 1835-1960 . . .* [Des Plaines, 1960].

X46 *The Des Plaines Historical Quarterly.* Des Plaines, 1939- .

X47 Wolfram, Clarence Albert. *When Des Plaines Was Young.* Reprinted from the Des Plaines *Suburban Times.* [1948].

(Dolton)

X48 Dolton-South Holland (Ill.) Woman's Club. *Dolton, Illinois, 1892-1976.* [Dolton, 1976].

(Downers Grove)

X49 Downers Grove, Illinois. Centennial Committee. *Downers Grove Centennial, July 4, 1932.* Downers Grove, 1932.

X50 Downers Grove, Illinois. *135th Anniversary Souvenir Album.* [Downers Grove, 1968].

(East Chicago)

X51 Indiana Association of Park Departments. *The City of East Chicago.* n.p., [1934].

X52 *East Chicago. Indiana Harbor. Twin Cities of Indiana: Political, Historical, Industrial Sketches.* n.p., 1913.

(Elk Grove)

X53 Wajer, Mary. "Elk Grove: The Land and the Settlers, 1834-1880." W.I.U unpub. M.A. thesis, 1976.

(Elmwood Park)

X54 Elmwood Park (Ill.) Historical Society. *Elmwood Park Reflections.* [Elmwood Park, 1976].

(Fox Lake)

X54a Steele, James W. *Fox Lake Country in Illinois.* Chicago, n.d.

(Franklin Park)

X55 Loebig, Geraldine Ann, ed. *50th Anniversary, Village of Franklin Park, 1892-1942, Golden Jubilee, July 1 to 5, 1942.* [Franklin Park, 1942].

X56 Village of Franklin Park. *Diamond Jubilee, 75th Anniversary.* [Franklin Park?, 1967].

(Glen Ellyn)

X57 Harmon, Ada Douglas, comp. *The Story of an Old Town - Glen Ellyn.* Glen Ellyn, c1928.

X58 League of Women Voters of Glen Ellyn. *This is Glen Ellyn . . .* [Glen Ellyn], 1955.

X59 League of Women Voters of North DuPage County. *Glen Ellyn, It's Your Village.* [Glen Ellyn], 1950.

X60 Weiser, Frederick S. *Village in a Glen: A History of Glen Ellyn, Illinois*. Glen Ellyn, 1957.

(Glencoe)

X61 Glencoe Historical Society. *Seventy-Five Years of Glencoe History, 1835-1944*. [Glencoe, 1944].

X62 Illinois Historic Structures Survey. *Inventory of Historic Structures in Glencoe, Cook County. Interim Report*. [Chicago], 1972.

(Glenview)

X63 Glenview Area Historical Society. *Glenview at 75, 1899-1974*. Melrose Park, Ill., 1974.

(Hammond)

X64 Beaudette, E. Palma. *Art History of Hammond, Indiana: A Review of Its General History and Its Present Status . . .* Chicago, 1913.

(Harvey)

X65 [Kerr, Alec C.], ed. *History, the City of Harvey, 1890-1962*. Harvey, 1962.

X66 Deleted

(Highwood)

X66a Wittelle, Marvyn. *28 Miles North: The Story of Highwood*. Highwood, [1953].

(Hinsdale)

X67 Baker, William H. *Picturesque Hinsdale: Forty Illustrations of Streets, Public Buildings and Private Residences . . .* Chicago, n.d.

X68 Dugan, Hugh G. *Village on the County Line: A History of Hinsdale, Illinois*. [Chicago], 1949.

(Kenilworth)

X69 *Kenilworth: First Fifty Years.* Kenilworth, 1947.

X70 Kilner, Colleen Browne. *Joseph Sears and His Kenilworth: The Dreamer and the Dream.* Kenilworth, 1969.

X71 __________. *Kenilworth Tree Stories: History Woven Around Its Trees.* Kenilworth, 1972.

(La Grange)

X72 Illinois Historic Structures Survey. *Inventory of Historic Structures in La Grange, Cook County. Interim Report.* [Chicago], 1972.

X73 *La Grange Diamond Jubilee, 1879-1954.* [La Grange, 1954].

(Lemont)

X74 Buschman, Barbara, ed. *Lemont, Illinois: Its History in Commemoration of the Centennial of Its Incorporation.* [Des Plaines, 1973].

X75 Illinois Historic Structures Survey. *Inventory of Architecture Before W. W. II in Lemont, Cook County. Interim Report.* [Chicago], 1973.

(Libertyville)

X76 *Libertyville Illustrated: Lovely Location, Wonderful Waters . . .* [Chicago?, 1898?].

X77 Price, Glenn. *Our Town: The Story of the Growth and Development of a Typical American Town.* Libertyville, [1941].

(Lockport)

X78 Centennial Celebration. Publicity Committee. *Lockport Has a Birthday: 1830-1930.* [Chicago?], 1930.

(Lombard)

X79 Dunning, Mildred Robinson. *The Story of Lombard, 1833-1955.* [Lombard, 1956?].

(Lyons)

X80 Benedetti, Rose Marie and Virginia Bulat. *Lyons: A History of a Village and Area Important for 300 Years.* Riverside, 1959.

X81 __________. *Portage, Pioneers, and Pubs: A History of Lyons, Illinois.* [Chicago?, 1963].

(Maywood)

X82 Maywood, Illinois. *Maywood and Its Homes.* Maywood, 1904.

(Mokena)

X83 Pitman, Florence. *The Story of Mokena.* Mokena, [1963].

(Montgomery)

X83a Ely, Salem. *A Centennial History of . . . Montgomery . . .* Chicago, [c1918].

(Naperville)

X84 Naperville, Illinois. Centennial Historical Committee. *Naperville Centennial, 1831-1931.* [Chicago?], 1931.

(New Lenox)

X85 Paustian, E. C. *Economic, Social and Educational Survey of New Lenox, Illinois.* [Evanston?], 1920.

(New Trier)

X86 *New Trier: Pictorial, Business, Professional, Municipal, Educational, Religious.* Wilmette, Ill., 1923.

(Oak Lawn)

X87 The League of Women Voters of Oak Lawn, Illinois. *Know Oak Lawn; Published in the Interest of Citizenship.* 2nd ed. Chicago, 1956.

(Olympia Fields)

X88 Olympia Fields Country Club. *A Brief History of Olympia Fields.* [Chicago, 1925?].

(Palatine)

X89 Paddock, Stuart R. *Palatine Centennial Book: History of Palatine, Cook County, Illinois*. Palatine, 1955.

(Palos Park)

X90 Mann, Roberts. *The Palos Preserves*. [Chicago], 1963.

(Park Forest)

X91 *Facts About Park Forest, Illinois*. [Park Forest], 1953.

(Peotone)

X92 Peotone Centennial Committee. *Peotone on Parade, 1856-1956*. [Chicago, 1956].

(Plainfield)

X93 Herath, Jean L. *Indians and Pioneers: A Prelude to Plainfield, Illinois*. Hinckley, Ill., 1975.

X94 Plainfield (Ill.) Bicentennial Commission. *A History of Plainfield "Then and Now."* [Plainfield, 1976].

(River Forest)

X95 Illinois Historic Structures Survey. *Inventory of Historic Structures in River Forest, Cook County. Interim Report*. [Chicago], 1972.

X96 River Forest Optimist. *Centennial Souvenir Number*. [River Forest], May 29, 1936.

(Riverside)

X97 Cameron, John M. *Riverside*. [Riverside, 1938].

X98 Illinois Historic Structures Survey. *Inventory of Historic Structures in Riverside, Cook County. Interim Report*. [Chicago], 1972.

X99 Fuller, S. S., *et.al*. *Riverside Then and Now: A History of Riverside Illinois Illustrated with Photographs, Maps and Old Etchings*. Riverside, 1936.

X100 *Picturesque Riverside, Cook County, Illinois*. Chicago, n.d.

(Riverdale)

X101 The League of Women Voters of Riverdale, Illinois. *Spotlight on Riverdale.* [Chicago?], 1958.

(St. Charles)

X102 Pearson, Ruth Seen. *Reflections of St. Charles: A History of St. Charles, Illinois, 1833-1976.* [St. Charles, 1976].

X103 St. Charles (Ill.) City Plan Commission. *The Official City Plan of St. Charles, Illinois.* [St. Charles, 1928].

(Schaumburg)

X104 Fletcher, Connie. "We Have Seen the Future and It is Schaumburg." *Chicago,* XXVII, 11 (Nov. 1978), 156-163.

(Skokie)

X105 The Life, Skokie, Illinois. *Skokie, World's Largest Village, Diamond Jubilee, 1963.* Skokie, 1963.

(Stickney)

X106 *Pioneers of Progress: The History of Stickney Township.* [Chicago, 1969].

(South Holland)

X107 Cook, Richard A. *A History of South Holland, Illinois.* South Holland, [1966].

(Summit)

X108 Summit (Ill.) Bicentennial Commission. *Summit Heritage.* [Desplaines Valley, Ill., 1976].

(Tinley Park)

X109 *Centennial of Tinley Park 1845-1945: 100 Years of Progress.* [Tinley Park, 1945].

(Warrenville)

X110 Schmidt, Leone. *The Life and Times of Warrenville: A Bicentennial History.* Warrenville, [1975].

(Waukegan)

X111 Gregory, Ruth W., ed. *Waukegan, Illinois: Its Past, Its Present*. Rev. ed. [Waukegan], 1959.

(Western Springs)

X112 Illinois Historic Structures Survey. *Inventory of Historic Structures in Western Springs, Cook County. Interim Report*. [Chicago], 1972.

(Wheaton)

X113 Gary, Olin J. "Wheaton Seventy Years Ago." *JISHS*, XX, 1 (Ap. 1927), 128-137.

X114 Herrick, Frank Earl. *Memorial Stars: A Book of Tears and Pride*. Wheaton, [1948].

X115 League of Women Voters of Wheaton. *Wheaton Profile*. Wheaton, 1956.

X116 MacVeigh, Franklin. *Facts about Wheaton, Illinois . . . with Indexed Street and House Number Map*. Wheaton, [1932].

(Winnetka)

X117 Dickinson, Lora T. *The Story of Winnetka*. Winnetka, 1956.

(Zion)

X118 Cook, Philip Lee. "Zion City, Illinois: Twentieth Century Utopia." U.Col. unpub. Ph.D. thesis, 1965.

X119 Fisk, Chester Ballou. "Zion City, a Modern Theocracy." U.C. unpub. M.A. thesis, 1930.

X120 Harlan, Rolvix. . . . *John Alexander Dowie and the Christian Apostolic Church in Zion* . . .Evansville, Wisc., 1906.

X121 Kusch, Monica Henrietta. "Zion, Illinois: An Attempt at a Theocentric City." U.C.L.A. unpub. Ph.D. thesis, 1954.

X122 Pokin, Frank N. "Zion: City of the White Dove." U.C. unpub. M.A. thesis, 1967.

Y
INDIANS

Indians used the Chicago area for hundreds of years before the white man arrived. The Winnebago, Illinois, Miami, Menominee, Chippewa, Ottowa and Potawatomi were among the tribes in the Lake Michigan area. Patterns of settlement changed and by the time the United States came to own the land, the Potawatomi were the dominant tribe in the area. There is still much unknown about Indians in the area and great care is needed in using the literature, both primary and secondary. See also: B3.

Y1 Anson, Bert. *The Miami Indians.* Norman, Oklahoma, 1970.

A sound history of an important tribe in the area.

Y2 Black Hawk. *Life of Black Hawk, Ma-Ka-Tai-Me-She-Kia-Kiak.* Edited by Milo M. Quaife. Chicago, 1916.

Black Hawk led the last uprising in Illinois. This is one of many versions of his life.

Y3 Blair, Emma Helen, ed. *The Indian Tribes of the Upper Mississippi Valley and Region of the Great Lakes.* 2 vol. Cleveland, 1911-1912.

An important collection of primary sources.

Y4 Blasingham, Emily. "The Depopulation of the Illinois Indians." *Ethnohistory,* III, 3 (Summer 1956), 193-224, 361-412.

Y5 Bourassa, J. N. "The Life of Wahbahn-se: The Warrior Chief of the Pottawatomies." *Kan. H. Q.,* XXXVIII, 2 (Summer 1972), 132-143.

Wahbahn-se was a war chief during the 1820s and 1830s and was present at the treaty of Chicago in 1833.

Y6 Brown, Lizzie M. "The Pacification of the Indians of Illinois after the War of 1812." *JISHS,* VIII, 4 (Jan. 1916), 550-558.

A narrative.

Y7 Chowen, Richard. "The History of Treaty Making with the Potawatomi Nation of Indians." N.U. unpub. M.A. thesis, 1941.

Y8 Clifton, James A. "Billy Caldwell's Exile in Early Chicago." *CH,* n.s., VI, 4 (Winter 1977-1978), 218-228.

A re-evaluation of "Sauganash's" career.

Y9 Clifton, James A. "Chicago Was Theirs." *CH*, n.s., I, 1 (Spring 1970), 4-17.

A brief description of the Potawatomi, their role in Chicago and their fate after being forced from Chicago.

Y10 __________. *The Prairie People: Continuity and Change in Potawatomi Indian Culture 1665-1965*. Lawrence, Kan., 1977.

A careful, well-written, well-researched, detailed monograph. One of the best books on Indians of the Chicago area. The material in the latter part of the book, however, has been sharply criticized. See a review in *J. Am. H.*, LXV, 2 (Sept. 1978), 389-411.

Y11 Deleted

Y12 Conway, Thomas G. "Potawatomi Politics." *JISHS*, LXV, 4 (Winter 1972), 395-418.

A discussion of organization within the tribe.

Y13 Eby, Cecil. *"That Disgraceful Affair," the Black Hawk War*. New York, 1973.

A strongly pro-Indian account of the last Illinois Indian War. Documented; good bibliography.

Y14 Edmunds, Russell David. "A History of the Potawatomi Indians, 1615-1795." U.Ok. unpub. Ph.D. thesis, 1972.

A narrative of Potawatomi political life in the period before the Treaty of Greenville when parts of the tribe settled in Illinois.

Y15 __________. "The Illinois River Potawatomi in the War of 1812." *JISHS*, LXII, 4 (Winter 1969), 341-362.

A well-documented account based on doctoral research.

Y16 __________. "The Prairie Potawatomi Removal of 1833." *Ind. Mag. of H.*, LXVIII, 3 (Sept. 1972), 240-253.

A short account of the growing pressure for removal and of the actual event.

Y17 Foreman, Grant. "Illinois and Her Indians." *Papers in Ill. H.*, 1939, 66-111.

A narrative of treaties with the various tribes.

Y18 Gerwing, Anselm J. "The Chicago Indian Treaty of 1833." *JISHS,* LVII, 2 (Summer 1964), 117-142.

A general overview of the making of the Treaty and its terms.

Y19 Grover, Frank R. "Indian Treaties Affecting Lands in the Present State of Illinois." *JISHS,* VIII, 3 (Oct. 1915), 379-419.

He deals with treaties of 1795, 1804, 1816, 1821, 1825, 1829, and 1833.

Y20 Hagan, William T. "The Black Hawk War." U.W. unpub. Ph.D. thesis, 1950.

A thorough study of the War and related matters. Hagan argues that later accounts led to ". . . the creation of a war that never took place. It served, too, to divert attention from the operation of the Federal Indian policy during a vital 30 year period . . . Neither the romances nor the polemics, however, succeeded in metamorphising the actors in this frontier force into shining heroes or bloody villans." The bibliography is complete to the time of writing. See the review cited in the next entry.

Y21 __________. *The Sac and Fox Indians.* Norman, Ok., 1958.

Should be used with care. See the review in *JISHS,* LI, 2 (Summer 1959), 214-219.

Y22 Hauser, Raymond E. "An Ethnohistory of the Illinois Indian Tribe, 1673-1832." N.I.U. unpub. Ph.D. thesis, 1973.

The power of the Illinois was great during the French period but declined greatly with the tribe's depopulation. The decline in numbers was due to the tribe's over-dependence on the French, who exposed them to dangers and who left them in 1765 in a much weakened condition.

Y23 Hickerson, Harold. *The Chippewa and Their Neighbors: A Study in Ethnohistory.* New York, 1970.

Y24 Indian Claims Commission. *Garland American Indian Ethnohistory Series.* New York, 1974.

"The Garland American Indian Ethnohistory series presents original documents on the history and anthropology of many American Indian tribes and groups who were involved in the Indian Claims actions of the 1950s and 1960s. These reports were written to be used as evidence in legal proceedings to determine the aboriginal rights of various Indian groups to certain geographical regions or areas within the United States In each case, the Indian Claims Commission issued a set of findings which are an important historical outcome of the proceedings and of the reports." Some of the volumes now published are:

Indians of Illinois and Indiana: Illinois, Kickapoo and Potawatomi Indians.
Indians of Northeastern Illinois.
Indians of Western Illinois and Southern Wisconsin.
The Piankashaw and Kaskeskia and the Treaty of Greeneville.
Winnebago Indians.

Y25 Kinietz, W. Vernon. *The Indians of the Western Great Lakes, 1615-1760.* Ann Arbor, 1940.

Y26 Landes, Ruth. *The Prairie Potawatomi: Tradition and Ritual in the Twentieth Century.* Madison, 1970.

Y27 Lurie, Nancy Oestreich. "The Winnebago Indians: A Study in Cultural Change." N.U. unpub. Ph.D. thesis, 1952.

Y28 Deleted

Y29 Miller, Otis Louis. "Indian-White Relations in the Illinois Country, 1789-1818." St. Louis U. unpub. Ph.D. thesis, 1972.

Essentially a narrative.

Y30 O'Connor, Mary Helen. "Potwawtomi Land Cessions in the 'Old Northwest'." C.U. unpub. M.A. thesis, 1942.

Y31 Ourada, Patricia Kathryn. *The Menominee Indians: A History.* Norman, Ok., 1978.

A narrative from the early 17th century to the present day.

Y32 Prucha, Francis Paul. *American Indian Policy in the Formative Years: The Indian Trade and Intercourse Acts, 1790-1834.* Cambridge, 1962.

Y33 Quaife, Milo M. "Documents: The Chicago Treaty of 1833." *Wisc. Mag. of H.*, I, 3 (Mar. 1918), 287-303.

Prints a copy of the Treaty, crucial to Chicago's history, with notes by an important student of the period.

Y34 Quimby, George Irving. *Indian Life in the Upper Great Lakes, 11,000 B.C. to A.D. 1800.* Chicago, 1960.

A well-illustrated introduction with a glossary and bibliography.

Y35 Radin, Paul. *The Winnebago Tribe.* Lincoln, 1970.

Reprints a classic source of material on the Winnebago Indians.

Y36 Shapiro, Dena Evelyn. "Indian Tribes and Trails of the Chicago Region, a Preliminary Study of the Influence of the Indian on the Early White Settlement." U.C. unpub. M.A. thesis, 1929.

A re-working of Sharf's M.S. work and other standard texts.

Y37 Smith, Dwight L. "Indian Land Cessions in the Old Northwest, 1795-1809." Ind.U. unpub. Ph.D. thesis, 1948.

Y38 Spindler, George and Louise. *Dreamers without Power: The Menominee Indians*. New York, 1971.

Y39 Steward, John F. *Lost Maramech and Earliest Chicago: A History of the Foxes and of Their Downfall Near the Great Village of Maramech*. Chicago, 1903.

Based on early French accounts, not many contemporary secondary sources used. Maramech was the battle where the French crushed the Indians.

Y40 Strong, William Duncan. *The Indian Tribes of the Chicago Region, with Special Reference to the Illinois and the Potawatomi*. Chicago, 1926.

Y41 Temple, Wayne C. "Indian Villages of the Illinois Country." *ISM Scientific Papers,* II, part 2. Springfield, 1958.

Use with care; it has been subjected to criticism because of errors of fact.

Y42 Whitney, Ellen M., ed. *The Black Hawk War, 1831-1832. Ill. State H. Lib. Collec.,* XXXV. Springfield, 1970.

A very useful collection of primary material. In particular, see the scholarly introduction by Anthony F. C. Wallace in vol. XXV, p. 1-51.

Y43 Winger, Otho. *The Potawatomi Indians*. Elgin, Ill., 1939.

Z
REFERENCE

Collective Biography

Most long 19th and early 20th century histories have much biographical material. Other important sources are the national biographical works of a particular group, e.g., the *Biographical Dictionary of American Labor Leaders*. See also: A27, 35, 46; B15; E6.

Z1 **Deleted**

Z2 *Bench and Bar of Chicago*. Chicago, [1883?].

Z3 Bennett, Frances Cheney, ed. *History of Music and Art in Illinois Including Portraits and Biographies . . .* [Philadelphia], 1904.

Z4 *Biographical Dictionary and Portrait Gallery of Representative Men of Chicago and the World's Columbian Exposition*. Chicago, 1892.

Z6 *Biographical Sketches of the Leading Men of Chicago, Written by the Best Talent of the Northwest*. Chicago, 1868.

Z7 *Black Book Directory*. Chicago, 1970- .

Z8 *The Book of Chicagoans*.

See Z20.

Z9 The Chicago, Rock Island and Pacific Railway. *The Chicago, Rock Island and Pacific Railway System and Representative Employees*. Chicago, 1900.

Z10 *Confederate Soldiers, Sailors, and Civilians Who Died as Prisoners of War at Camp Douglas, Chicago, Ill., 1862-1865*. Kalamazoo, [1968?].

Z11 Flinn, John J. *Handbook of Chicago Biography*. Chicago, 1893.

Z12 Municipal Art League of Chicago. Exhibition Committee. *Artists' Directory. Painters and Sculptors*. Chicago, n.d.

Z13 *Notable Men of Chicago and Their City*. Chicago, 1910.

Z14 Poole, Ernest. *Giants Gone: Men Who Made Chicago*. New York, 1943.

Z15 *Portraits and Biographies of the Fire Underwriters of the City of Chicago*. Chicago, 1895.

Z16 Society of Medical History of Chicago. *Bulletin*. 5 vol. Chicago, 1911-1940.

Contains many short biographical sketches.

Z17 Sparks, Esther. "A Biographical Dictionary of Painters and Sculptors in Illinois 1808-1945." N.U. unpub. Ph.D. thesis, 1971.

Z18 *Unrivaled Chicago: Containing an Historical Narrative of the Great City's Development and Descriptions of Points of Interest*. Chicago, 1896.

Z19 Waterman, Arba Nelson. *Historical Review of Chicago and Cook County and Selected Biography*. 3 vol. Chicago, 1908.

Mostly a collection of biographical articles.

Z20 *Who's Who in Chicago; The Book of Chicagoans, a Biographical Dictionary of Leading Living Men and Women of the City of Chicago and Environs . . . 1905, 1911, 1917, 1926*. 1st-8th ed. Chicago, 1905-1945.

Title varies: 1905, 1911, 1917, *The Book of Chicagoans, a Biographical Dictionary of Leading Living Men of the City of Chicago . . .*; 1926, *Who's Who in Chicago; The Book of Chicagoans . . .* Editors: 1905, J. W. Leonard; 1911, 1917, 1926, A. N. Marquis.

Z21 *Who's Who in the Midwest; a Biographical Dictionary of Noteworthy Men and Women of the Central and Midwestern States*. Chicago, 1949- .

Z22 *Who's Who in Radio*. Chicago, 1925.

Z23 Wilkie, Franc Bangs. *Sketches and Notices of the Chicago Bar: Including the More Prominent Lawyers and Judges of the City and Suburban Towns*. Chicago, 1871.

Z24 Deleted

Z25 Deleted

Z26 Deleted

Bibliographies

This list of bibliographies includes only the lists that were found to be most useful. There is no pretense that it is complete.

Z27 Andrews, Clarence A. "GLR Bibliography of Place - Chicago (Part I)." *Great Lakes R.*, V, 1 (Summer 1978), 67-92.

Z28 Bridges, Roger D. "A Bibliography of Dissertations Related to Illinois History, 1884-1976." *JISHS*, LXX, 3 (Aug. 1977), 208-248.

Z29 Brook, Michael. "Annual Bibliography of Periodical Articles on American Labor History: 1965." *Labor H.*, VIII, 1 (Winter 1967), 71-86.

Additional annual bibliographies by Brook appear in these issues of the journal: Fall, 1967; Winter, 1969; Fall, 1969; Winter, 1971.

Z30 Buck, Solon Justus. *Travel and Description 1765-1865 . . .* Springfield, 1915.

Z31 Buenker, John D., *et.al.*, ed. *Immigration and Ethnicity: A Guide to Information Sources*. Detroit, 1977.

Z32 Chicago. Bureau of Social Surveys. *Selected Bibliography on Housing, Zoning, and City Planning in Chicago*. Chicago, 1926.

Z33 Chicago. Municipal Reference Library. *Catalogue of the Chicago Municipal Library*. Chicago, 1908.

Z34 __________. *Check-List of Publications Issued by Local Governing Bodies in Chicago and Cook County*. Chicago, 1936-1954.

Z35 __________. *Checklist of Publications Issued by the City of Chicago*. Chicago, 1958- .

Z36 Chicago. University. Center for Urban Studies. *A Directory of Urban and Urban Related Master Theses and Ph.D. Dissertations of the University of Chicago*. Chicago, 1970.

Z37 Chicago. University. Chicago Community Inventory. *Index of Sources of Data for the Chicago Metropolitan Area. Prepared by the Chicago Community Inventory, University of Chicago, for the Chicago Plan Commission and the Office of the Housing and Redevelopment Coordinator, City of Chicago*. Chicago, 1954.

Z38 Chicago. University. Library. *Chicago and Cook County: A Union List of Their Official Publications, Including the Semi-Official Institutions. The University of Chicago Libraries, Document Section*. Chicago, 1934.

Z39 Chicago. University. Library. *Private Civic and Social Service Agencies of Chicago: A Union List of Their Reports and Publications.* Chicago, 1936.

Z40 DePaul University. Library. *Chicago: Then and Now.* Compiled by Ernest Butt. [Chicago, 1978?].

Z41 *Dissertations in Urban Studies: The Historical Dimension.* Compiled by R. David Weber and Donna C. Bell. Ann Arbor, n.d.

Z42 Heater, Nancy L. *Commodity Futures Trading: A Bibliography.* Urbana, 1966.

Z43 Deleted

Z44 Jackson, Kenny. *A Critical Bibliography of Novels Written About Chicago: 1900-1948.* Chicago, 1950.

Z45 Kram, Regina I. "The Foreign Language Collections of the Chicago Public Library, 1872-1947." U.C. unpub. M.A. thesis, 1970.

Z46 McBrearty, James C. *American Labor History and Comparative Labor Movements: A Selected Bibliography.* Tucson, 1973.

Z47 U. S. Office of Community War Services. *Chicago, Community Resources and Problems: A Bibliography of Source Materials from January 1940 to March 1945.* Chicago, 1945.

Z48 Monaghan, Frank. *French Travelers in the United States, 1765-1932: A Bibliography.* New York, 1933.

Z49 Neufeld, Maurice F. *A Representative Bibliography of American Labor History.* Ithaca, 1964.

Z50 Northeastern Illinois Metropolitan Area Planning Commission. *A Selected Bibliography on the Chicago Metropolitan Area.* Urbana, 1964.

Z51 Richardson, Helen R., comp. *Illinois Central Railroad Company: A Centennial Bibliography 1851-1951.* Washington, 1950.

Z52 Simpson, Vernon and David Scott. *Chicago's Politics and Society: A Selected Bibliography.* DeKalb, 1972.

Z53 Stratman, Carl J. *Bibliography of the American Theatre, Excluding New York City.* Chicago, 1965.

Z54 Wodehouse, Lawrence. *American Architects from the Civil War to the First World War: A Guide to Information Sources.* Detroit, 1976.

Z55 Wodehouse, Lawrence. *American Architects from the First World War to the Present: A Guide to Information Sources*. Detroit, 1976.

Z56 Writers Program. Illinois. *Selected Bibliography: Illinois, Chicago and Its Environs*. Chicago, 1937.

Z57 __________. *Chicago in Periodical Literature, a Summary of Articles 1833-1871*. Chicago, 1940.

AUTHOR INDEX

INDEX OF NAMES

This is not a subject index, but a list of important names mentioned in the entries and their annotations.